Virtual Money

Virtual Money

Understanding the Power and Risks of
Money's High-Speed Journey
into Electronic Space

Elinor Harris Solomon

New York   Oxford
Oxford University Press
1997

Oxford University Press

Oxford   New York
Athens   Auckland   Bangkok   Bogotá   Bombay
Buenos Aires   Calcutta   Cape Town   Dar es Salaam
Delhi   Florence   Hong Kong   Istanbul   Karachi
Kuala Lumpur   Madras   Madrid   Melbourne
Mexico City   Nairobi   Paris   Singapore
Taipei   Tokyo   Toronto

and associated companies in
   Berlin   Ibadan

Copyright © 1997 by Elinor Harris Solomon

Published by Oxford University Press, Inc.
   198 Madison Avenue, New York, New York 10016

Oxford is a registered trademark of Oxford University Press

Library of Congress Cataloging-in-Publication Data
Solomon, Elinor Harris.
  Virtual money : understanding the power and risks of money's
high-speed journey into electronic space / Elinor Harris Solomon.
     p. cm.
  Includes bibliographic references and index.
  ISBN 0-19-509747-5
  1. Electronic funds transfers. 2. Capital movements.
3. Banks and banking—Data processing. 4. International finance.
i. Title.
HG1710.s65 1997   332.1'0285—dc21   97-6556

9 8 7 6 5 4 3 2 1
Printed in the United States of America
on acid-free paper

This volume is dedicated, with much love,
to my husband, Richard A. Solomon

Contents

Preface

Money big and money small
Money long and money call
Money thin and money tall
And sometimes money not at all

    —In the style of Christopher's bedtime story by Sandra Boynton
    Oh My Oh My Oh Dinosaurs!
    (New York: Workman Publishing, 1993)

This is a book about virtual money—money never to be touched, held, or seen. It is a book about money in motion, money messages in the form of brief pulses of light that glide outward through cyberspace like ripples in a pond. It is a book about money at rest, its form and shape, the magnetized memory bits on a "smart card" or just your ordinary PC. It is a book about the tailoring of financial markets to the new reality of cyberspace.

Included in this tale is plastic money, credit and debit cards, and the newly hatched e-money that plies the Internet trade. Also ubiquitous are the money quarrels, as banks and nonbanks wrestle for a rising place in this new era. Clandestine money of the underworld and the ensuing lawmakers' travails are part of the story. This is a book about a universal medium of exchange that befits the reality of today's global village, linked by invisible electronic threads that move money value around at mind-numbing speed.

The new technology is imaginative and indispensable, yet in many ways awesome. The directions that technology will take, in the areas of money and finance, are uncertain, their implications profound. In money and finance, the new creatures of technology proliferate and changes are irreversible—and unforeseen. This book looks at some of these changes, and what they may be doing for and to society.

In this odyssey, I have sought the views of bankers, operations and technical people, computer experts, policymakers, money users of all ages, and others active in the evolving drama. These interviews have generated many compelling and provocative ideas. Shared conferences and meetings have also been greatly helpful in conveying a feel for much of the present forward thrust, as well as its innate controversy.

The volume draws from my work-related experiences over the years and the interplay of ideas with former and present colleagues at the Federal Reserve Board, the Antitrust Division of the Department of Justice, and George Washington University. With never-failing enthusiasm spiced with critical comment, my students and wonderful family have contributed more than I can say. To my husband, Joan, Bob, and Tom and Benita I express my deepest gratitude.

My object is to write for the general reader, student, potential money user (aren't we all?), and technical expert alike and make some very complex phenomena a little bit easier for people to understand. The reader can pick and choose between, or even within, chapters according to interest.

The benefits of electronic money are enormous yet erratic. The electronic revolution is doing some quite peculiar and not readily understood things to financial markets and to those who own financial assets. *Virtual Money* talks about these issues and shines the spotlight on the more successful, as well as the more bizarre or vexing among them. It seeks to analyze the wonders, players, and mysteries within the ever-changing panorama that is modern money.

Washington, D.C.   E.H.S.
January 1997

Acknowledgments

Many people have given generously of their expertise—and time—and I am very grateful to them all. A number have commented on earlier drafts. The Federal Reserve Board and American Bankers Association have provided data and a wealth of knowledge. I wish to express my special thanks to Stephen Rhoades, Jeff Marquardt, Jeff Stehm, Heidi Richards, Edward Ettin, Linda Moore, and Kawika Daguio. Donald I. Baker lent his impressive legal talents, as did Rebecca Dick and other former colleagues at the Antitrust Division and of the early private EFT community, including Dale Reistad and Wayne Boucher.

Discussions with Chera Sayers, Ted Jaditz, and Tom Solomon have explored the interesting finance-oriented nuances of chaos theory, and helped me to understand a little of its possibilities. Michael Nelson, Paul Henderson, Florence Young, Kenneth Buckley, Carl Howe, Henry Geller, Joan Winston, and Vary Coates explained difficult operational, security, and technical issues with clarity and patience. The wisdom of Penelope Hartland-Thunberg, Robert Solomon, Thomas Simpson, and John Ammer was crucial to the international analysis. Some of the names of the many others interviewed, who significantly contributed to the eclectic mix of ideas, are to be found in the Notes.

I very much appreciate Claudia St. Clair's fine contribution to the art, and the photos generously supplied by the Bank of Japan and the Federal Reserve Banks of New York, Philadelphia, and Chicago. Thanks are due to Zachary Rolnik and Kluwer Academic publishers for permission to use some of the ideas worked through in our earlier books. I have been most fortunate to have had the enthusiasm and great help and support of Oxford University Press and its Executive Editor, Herbert J. Addison, long before e-money became a household word.

Finally, I wish to thank Professors Anthony Yezer and Frederick Joutz and my other George Washington University colleagues, including Scott Stebleman of our Gelman Library and the talented technical staff of CIRC (Computer Information and Resource Center). A debt of gratitude is owed to the Economics Department and its students whom I have had the privilege to teach. They have displayed a rare willingness to consider the unthinkable and challenge ideas, both old and new, in equal measure. Needless to say, any errors of omission or commission that may be present are mine alone.

Virtual Money

Part **I**

The Road to the Present

An Introduction to the World of Electronic Money

The decade was the sixties and the word "automation" was creeping into the banking vernacular. Federal Reserve Board Governor George Mitchell and Dale Reistad of the American Bankers Association called the world of the future the cashless/checkless society. The phrase stuck, but the vision didn't. Some electronic inroads were made into the traditional paper medium of exchange, but consumers rejected out of hand any notion of a wholly paperless money system.

Bill Gates of Microsoft fame was scarcely out of kindergarten then, as the Antitrust Division of the Department of Justice sallied forth to scrutinize this nascent technology. Some new laws were passed that made the Justice presence in banking matters obligatory. It was at that time and place that I became introduced to the fascinating lore of high-tech banking—EFT we called it then, for electronic funds transfer. The largest money flows (the wholesale payments) were to be sloughed off from their heavy physical paper journeys. Shortly thereafter the "plastic" of credit cards emerged to change the face of the retail money scene.

In 1963, quite by accident, meteorologist Edward Lorenz of M.I.T. discovered the tracings of chaos theory. Given certain initial conditions, the computer paths of three interlinked trajectories were found to track out a pattern very like a butterfly's wings. Order of quite beautiful nature emerged, unexpected, out of apparent chaos. That fascinating discovery was to lay the foundations for the later search for structure in financial markets. The fact that no one has ever been able to find any distinctively useful predictive patterns has not stopped traders from applying less elegant cousins of chaos theory to these markets.

In 1969, Bolt Baranek & Newman, a technology company in Cambridge, Massachusetts, won a contract to develop a fail-safe military communications network. Based on earlier work coming out of several universities, this network was designed to send out fragments of information in packets, to be reassembled quite literally from thin air at their point of destination. This prototype Net was deliberately conceived as anarchistic, without central direction. Its splintered nature would add to the security of what was then called ARPANET, and vital military secrets could be transmitted and recovered even if half the country were blown to bits by nuclear attack. Thus was born what was later to become the Internet, the most recent central player in our money story.

Some thirty odd years later, all these strands have improbably come together. Their juxtaposition has been a process of slow evolution, mutations, births, and deaths in a strange yet riveting tale for everyone involved. Some of the offshoots have fallen by the wayside. Others like ATM and credit cards have survived to succeed well beyond the modest anticipation of people whose construct they originally were.

Dale Reistad now believes it will be another thirty-five years before the checkless/ cashless society becomes reality in the sense that we have substantially reduced paper in the system.[1] But, no matter. The financial landscape is already transformed, evolving in a manner that staggers the early imagination.

Payments have always been interconnected. When you want to pay someone, there's a buyer and seller, often with different banks, and the money must always get from here to there; however, in the age of cyberspace and the Net, the term "interconnected" takes on a different cast.

The Internet Connection

The Internet has shaken up the world of high finance, visibly and in a manner that dazzled the financial press. With per-item fees and royalties as the potential prize, the present gleam of dollar signs is irresistible. But long before its intertwining with finance, the Internet was quietly evolving, in a rarified and definitely nonprofit-generating mode.

The Internet typifies a perfectly democratic institution where the fifteen-year-old computer whiz receives equal treatment with the powerful. No one is in charge—no one can claim sole credit for its invention. Pieces of the Net were spliced on, such as Gopher, named both for the football team of its host university and its prodigious digging capabilities. With the Gopher, and also free of charge, came software tools with such names as Veronica, Archie, WAIS, and Jughead. They allowed the Net to be increasingly used by nonspecialists, and opened up libraries around the world—assuming you could get through, a real problem in the early days. Research efforts improved vastly when the World Wide Web appeared with its graphical point-and-click interface capable of being used by even the most techno-phobic person.

The World Wide Web was invented by an idealistic scientist who sought no monetary reward, Tim Berners-Lee. Its place of birth was CERN, in Switzerland, where high-speed energy collisions fracture atoms into new and short-lived virtual particles. Scientists in the field could now more easily speak with each other. Still, it wasn't always easy for the novice to get around.

The Web's original navigation system, MOSAIC, was first developed at the University of Illinois by the then twenty-one-year-old Marc Andreessen, now head of Netscape Corp. The Netscape Navigator became early on almost the Web standard, although Microsoft's Explorer would later challenge its predominance. Originally given away, the "browsers," as they are usually called, have transformed the way we can advertise and communicate on-line. With jazzy graphical interface and colorful pictures, the Web's potential has paved the way for buying and paying for items on the Net—"electronic commerce," if you will.

Given the necessary "handshaking" protocol so the bits and pieces can talk to one another, the Internet's structure and control are said to be the closest thing to effective worldwide democracy across national borders that one can imagine. A home page, whether placed by cottage industry or multinational firm, projects a wonderful global selling platform. Advertising markets now can encompass the planet.

Inexorably, the Net is proceeding to center financial stage. The Net becomes a medium for moving everything from data to money. On-line systems have found it cheaper and more surefire to work through the Net rather than compete with it. Rivals' cries of monopolization attempts reach the very pristine temple of the Internet itself. They also reach the ears and eyes of antitrust authorities.

The Net's character is constantly undergoing metamorphosis. Core financing of the Internet's backbone infrastructure, NSFnet, and of the regional networks that got their start on college campuses in the 1980s, has mostly been withdrawn—the National Science Foundation no longer pays the major bills. Private suppliers pick up some pieces and supplement others.

In the wake of these changes come complaints. Some smaller or cash-strapped colleges fret that they may not have access to the same quality of services at the same cost. Some fear pressures to change the Net's nature, at the worst turning it into a version of a utility with regulated rates and charges. Capacity can also be a worry since graphics and tele-conferencing occupy large chunks of space compared with the original rather simple exchange of mere digital information.

At the same time, for the average only mildly computer-literate consumer who uses the Net for private information, a world of new opportunities now exists. Once the access provider is paid, individual consumer use appears to be free. Of course someone picks up the rest of the tab, in this case the telecommunications companies who handle the bulk of the traffic. They will be reimbursed for their costs, unless competition forces them to eat a portion. The charges may be passed back, but only indirectly. Users of the Net presently get a lot for very little.

Electronic Money Hookups

The eventual merging of the two vastly different worlds of cyberspace and finance was once the stuff of fantasy. Technology, along with the jagged "virtual" paths carved out by computer systems with their dynamic high-technology tools, have coalesced with the money systems. How did this happen? Again, we go back in time to the days of the early Net.

Electronic bank delivery programs have been around for as long as the Internet—over three decades. Early on, a label was attached to these mechanisms that permit money to fly through the air without benefit of airplane. The clumsy nomenclature, which seems to have stuck, was electronic funds transfer (EFT).[2] EFT didn't do any money creating; it merely moved around what was already there in bank accounts in deposit form, but much faster. EFT gave us "fast money flows" and eventually "virtual money." Its evolution followed a path similar to the Internet's—not anarchy surely, but market motivated without a deliberate pre-mapped plan. And, with persistent linkages, its swath and influence kept growing.

For the original money transfer systems, as for the Internet, their virtual nonphysical paths were developed by computer-savvy people working in tandem with banking pioneers. Visa and MasterCard led the retail plastic way. These plastic coalitions spread from local then regional to the international bank card systems we now know and use. The overriding need to gain universal acceptability of any money form shaped the coalitions, and the retail system partners—not without some difficulty —forged mutually acceptable rules.

With some weeding out, the large (wholesale) EFT systems quietly thrived, too. Prime among them have been electronic networks operated by central banks or private bank partners worldwide (e.g., the New York-based CHIPS). Together, they handle large foreign exchange and other wholesale operations. They also disseminate the fast money flows, far and wide.

Given the extraordinary speeds, money's daily travel reaches quite staggering amounts. The Federal Reserve's Fedwire and CHIPS send out well over $2 trillion daily. Retail systems such as credit and debit cards deliver several hundred billion more. Daily, the recorded flows are running about half the entire broad money (M3) stock of the United States. The combined dollar flow *in one day* equals over one-third of our gross domestic product for the entire year.

A decade or so ago, while the large payment flows sloshed stealthily under and over, most ordinary citizens remained disinterested. We were largely unaware of the dramatic implications of electronic money transfers in our daily lives—most people found the whole subject boring. To avoid becoming social poison, those who did know rarely talked about electronic money much, except to kindly captive audiences such as family, colleagues, or students. The issues seemed too complex and far removed. People got their credit cards and liked what they could do, but the unseen unfolding of the grander e-design could have been taking place on Mars, for all the general public cared.

Of course, everything is changed now. With journalistic flair, the popular press trumpets e-money details. Each time Microsoft embarks on another venture, the world listens and waits, and the travails and intertwining of banks and telecommunications and computer people are the stuff of popular press and animated discussion. People wonder how the wave of bank mergers may affect them, whether banks should acquire the useful e-money partners, or vice versa, and what the proper legislative fix might be.

This consolidation process is a necessary and continuing one. Interindustry links between finance, computers, and telecommunications are being forged, and the fortunes of these disparate megagiants are melded, with inevitable friction, like those of mutually interdependent family members who must get along. Banks and credit card systems align with Netscape, and/or Microsoft, RSA, IBM, Sun Microsystems, or Oracle, among innumerable others. It's difficult to keep track and to stay current. Fledgling software and security (encryption) systems are brought on board to assure the money's safe delivery, in the manner to which we are accustomed. But what is new about any of this? The size, yes; the unbelievable diversity of the partners and their open wrangling, most surely. But not the process. For finance, the current intertwining is an extension of the past.

Now, with the Internet beckoning, the interweaving process is extended. The nonbanks grab the bait: computer firms, phone companies, cable and TV, encryption people—you name it. The creative juices are flowing. Sounds from the explosion of the new money forms can be quite deafening.

A Cambrian Money Explosion

As I talk to people, one perception stands out: they are all astonished by the metamorphosis in the money vista. It was as if you opened a closet door, and everything—you knew not what—suddenly fell on top of you. It all evokes the Cambrian explosion of life forms in great profusion that geologists think dates back about 600 million years ago.

For high-tech banking there had been a lull of about a decade, and some segments appeared quite comatose. No one had much appetite for home banking; the early glitches certainly ensured that. One made the transfers quite handily, but when a problem arose and evidence of payment (such as a lowly check) was requested, the correction process could grind to a screeching halt. After the credit card technology was digested, banks wondered why consumers shunned merchant-based payment at point of sale (POS) or home banking. To be lost was the credit card float—what was its advantage? Did anyone really want the smart card as a substitute for cash? In the 1980s, there were few if any takers.

Bank Collisions with Other Cultures

Then the newest money creatures appeared, as if out of the blue. Popular acceptance of the Internet and its possibilities was the catalyst—the Net produced a ready-made delivery vehicle along with an addicted cult of talented creators and avid enthusiasts. EFT and the Internet were to blend their fortunes. The true innovations now come thick and fast and continue to emerge as this book is being published. And this time they can properly be characterized as virtual money, money in a stream of digital bits, the "ons" and "offs" of computer lingo, some, as we will later see, without any reserve base or monitoring or measurement feature of the customary banking kind.

The Internet is gearing up to carry e-cash, or digital money. But are computer people willing or able to provide the necessary safeguards?—an issue highlighted by recent lapses in security. Will digital money be redeemed in real money on demand? And what do high-tech sellers know about banks and financial markets anyway? has been an outcry.

The "electronic wallet" of the computer genre looks to be a multipurpose record keeper, communicator, money keeper, and payment maker all rolled into one. In alarm, bankers engineer their own plans. One example is a plastic electronic purse that looks very much like a pocket calculator, with infrared mechanisms for beaming money instructions outward. Credit-card purveyors have similar plans—the smart or stored-value cards, that are being tested in far-flung places, currently with limited success. More computer experts are then hired to help develop bank technology and the result is a very new type of man or woman already just below (or in some cases at) the highest bank management level. You see them quietly at work at conferences and within the halls of the Federal Reserve. They will say they aren't economists; their approach is fresh and they talk with candor and in clear detail. Within a bank, or outside it, their influence is powerful.

Microsoft, meanwhile, has grappled with the Antitrust Division of the U.S. Department of Justice in its attempts to acquire an established gateway to electronic commerce and e-money, with the popular Quicken program. Rebuffed, Microsoft promptly set its sights elsewhere toward its own home-brew personal finance system, with implementing banks and encryption firms signed up, to secure the whole operation with mathematical locks and keys.

From the untried and the new the buyer must pick and choose. Many vendors come and go; a lot of mistakes have been made and exaggerated claims abound. In the words of EFT pioneer George White, if there is a lesson for users, it is to think critically about everything.[3] And, of course, some who have emerged from the firestorm of innovation will survive; others won't.

Creation and Survival

The distinguished paleontologist Stephen Gould discusses the process of weeding out the inefficient, those who are not suited in one way or another to the environment as it shapes itself over time. Of course, adaptability has always been the nature of money and banks, and the reason why these institutions have managed to bend with the changing times.

Gould points out that Darwin in his great work, *The Origin of the Species*, brought economics into his discussion of natural selection. In July 1837 Darwin started his first notebook on transmutation. He later wrote in his autobiography

"On October 1843 . . . and being well prepared to recognize the struggle for existence which everywhere goes on, it struck me that favorable variations would tend to be preserved and unfavorable ones would tend to be destroyed, so that this would be the formation of new species."[4]

According to Gould, Darwin argues that evolution has only one purpose; individuals seek to increase the representation of their genes in future generations. If the world displays any harmony and order, they arise only as the result of individuals seeking their own advantage. Moreover, evolution has no direction and does not necessarily lead to higher or better things—organisms simply become better adapted to their local environments. It is the classical market theory of Adam Smith adapted to nature.[5]

Something of that sort appears to be going on right now. Markets adapt. We almost forget the names of those many well-respected concerns that didn't quite make it. Carte Blanche, Diners Club, then Choice, were all absorbed into Citibank. In the early 1980s the promising New York-based settlement mechanism, Bankwire, yielded to Fedwire and CHIPS. Shortly thereafter, the debacle of the savings and loan institutions wiped out much of a cherished post-World II savings and home financing tradition. With the official advent of interstate banking, the bank merger wave takes on tidal proportions.

A similar swell occurred in banking some thirty years ago. Markets digested and adapted. The regulators and Congress took a closer look, and the surge tapered off—for a time. New products and firms were developed, and accepted, in due course. Now it all begins again, explosively.

Money's Many Faces

There is a pretty good textbook definition of money that still makes sense. Money—if it is to be worth its salt as a medium of exchange—must be generally acceptable. It must provide a unit of account with a lasting store of value. The money unit must be guarded against unbridled overissue and inflation—that is, against erosion of its value. Whether "narrow" (retail) or "broad" (wholesale), it must be fully redeemable for other kinds of money.

Given the switch underway from the tangible to the esoteric, can you recognize money when you see it? Does it move around on armored trucks, lay hidden in satchels, walk down the street, or fly through the air? The answer is not as simple as you might imagine.

With the use of paper checks, the money or deposit transfer is expressed in writing. A check provides the promise of future value exchange once it clears the system. In contrast, electronic systems convey intangible and close to immediate value exchange. In either case, money is defined as a store of value, but its most necessary characteristic is its general acceptance as a medium of exchange. People must be willing to accept the money form, either tangible or ethereal, in return for goods and services. Given that broad definition, many kinds of money now exist, each superimposed on preexisting money forms.

The New E-species

A strange computer cybermoney awaits our bidding, provided the consumer confidence level becomes sufficiently high. Limited-use "prepaid media" have existed for some time, of course. They are handy for telephone calls and subway rides or toll roads, or to use at places like Club Med, universities, or army bases. The plastic card contains spendable value, transferred from bank account or wads of bills to magnetic strip.

Yet the prepaid forms, whether a telephone card or Metro pass, are not a true money form unless they are generally acceptable. You can only use a D.C. metro card at the D.C. metro station; prepaid telephone cards will only buy phone calls. Most merchants cannot or will not accept the prototype smart cards currently in existence. However, the technology for making such a leap to a true money form is present and test marketing is well under way.

Initially, the primitive smart card most likely will take the place of currency and coin, at vending machines, say, then move on to serve as general record keeper and banking vehicle within the hand. Perhaps the smart coin may be coated in a thin layer of gold to provide a more traditional feel. The next generation of electronic wallets may transfer money between themselves without any terminal or other bank interface—or they might exist on a chip and memory form within the one ubiquitous piece of plastic.

In the extreme, there may be no physical manifestation at all, merely a transfer of value from computer to computer, the cybermoney of this volume. How, then, may money and banking evolve?

From Goldsmith to Virtual Banker

The concept of a bank may have changed a great deal over the years, but its basic idea is still pretty simple. A bank initiates money transfer from one person (payor) to another person (payee). A bank makes loans and creates money based on some reasonable ratio between reserves and customer deposits. A bank takes in deposits from its customers, and converts (intermediates) these deposits into interest-earning assets.

In return for the use of money, the bank will pay interest and also provide useful services such as loans. In performing these services, a bank need not have brick and mortar walls. It may inhabit cyberspace and be unlike any bank ever before seen. It may look and think like a computer company, with a definitely nonbank-like corporate culture. It may pronounce its own form of reserve base, as long as people are happy with the choice. Within a diverse money-creating conglomerate, the officially designated banker may be the tail wagging the dog, rather than the customary reverse.

The cast of characters changes apace, and in unusual ways. The theme of surprising contrast in players, places, and relevant subject matter—all entwined—recurs throughout. Please feel free to read or browse according to your interest—each chapter is designed to be self-contained.

The Road to the Present

The Format of This Book

Virtual Money traces the road to the present (Chapter 2), with a little money history from gold to photons, then peers within the money machine that puts the pieces together (Part II). From the most successful pioneers came the wholesale or big-value private e-flow money trail (Chapter 3), now fanning out with some trepidation to the open Internet.

The tale shifts focus to the retail plastic, with gradual permeation into almost all layers of society via the ubiquitous credit and debit cards (Chapter 4). Discussion of the exotic e-monies (smart card, e-cash, and cybermoney) and how they work (Chapter 5) is followed by a chapter on the question of money's nature today, both in scientific and economic terms (Chapter 6).

Part III highlights the role of government. Present official money definitions may be obsolete when the effective medium of exchange exceeds the official money aggregates by staggering amounts. The value that people actually may spend is perched, expanding, on a thin sliver of a base. In such cases, links between the reserve base and what serves as a medium of exchange are eroded, perhaps severed altogether (Chapter 7).

Around the world, monetary policy adapts, as the monetary control fundamentals change. So also do the able suppliers for banking services, as discussed in Chapter 8. The Justice Department, after a decade's hiatus, has sharpened its focus in order to halt the onset of any market power by the giants at critical chokepoints. Private competitors throw down the gauntlet to protect their competitive turf as other players have before them (Chapter 9).

Financial globalization becomes reality, in the seamless web depicted by Chapter 10, which provides an overview of the international capital markets-oriented Part IV. These days, money's creation bypasses both national boundaries and currency borders, while the architects of efficient money laundering schemes benefit from a vast electronic "pipe" that commingles the dirty and the clean. That high-tech washing also helps the perpetrators elude detection (Chapter 11). This tortuous journey of clandestine money presents a tale unto its own, which the authorities—now also global—seek to unravel and uncover.

Meanwhile, dipping legitimately in and out of markets around the world with great sophistication are the global banks, traders, and chaos-schooled mathematicians and scientists—strange bedfellows all (Chapter 12).

And, of course, a book on virtual money wouldn't be complete without a look at the amazing real-world influence of the tiny virtual quantum or particle that projects the known forces of the physical world. Both physical and money analogy enjoy transitory existence by benefit of spontaneous overdraft, from either physical or financial world, and ultimately to be repaid like Cinderella money (Chapter 13).

Part V concludes with technology's consequences, the privacy and security issues, and the mathematical locks and keys of arcane encryption (Chapter 14). The money whole is reconstructed, along with updated concepts framed to help us along in the task of understanding the future money stage and its players (Chapters 14 and 15).

––––––––

Our odyssey begins with the story of how banks came to realize that the hard money in their vaults was not the most important kind of money they had to lend. Now it more likely takes the form of computer entries.

A Tale of Money and Banks

Money has value because, given our society, something about it is much prized. Whenever times change, the money form moves on. And, whatever it is that the state of the art has to offer, money and its purveyors also march on. Sometimes the money is very beautiful, sometimes it is a little strange.

Most central banks and many large banks have currency museums that house a collection of items people have been willing to accept in return for the fruits of their labor—everything from huge and decorated slabs of pure gold to tin coins, feathers, and wampum. We may see beautifully engraved pieces of paper and delicate works of art, some passed on from long-gone civilizations. From pre-history to space-age society, these exciting and unusual money collections tell the story of our lives as human beings.

Barter

The narrative of money begins with a most primitive instinct—acquiring something we don't have and can't find or produce ourselves. Primitive people wanted many things that were owned by others, who, in turn, wanted items they couldn't produce or find. When our ancestors first matched mutual wants by exchanging goods, *barter* began. Archaeologists believe that European and Asian tribes routinely met to exchange goods in the Ural Mountains about 12,000 years ago.

This kind of primitive barter worked fairly well for thousands of years, but was nonetheless troublesome. Wants had to match exactly—an early farmer offering wheat for a cow had to find a cow owner who wanted wheat. If the cow swapper wanted a copper tool instead the farmer was out of luck. The farmer could search for a tool maker who would take wheat for his copper, then trade the copper for the cow, but searching took time and didn't always work.

Price was also a problem. One day, three axes might be exchangeable for a small cow, but not for a bushel of wheat. Two weeks later, a hungry toolmaker might willingly swap three axes for the wheat. If there was a drought, you might have to supply five axes for the wheat with maybe a few flints thrown in for good measure. Under these circumstances it was hard, if not impossible, to agree on a "standard of value" or a yardstick for making swaps. Nor was it easy to save—to store up purchasing power for future use on a rainy day. Many commodities that people needed would spoil. Apples might be valuable in the fall, but, if held too long, no one wanted them.

As permanent communities and nations developed, and numbers of transactions grew, barter on a large scale became unworkable. Its difficulties, or transactions costs, increased by leaps and bounds.[1] Barter hasn't totally disappeared, however, and we still use it to some degree. In some communities people often provide their services in exchange for food or housing or specific things they may want. Even in the electronic money marketplace, barter has its place. You may transfer your electronic credits for my electronic credits, or for goods for future delivery. In the interim between money's transfer and final settlement into national currencies, no "real" money changes hands. Or, to cite another example, some test runs of digital cash are conducted in "funny money" or barter on the Net.

Electronic money will always need to be converted (settled) finally into some form of base or commodity money that has intrinsic value or worth, or else it wouldn't be worth much as a long-run standard of value.

Pigs, Cows, and Gold

One by one, early societies realized this and adopted prized commodities as standards for their wealth. They recognized that solving barter's problems meant adopting a medium of exchange, something everyone wanted and accepted. These objects of money standards were generally accepted because they were usable and useful, and thus valuable in themselves. Yet, many commodities had built-in drawbacks that limited their usefulness as money. A good money must be easy to handle—a cow doesn't fit that requirement. It must serve as a standard of value—a uniform measurement of relative worth. It should be capable of being easily subdivided to buy fractions of things, or those less valuable.

Despite their drawbacks, commodity monies have been around for thousands of years. Grain, fish, gunpowder, and shot, for example, were some popular American commodity monies. Indian wampum, feathers, and tobacco are on display in the Continental Bank's collection of moneys. Cigarettes were a commonly accepted medium of exchange in American prisoner-of-war camps during World War II. Tribesmen of New Guinea by tradition accept pigs as a universal money form; they are circulated among the community at communal feasts. The Masai warriors of Africa buy brides with cattle. Of lesser practical utility, the Yap Islanders of the Pacific used massive stone "money" wheels until World War II, while the Bank of Japan displays some remarkably beautiful six-foot iridescent shells that served as early money in the Far East. Massive tablets of pure gold, most artistically carved, can also be seen in that collection, along with engraved ancient coins and early forms of paper currency (Figure 2.1).

It comes as no surprise that gold and silver, the so-called precious metals, became the more enduring commodity standard after they were introduced. Because they were difficult to obtain and many people wanted them, someone offering a precious metal could command more goods than when dealing with with most other commodities. Relative to value, precious metals are light and durable compared to cows, tobacco, or apples. They can be subdivided; they do not spoil or need to be fed or nurtured. Given fixed weights, they can become a commonly agreed on unit of account—you could express prices of what you have to offer in terms of a fixed weight of gold.

Coinage is traced back at least to Egyptian and Greek civilizations, and ancient coins of Alexander the Great from the mid-4th century B.C. are shown in Figure 2.2 (a) from the Philadelphia Reserve Bank's coin collection. By way of contrast, some modern bricks of stamped gold, and their means of rather laborious transfer, are displayed in Figure 2.2 (b). Scrupulous supervision by auditors is required every step of the way to make sure each exchange is exactly correct.

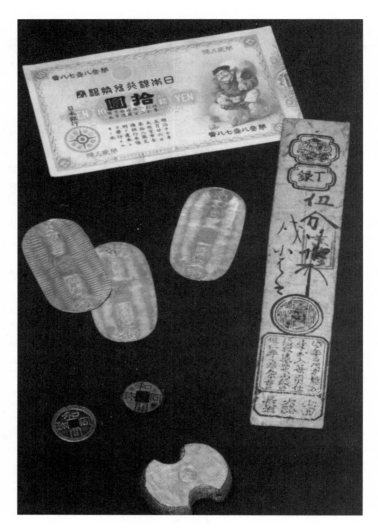

Figure 2.1 The beautiful money forms of Japan, antique and modern. (This photograph was provided by the Currency Museum, Bank of Japan, 1996, and reprinted with their permission.) Clockwise, from top to bottom: 10 Yen Bank of Japan Note: first note of Bank of Japan convertible into silver, 1885; *Yamada Hagaki*: first paper money in Japan, ca. 1600; *Taiko Fundokin*: stamped gold ingot stored for emergency use, late sixteenth century; *Koban*: standard gold coin, seventeenth to nineteenth centuries; *Wado Kaichin* or *Wado Kaiho*: first coins minted in Japan, A.D. 708.

Figure 2.2 Money of Western civilizations, old and new. (a) Coins from the fourth century B.C. *From left to right*: The front of Alexander the Great's tetradrachma bears the head of the young Hercules, and on the other side is shown the seated image of Zeus. Ptolemy I of Egypt broke with tradition to become the first to mint coins with the likeness of a living mortal, himself, on the face of the coin that follows; the eagle on the back is strongly reminiscent of the American symbol. (Photographs were provided by the Federal Reserve Bank of Philadelphia, from their collection as shown in *Coins of the Ancient Mediterranean World*, October 1987, written and researched by John P. Mulcahy.) (b) Supervising a gold transfer. This photograph was provided by the Federal Reserve Bank of New York.

Not to be missed is a trip to the gold vault of the New York Federal Reserve Bank, which acts in custodial capacity for the gold of many central banks. It is quite impossible to express the feeling one encounters when entering its inner sanctum. Once past the guards and multilayered locks in the Bank's sub-sub basement, you get to see the gold, which surprisingly looks and stacks just like ordinary bricks. However, the luminous sheen of 24-kt gold surrounding the walls is something you don't forget—it's a bit like a psychedelic experience. King Midas was not alone—I suppose the rulers of the realm got their fix of the day by gazing on the splendors of this metal. It comes as no surprise that gold survived longer than any other money medium.[2]

Paper Proxies

Of course there wasn't enough gold to go around as societies evolved, and gold also had its own problems: weight, theft, and delivery costs. A critical next step in money's evolution were the paper IOUs, gold certificates, or bank notes from the days of the Renaissance. Often elaborately engraved to help prevent counterfeiting, paper surrogates for gold and silver kept the gold standard alive until well into the twentieth century. Gold as a money standard fit in nicely with the European seventeenth-century philosophy known as mercantilism, which held that nations remained powerful and wealthy by amassing gold and silver and selling more merchandise than they bought. The mercantilists established colonies and took raw materials from these new lands while selling them goods from the home country. As is well known, their explorers also plundered gold from the new lands and brought it back to the kings to spend as they fancied.

Some odd things, however, occurred in Spain that caused a questioning of this practice. In 1776, Scottish philosophy professor Adam Smith published *The Wealth of Nations*, which argued that the source of national power and wealth wasn't gold and silver but the production of goods. Smith showed that the introduction of vast quantities of gold into the money stream at home was not very wise. Without a corresponding rise in the nation's productive capacity, an increase in gold could produce ruinous inflation and depreciation in the money's value. Yet people still craved gold.

Polyglot Money

Gold lived on, but not forever. Its usefulness as a standard of value remained well entrenched until the early 1930s. Then, nations determined that they needed a more flexible money base, one more easily able to be expanded than bricks of pure gold. Gold remains something that people want and use for a variety of personal and industrial purposes, but it is no longer a medium of exchange. It is simply worth too much. Expressed in paper money or deposits, it trades at a higher value than it did before nations abandoned the gold standard.

Meanwhile, we construct our own money pyramids. Each new money form builds on those that already exist. First and still foremost in terms of frequency of use is the garden-variety *physical* money, coins or paper currency, that one can touch and hold.

Accounting money, or bank deposits, became suddenly very important following the Civil War when the National Banking Act of 1963–64 taxed the note issue of state banks. What those who drafted the Act really wanted was to kill off the state banks, with their unfortunate tendency to issue too many notes without proper backing. The goal was to end "free banking" and give the Comptroller of the Currency and Treasury complete control over money and note issue.[3] Exactly as expected, when the government imposed a 10 percent tax on any state bank that issued its own note, the state banks then found it too expensive to do so. Instead, they created their own deposit IOUs, expressed as balance sheet liabilities, that indicated what they owed to deposit customers. Eventually, customers came to accept the bank's IOU to redeem their deposits on demand. Deposits of state banks replaced their bank notes as a form of accounting money that existed only on a bank's ledger. This bookkeeping deposit adaptation was brilliant and state banks greatly increased and thrived. Congress's clumsy attempt to kill them off by taxation and regulation failed miserably.

A similar money transformation is now in progress. A true *computer money* is on the horizon, once people get used to it and believe this e-money to be safe.

Consider how far we've come. Look at the difference between gold and e-money (Figure 2.3). An e-dollar bill (a) weighs nothing and can't be seen except in artist's rendition; a brick of gold (b) weighs 400 troy ounces and dazzles the visual senses. The New York Fed's gold from

Figure 2.3 Gold bricks and e-money. The figure contrasts heavy gold bricks with the weightless e-money form. (a) A representative e-dollar bill. (With permission of the Federal Reserve Bank of Chicago, from *Electronic Money*, August 1996: cover page); (b) Gold bars of many countries held at the Federal Reserve Bank of New York. (This photograph was provided by the Federal Reserve Bank of New York, from *The Key to the Gold Vault*, 1991: cover page.)

many countries is secured in an impressive vault nearly half the length of a football field; the e-bill occupies a mere fragment of space on computer memory.

A "smart card" holds your money in bits and bytes, within a plastic shield that may also serve as credit and debit card and conventional banks are begining to offer it. Often, however, the vendors that supply the unusual "money" or e-cash are not even banks, in any conventional sense. If not linked formally with a bank, they may not presently be regulated, nor required to disclose their money's backing. Their mission is too new, the money's shape too unfamiliar. So it is with banks.

These new vendors of e-money may not resemble the other banking forms we have known over time and work in a different medium entirely. Their expertise may be computer science and mathematics and the fashioning of secure invisible locks (the science of encryption), and safe digital signatures. The metamorphosis in the nature of banks is as great as the drastic change in the invisible money they produce.

Banking's Beginnings

The fundamentals of banking go back thousands of years, and bankers have changed quite a bit over that time. Where and when did banking begin? The Assyrians, Babylonians, and ancient Greeks all practiced simple forms of banking—safekeeping, exchanging foreign coins, and making loans—mainly in connection with trade. Ancient Rome had two types of banks: those that made loans and those that exchanged foreign monies. Banking grew rapidly in the Middle Ages when trade began to flourish. Italy has one of the oldest banking systems; banks were established in Venice in 1171 and in Genoa in 1320.

British banking began almost by accident in the mid-1600s when King Charles I was said to have helped himself to the money that merchants left in his protection in the Tower of London. Although the King later returned the money, the merchants didn't trust him and instructed their clerks to protect their money. But the clerks were not all that honorable either and often secretly borrowed the merchants' money and lent it to goldsmiths, the early bankers of the European Renaissance.

The goldsmith was custodian of the gold that people brought in. He paid a low interest rate for the borrowed money and lent it out at a higher rate. Borrowing and lending this way became so profitable that goldsmiths expanded their operations by soliciting gold coins from the public. They promised safety and an interest return.

Their resourceful sales pitch was well received. The times were ripe for innovation and goldsmiths filled a special need. Merchants were trading in that flourishing era, with countries as far away as the Far East. Gold was a common medium of exchange, the universal money standard, but it was rather dangerous to carry on stagecoach or sailing ship. A new and most promising business was born.

The goldsmith was generally a respected and shrewd man, with pretty good merchandising skills and an admirable track record of delivering the gold back when its owner wanted it. Perhaps the sales spiel for what would be the forerunner to the modern paper bank note went somewhat as follows. "Why carry all that gold around, when you might get robbed, or maybe murdered. Leave the gold with me, in my strongbox. It will be safe—have no fears. To seal the bargain, I will give you a paper IOU that proves that you have *x* number of florins or pounds sterling in pure gold in my strongbox. You can come back for the gold when you finish your long voyage, exhausted but even richer no doubt. Or, you can pass the IOU to someone to whom you owe money and he can get the gold for himself from my vaults. Either way, the gold is safe until it needs to be used. Not to worry."

The goldsmith's IOU, his liability, became a money form—a very significant step.

An Alchemist's Dream

This myth depicts the genius of multiple money creation: an alchemist's dream come true. Very soon the goldsmith figured out a new strategy, phased in at different times and in various ways. The goldsmith, so the story goes, did what any aggressive profit-seeking entrepreneur might do: he took surplus gold and loaned it out for profit at what came to be known as the rate of interest.

But the goldsmith didn't want to go out of business either, in case gold depositors all came in seeking cash in a sort of medieval run on the bank. He calculated customers' habits and how much depositors were likely to require in the way of gold redemptions at any given time. Of course, in order to survive, a goldsmith had to work things out pretty carefully. He needed to compute the ratio of untouched gold in his strongbox relative to all his customer IOUs. Reserves of gold had to be large enough to meet all feasible drains on gold whenever their owners wanted their rightful money back.

It took a while for depositors to realize that the goldsmith was making a good profit on their hard-earned money. When they did catch on, the goldsmith/banker told another valid and equally persuasive story. "Of course I loaned out your money; it would be foolish and wasteful of resources not to. But again, I'll tell you what I will do to make you happy. You will share in the profits. I'll pay you a suitable return or interest. Furthermore, to make you even more financially secure, when you need money for your business ventures, I'll promise I will make a loan to you. It will be very advantageous for us both. Trust me."

Commercial Bank as Friend

From those early and rather crude beginnings today's commercial bank emerged. So also did the hallmark of full-service banking, the traditional customer-banker relationship. "You have a friend at Chase" is a familiar slogan. The concept promises the full menu of loans and services in return for deposits, and dates back many centuries.

The most trusted bankers in the seventeenth and eighteenth centuries claimed to play things conservatively. They took in customer deposits just as banks do today and made loans to their good customers, but these loans were mainly "self-liquidating" commercial loans—short-term loans expected to be repaid within a reasonably brief period. Favorite candidates were farmers seeking to plant and harvest goods or merchants needing to build up inventory for future sale. The conservative cast of these loans helped protect the banker from illiquidity or other disaster and, since the portfolio was mostly loans for commerce, the institution was called a commercial bank.

For most respected banks, this lending caution persisted. Throughout the nineteenth century, many commercial banks sought out safer kinds of agricultural or inventory loans. When the venture paid off, say at fall harvest or after the peak Christmas selling season, the loan was repaid. At that time, the banker's stores of gold and silver, or reserves of the day, were replenished.

But over time many banks revised their strategies. They strayed further and took more risks to make more profits and stretch their range of services. By the early twentieth century, bankers decided that it was perfectly prudent to invest in such short-term assets as Treasury bills or short-term commercial paper of well-known firms. These could be sold quite easily in the market when depositors came to collect their funds and became a form of secondary reserves for the banks. Bankers dabbled in other investments, such as municipal and utility bonds, while still making good on their promise of offering priority loan services to dependable customers.

Of course, this history is also replete with stories of banks that took unjustified risks and of state banks that issued close to worthless paper and helped to fuel banking panics. Wildcat banks of our pre-Civil War era were so named, not entirely in jest, because they inhabited remote areas where wildcats were more numerous than people. These banks had a high mortality rate, but some survived to help finance the West's risk-prone development.

Meanwhile, a most useful kind of shared relationship with other banks, called correspondent banking, developed. The interbank networks of great numbers of independent banks did the work of the branch banking networks that were then prevalent in other countries. Large city banks made reciprocal deals with smaller country banks and loans and services were swapped between big city correspondent and country respondent. Balances of the smaller bank became a sought-after form of deposit and earned a return that was both tangible, such as clearing services and loans, and intangible, in the form of advice.

These informal correspondent networks for the most part performed the job of nationwide branching, and made it easier to exchange information and capital. Thus linked, the numbers of independent commercial banks reached over 30,000 just before the Great Depression annihilated at least half of them. This fractured banking system, an accident of history, has received a great deal of criticism, but it did work. Correspondent banking arrangements also provided some lessons on sharing, useful for the EFT arrangements about to emerge.

Banks of the Electronic Revolution

Innovations came thick and fast in the 1950s and 1960s when computers made their presence abruptly known. Among the most striking were the Eurodollar, federal funds markets, and Citibank's negotiable certificates of deposit (CDs), first tucked into press accounts barely larger than a footnote.

When the early EFT (then called automation) began to supply more speed and flexibility in the mid-twentieth century, banks coined the newer managed-liabilities concept of bank management. As its nomenclature suggests, this technique made possible a more aggressive approach. If you were a large and well-known bank, you might not wish to wait patiently for funds to flow in from those with whom you had long-standing customer relationships. Rather, an astute banker sought to develop funds from sources around the globe through marketable CDs and other means. This strategy was especially useful to banks of the Midwest "unit banking states" who were forbidden by state law from adding branches beyond their principal place of business, and hence were restricted in their ability to attract deposits.

However, after the 1978 failure of Chicago's mighty Continental Bank, which relied too heavily on impersonal external sources of funds such as CDs, the trend has returned to a more balanced form of bank management—assets/liabilities management. The banker attempts to tailor balance-sheet assets more closely to liabilities of similar size and dates of maturity. Large commercial loans in particular have short—sometimes overnight or weekend—maturities; they roll over frequently and automatically at prevailing rates of interest—a safer strategy.

This general philosophy also includes a focus on "off-balance sheet" (nonlending) activities that provide hedging and risk-management services. The good banker thereby hopes to protect both customer and bank against interest and exchange-rate risks and the door is left open for very innovative services that can piggyback on the speed of the electronic flows. The possibilities are many. However, if not properly supervised from within the bank, the newest techniques can lead to unexpected consequences for customers who are seeking safety rather than involvement in modern financial engineering, that they may not fully understand.

Current Banks and Systems

Banking is a little like money in its evolution—the old forms don't go away and we simply see more superimposed layers of the new. The oldest form is the *community or local bank*. It is usually small and closest in concept to the goldsmith and his early descendants, eighteenth-century commercial bankers. A community banker takes in deposits and offers new and traditional banking services to deposit customers as part of a deposit/services package. She offers friendly advice and loans to established customers in the community with whom she lives and works. More elaborate electronic services may also be provided through a big city correspondent or shared network. The customer feels comfortable dealing with a friend, based on trust and long-standing relationships.

Of similar staying power has been the financial *boutique*, which provides services to a limited group of customers who appreciate the specialized skills. In form and function it too is an early and enduring banking offshoot, unlikely to disappear.

More all-encompassing are the *department stores* of finance, who sell many different banking products, as their name suggests. They usually function as affiliates under the bank holding company umbrella of existing banks and may also offer services closely related to banking with Federal Reserve approval and supervision. They provide a great variety of customer services, including foreign exchange, investment advisory, and other non-lending activities. And they have initiated the formation of the modern EFT systems, along with other partners, large and small.

Finally, the *electronic systems* surface as a kind of modern banking phenomenon. Visa and MasterCard, and regional ATM systems, currently provide the standard credit and debit card services, which can get to look a lot like banking. It seems quite possible that these computerized bank-run systems eventually may pull some important services away from their individual bank members such as home banking or the "electronic wallet," a kind of prepaid value. The bank's name may still appear "branded" on the card so the consumer knows who issues the card and who will handle complaints.

However they are fashioned, these alliances will significantly change the banking climate. The electronic system has its own joint needs; the member banks have their own separate ones. These separate goals between systems and members are not necessarily the same, or even compatible. This conflict has generated novel antitrust questions—for example, between founding system members and any newer entrants with different profit-maximizing strategies. These systems make their own rules, as of course they must; yet they don't have the powers to back them up.

Nonbank "Banks"

The real novelty, for banking markets, is the entry into electronic banking of *nonbank systems*. One example from a decade ago is the Discover card, offered originally by a retail merchant, Sears, and later sold to Dean Witter, a large brokerage firm. With the merchant focus already in hand from its Sears' forebears, the Discover card got a solid market following. A few years later AT&T's Universal credit card followed, which offers Visa or MasterCard through a cooperating bank (Universal Bank); the card quickly rose to a prominent credit card position just behind Citicorp and First Chicago.

Some computer and telecommunications firms may believe they have the capacity to supersede banks in marketing prepaid cards, essentially a money substitute. However, Citicorp and other major banks have retaliated by engaging in active global competition for the smart card business—now given the name electronic wallet—and for ATM-generated home banking links around the world.

Why are we suddenly seeing some familiar but definitely unbanklike names surfacing as active participants in the money and banking arena? Specialized nonbank people were always there to deliver the varied pieces of paper, checks or cash; trucks, trains, or airplanes were readily available. In this limited sense, nothing new is added to the equation. But these ancillary suppliers didn't have much clout on their own. Armored delivery trucks were a transportation medium without ambitions; the airlines had their own business priorities. The telephone company in the early days focused on its research and its own very ambitious but nonmoney-related plans. After the AT&T breakup in 1974, fragments of the former vast monopoly were busily preoccupied with establishing their position in telecommunications.

Now advanced technology brings the functions of all these unlikely players closely into the money delivery business, which, of course, has grown larger. Telecommunications firms, here and abroad, deliver the vast flows and have replaced a good portion of the work of the armored vans and the airplanes. They are an integral part of the process. Whether Baby Bells or mother AT&T, they have the deep pockets and imagination to form their own niche in the payments process and are making plans to do just that.

Nor are the computer people, analogous to the check printers and accountants who kept track of things in the old days, about to sit idly by. Computer processors have developed a knowledge of the business from two decades ago when they silently routed our credit card and ATM payments. They are already very active in establishing electronic terminals of their own, at 7-Eleven stores, for example. It is quite possi-

ble that these and other nonbanks may eventually take away from traditional brick and mortar banks a portion of the kinds of bank services
easily switched to an electronic mode. Lost may be some kinds of services that don't require much human interface—or, the human interface
may be supplied on-line, perhaps through an interactive desktop PC or
server on the Internet.

Microsoft has thrown its hat into the Internet ring of electronic commerce and money payments with great fanfare; within a consortium
(which generally includes a bank), many other computer leaders follow.
Banks are particularly wooing Quicken and Netscape along with
Microsoft's Money, and making some tentative choices. In this latest
E-money permutation, where computers get to deliver the money and
possibly manipulate it as well, banks and computer people recognize
their mutual interdependence.

Money Revolutions

Figure 2.4 depicts money over the ages, with its many phases. An appropriate time span occurs between each—physical, accounting, EFT, and
e-money—to allow for the usual innovation, marketing, and digestion
of technologies. Needless to say, that time span has recently shrunk, but
even electronics can take a decent twenty years or so to mature and capture market interest.

Electronic funds transfers (EFT) as wave began to swell in the late
1960s, before it assumed today's tidal proportions. Let's call it the "fast
flows" or "wholesale e-flows" era. For these flows the underlying
money remains the same as always, but can enjoy a much faster ride.
Instructions ordering delivery of the money can convert from clumsy
paper check to nonphysical electronic form—EFT takes our ordinary
money, bank deposits, and gears up instantaneous delivery speeds.

A few years later, and for different reasons, we entered the "plastic
money" era. The fast flows were a *wholesale* event, the flows of the big
money, currency and foreign exchange transactions, intermixed occa-
sionally with some high-value physical goods such as land and corporations.

But plastic was a *retail* phenomenon, and though it got started rather
slowly, it became absorbed into the payment structure around the world
in a matter of two decades. Plastic is now a common medium of
exchange. Underlying it are conventional deposits, either in the form of

MONEY OVER THE AGES

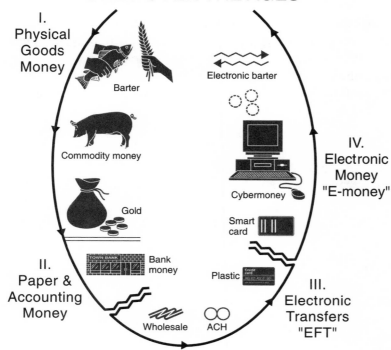

Figure 2.4 Money over the ages. Money's permutations—that is, what people will accept in payment for goods and services—run the gamut. Included in the figure are the physical goods, paper and accounting, electronic transfers (EFT), and electronic money phases. At present, virtually everywhere, all coexist and are blended according to the ways in which we wish to pay (or receive payment) for things we buy from others.

a line of credit (the credit card) or immediate cash (the ATM or debit card). Once again, the underlying money doesn't change—what is different is the manner of its access and delivery. Plastic, not paper, is the access form; electronics, not airplanes or trucks, is the delivery form.

So what is new? You could always take your money from banks and stuff it under the mattress. Now you can pull your money from banks and stuff it into computer memory on electronic purse. Your stash could also be comfortably laid to rest in a computer system owned or stitched together by a nonbank group of collaborating companies. When extracted from its normal resting place, the money may traverse cyberspace like the wandering Dutchman, weaving in and out and never returning.

Money transfer messages move as directed waves or little particles of light—photons. Physicists call them electromagnetic waves; engineers refer to them as signals. Whatever their nomenclature, the nature of money and its transfer (payments) is greatly altered. It has been a long and interesting journey from gold coins to weightless money bits and bytes.

Part II

Inside the Changing Money Machine

Money on the Move

"One, if by land, and two, if by sea; And I on the opposite shore will be." So said Paul Revere in Henry Wadsworth Longfellow's *Paul Revere's Ride*. For Paul Revere, the beam of light provided the means of communicating that the British were riding to Lexington and Concord. The code was the binary set of light flashes, his medium the simple beacon of light hurling messages across the Charles River from a church steeple.

Light and Money's Transfer

Paul Revere's use of the lantern's light waves was strictly limited in space and time. To get to the minutemen assembling in Lexington and Concord, the message that the British were coming required further trips by horseback. Today, the beam of light is the jostling forward of a stream of elementary light particles, or photons. You can also say that the messages to transfer money move as rippling waves of light, since photons exist in dual form as both wave and particle. The on-and off signals of the simple beacon translate into the binary one and two code of computer language. What's substituted for the human eye is the sightless computer on the satellite's transponder that drops the signal back to earth for human reception. For this process at least, the horse is obsolete. Today's gross payments flows travel directly to intended recipients over vast distances and almost instantaneously.

Let's look at other changes wrought when digitally encoded money messages move as flows of light or electricity rather than as bags of checks, with their pen and ink-conveyed instructions. In the olden days at a Fed bank, many women manually sorted the checks and read the writing and signatures; others felt the currency to detect counterfeits. They were proud of their work. How can you tell a counterfeit bill, was the typical question. It's easy, you can feel the difference—you just know, was the answer. If that was how you made your living, your fingertips got to be very sensitive. For check clearing, with its bags and batches of paper, your eyesight was also pretty good.

Encryption, a mathematics branch that we have heard a great deal about recently, now provides the security for e-flows. For the daily trillions that move the cyberspace route, computers and mathematicians do the work of my earliest friends at Boston's Federal Reserve Bank.

Wholesale Megamoney

Computers and EFT systems move the large and distant money flows, and have for the past two decades. Between them, the Federal Reserve Fedwire and CHIPS (run by private New York clearing banks) transfer over two trillion dollars daily, on average. When you add the retail wires to that, we see money traffic on the electronic superhighway—that we know about—equal *in only one day* to over one-third the U.S. GDP (gross domestic product) for the entire year.[1]

Most central banks now have, or are building, electronic systems of their own. So too are the largest multinational corporations, often from leasing bits and pieces of public and privately fashioned links. There are private "virtual" links, carved out from cyberspace according to need. Many firms use electronic data interchange (EDI), which "bundles" and sends all manner of useful corporate information. Small retail consumers also have worldwide links—globally compatible ATMs or automated clearing houses (ACHs). Through them we can get instant cash halfway around the world, in Moscow or Tokyo, from the same kinds of machines we use in Washington or New York.

Invisible and impermanent threads bind us all through cyberspace. The overhanging maze includes the interlinked computers, the Internet, private networks, cable, TV, and even cellular phones. Together they make up the Information Superhighway. Call that the I-Way if you wish to go the slang route, or the National Information Infrastructure (NII) or the Global Information Infrastructure (GII) if you want to be more formal.

The term cyberspace, borrowed from the science fiction writings of William Gibson, includes the entire web of invisible and intangible paths generated throughout the space continuum. Cyberspace well explains the essential idea of the latest and most improbable payments medium.

From Cave to Space Age

When we talk about payments systems, what exactly does that term mean? Quite simply, a payments system is an agreed upon way to transfer payment between buyer (payor) and seller (payee) in a transaction. The system can be slow or fast, physical or virtual.

From prehistory to the present, our payments media span an impressive range: from canoe and sailing ship, to truck, train, and airplane, from the clumsy to the swift. They all are part of the paper payments mechanism that by definition gets money from me to you. In the last half of the twentieth century, we graduated to magnetic tape, hard-wired telephone cable, or microwave relay bouncing its way forward. The next step was to beam the money message to a transponder on a satellite 22,000 miles up, then down to a distant earth station near or at the site of recipient payee. The most thoroughly modern of the lot is fiber optics technology, which can wire cities or link nations beneath oceans. It has speeded up money's use and rendered some profound changes.

The contrasts are startling. The paper-based mode of shipping money involves the physical moving of billions of pieces of paper, or checks, through the payor bank and its clearing house, and/or the Federal Reserve Bank. The check you write is bundled up with other checks. Today, that piece of paper, with many companions, will probably travel by airplane if the payee who is due to get your money happens to live some distance away. It is an improvement over truck or sailing ship. Still, the journey can be very long and expensive. The paper check enjoys a nice tour around the country, perhaps the globe, before arriving back at the originating payor bank for appropriate deduction from your bank account.

When the Federal Reserve System transfers paper checks or cash by conventional means—trucks, trains, even airplanes—the process is stodgy. The money cannot turn over very fast, especially when the transfer is between countries, and the many steps the check may take along its physical route from buyer to seller are tiresome. In a variety of transportation forms, the simple check ricochets from bank to bank.

During all the time the money moves between banks from check writer (payor) to end receiver (payee) it is said to undergo clearing, and usually a clearing or Federal Reserve Bank enters into that process as well. There are bags of cash to move around and put into the right piles for delivery. Transportation delays, rain or snowstorms, tornados and the like can slow things. One or two weeks may elapse before the checks are eventually collected or "settled"—that is, deducted from the check writer's (payor's) bank account and credited to the seller's (payee's) bank account in a useable form.

Money Superhighways

With EFT, transfer delays are minimal and there are many possible payment paths. Payments may proceed over hard-wired telecommunications links such as the early Fedwire or private "dedicated" lines. Using hard wires, dug in a trench, or strung on unsightly poles, such payments move only at the speed of electricity. However this transmission mode, which looks fast when matched with paper-based standards, is also going the way of the dinosaur. Satellite or fiber-optics are fast conquering the electronic wholesale market where money messages streak above or below us as pulses of light.

Payors and payees may also use microwave relay facilities, but these are now somewhat outdated because microwaves only travel for line-of-sight and require relays of towers to transmit a message over longer distances.

The newest technologies thus make possible an almost instantaneous delivery of vast amounts of an electronic proxy for spendable money and can carve out the most efficient and cheapest virtual routes as well. They are also being used increasingly for long-distance wholesale transactions. Why, then, did it take so long for the technology to begin to penetrate?

Schizophrenia, Wholesale vs. Retail

There is a dichotomy between the average retail consumer, the small dollar payor, who—despite some recent avid wooing—is still mostly wedded to paper (or plastic), and the multinational corporation or financial institution or trader, whose money streaks almost entirely via satellite and the fiber-optic routes.

How can one explain the difference in choice? One important reason is the cost of the private bank wires, the Rolls-Royce of money transfer forms. In addition, there are such matters as interest earned and foregone, float, and the security of the message transmission.

Right now, our physical money—coin and paper currency—still accounts for the bulk of individual money transactions *by number*. Coins tend to be dropped into machines, and dollar bills still buy things for those without checks, credit cards, or any other options. This is shown graphically in Figure 3.1. It depicts two triangles, one for the *volume* of transactions (on the left) and one for their *dollar value* (on the right). With electronics (on top), checks (the center), and currency and

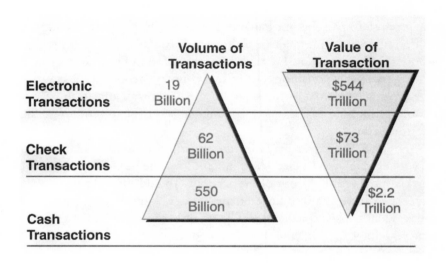

Figure 3.1 U. S. payments structure. Portrayed are the major ways we now pay for things: through currency and coin, paper and check, and electronic payments. When we look at the *values* of transactions, electronics predominates, since the very large or wholesale amounts are transferred to others by electronic wire. However, when we examine the *numbers* of transactions, currency and coin still overwhelmingly come out ahead. (Figures and data for 1995 were provided by the Federal Reserve Board of Governors, Washington, D.C.)

coin (the bottom), the two pyramids shown in this format are an inverse of each other. It is obvious that electronic modes overwhelmingly predominate for large payments, and represent close to 90 percent of all payment *value*.

When we look at payment transactions by *number*, however, the story is quite different. Currency such as dollar bills and coin overwhelmingly win out. Coins in vast numbers are swallowed up by traffic meters, soft drink machines, highway tolls, and the like. The folding bills that date their history back to the early Renaissance goldsmith are not going to go away very soon either, despite talk of the emerging checkless/cashless society. They are easy to use and can yield psychic satisfaction in the manner of well-counted stores of glittering gold.

Moreover, we still tend to want to *access* our deposits through the paper check, when the amounts are relatively small as, for example, when the plumber comes to fix a leaking faucet. Repairers of laser printers and fax machines also like to be paid by check. The check represents our promise to pay, via our bank and on through the seller's bank that will reimburse the plumber or technician through crediting his or her account. This indirect, rather time-consuming form of payment is called a debit transfer, and is popular. In this country, people don't want to give up either the float or the safety of the paper trail and so the check retains a firm hold at the center. But big-value payments tend to go the electronic route.

Of course, the buyer may not like the idea of fast EFT transmittal very much. He may be charged quite a lot for the dubious privilege of quickly moving money out of his account. To add insult to injury, the buyer also loses the free float normally associated with payment by check. Float consists of the money you retain to play with between the time you draw, or make up, the check and the time it actually is debited from your bank account some days after. The delay can be quite long, especially in far-flung transactions, and the float is an attractive subsidy. So when you pay someone, why should you choose anything other than paper?

The answer is that there are the two sides to consider. The person getting paid, the seller, may take a quite different view. It is certainly not in her interest to delay payment since she loses the interest the money might earn if delivered promptly. She may insist on payment by wire transfer, in, for example, large real estate, merger, or financial transactions. She will then get her money at the same time that title to the assets is transferred from the buyer. For her, electronics is the best route.

The problem does not exist to this extent in most other countries. The European payment structure is already mostly direct or credit-based, with direct wire transfer taking the bulk of the payment value, or 78 percent. Indirect and debit-based checks are a relatively small amount, only 2 percent. The use of credit transfer payments instruments such as GIRO (19 percent by value) is substantial. With a credit transfer, the money goes directly from the buyer's account to the seller's, whether GIRO or electronic wire. The transition from GIRO to electronic wire is easier since the check payor's subsidy of float is not a factor.

Overall, the main differences between the United States and Europe are: (1) Europe has more credit transfers including GIRO (reducing risk because payment times are greatly shortened); and (2) Europe uses more electronic transfers (reducing cost as well as time). As Fedwire, CHIPS, or even Internet usage grows, we too will move toward the credit-based European GIRO system: payment will go from buyer (payor) to seller directly, eliminating paper-based float and the implicit check-based subsidy.[2]

A Primer of Wires

The Federal Reserve defines Fedwire as its electronic facility that transfers reserve balances (deposits at a Fed Bank) in real time (or immediately) by dedicated wire. Fedwire transfers the balances among private banks in Federal Reserve Bank deposits, or legal reserves, and is the favored wire for domestic large-dollar transfers. The transfer of value on Fedwire is always direct, final, and irrevocable, and it has grown from $2.6 trillion in 1977 to well over $223 trillion today.

Shortly after the Fed opened shop, it introduced its first dedicated funds transfer network in 1918. Proudly featured was the latest available technology—a Morse code system, coexisting with some actual hard wires. But telegraph operators weren't easy to find, and the Fed converted its Morse code network to a teletype machine system during the 1930s. After World War II, funds-transfer activity moved to much higher levels, which unfortunately made transmission delays more common, and in 1953 the Fed replaced its teletype network with an automatic message system.

Still greater innovations awaited. In 1967, the Federal Reserve burrowed its message switching center securely into the side of a nearby mountain. Meanwhile, old portions of the system were replaced with computerized, high-speed electronic telecommunications and processing systems. The Internet-type packet switching techniques were introduced in the late 1970s, to make the message transfers more secure and glitch-free. I first heard about packet switching at an intergovernmental meeting from Henry Geller, then Assistant Secretary of Commerce for Telecommunications, and wondered what it was supposed to do. The notion that you could send messages out in scattered bits and pieces and expect them to rejoin at their destination seemed improbable then. Fedwire was no longer just a wire, but becoming a constantly changing computer-directed path, through fiber-optics strands. But that continued to be its name.

CHIPS (Clearing House Interbank Payments System) is run by private banks, out of New York. Its focus is international, and its dollar value has jumped from $16 trillion in 1977 to over $310 trillion today. CHIPS usually handles foreign exchange and other large-value international transfers. Net settlement is in dollar reserves through the Federal Reserve Bank of New York. The approximately 130 CHIPS participants control their risk through a combination of bilateral net debit caps and aggregate net debit limits. There is also a formal loss-sharing agreement backed by dedicated collateral held on a custodial basis by the Federal Reserve Bank of New York. The major work is done by thirty-nine or so members, for the accounts of the others, including some major foreign banks.[3]

Common Carriers and Private Patchwork Quilts

But the story doesn't stop there. Actual money transfer occurs, and it doesn't usually take the form of moving gold bricks from one pile to another. What do CHIPS and Fedwire do with their member money messages after they are entrusted with the valued information contained in them? Abruptly, we enter the difficult realm of telecommunications with its mysteries.

Someone has to do the work of sending and receiving, of converting electronic signals for money transfer to pulses of light. Banks hire telecommunications people for this job, and may lease the lines of domestic or foreign carriers to provide transportation routes. It is as if the banks were hiring armored vans, or buying dedicated planes, to transfer the heavy bags of checks.

And, since you go farther and faster, cooperation is very often the name of the game. International transmission "lines" are generally provided by the joint investment of communications companies; when two or more countries use the facility, switching remains in national hands at either end. Transoceanic cable systems have consortium ownership that traditionally reflects the degree of national use of the cable. Satellite transmission facilities are collectively owned and operated by the world's governments through Intelsat, also with shares proportional to national use of the system. A series of intergovernmental agreements effectively divided transmission between satellites and cables. The Federal Communications Commission (FCC) authorizes competitive international satellite systems and allocates scarce slots in space to bidders.

All these public or common carrier networks afford universal access to highly standardized services at regulated rates or tariffs. As the "shipper" of bank services overseas by wire, you know that AT&T and MCI must take you, at a somewhat regulated price. Nonetheless, many banks have chosen to create their own communications networks. A bank might start off by leasing international cable circuits and satellite capacity, then interconnect to some public network and its in-house terminal and back-office lines. The bank then enjoys full control over network operations. Only a few very large financial institutions can afford this luxury of elaborate international private data networks, but many institutions have some strategically placed point-to-point leased circuits to tie together their far-flung locations.

The Commerce Department's NTIA (National Telecommunications and Information Administration) elaborated on this theme almost ten years ago, and the Twentieth Century Fund followed up in 1995.[4] Financial firms often lease private networks to interconnect many local area networks (LANs). It has been difficult for telephone operating companies to provide these specialized connections with standard equipment because of frequent incompatibilities between computer and communications architectures. The patchwork quilts of private lines fill in the gaps. For example, the Office of Technology Assessment states that Manufacturers Hanover Trust in 1992 had a T1 (high-speed) backbone network providing transport between its U.S. locations, and a global X.25 packet-switching network based on Telnet (now Sprint hardware and software) connecting fifty-two cities in twenty-seven foreign countries.[5]

Let's look at other examples of network architecture. During the 1980s, Citibank developed 100 separate private networks covering 92 countries. Each Citibank business unit developed networks, or contracted for them. Beginning in 1992 they combined into one global information network, or GIN. Citibank's goals were seamless technology integration, with common architecture across national boundaries. Also at about this time, Citibank developed compatible ATMs around the world .

Chase, on the other hand, has used a private packet-switched network provided by Tymnet, which is owned by British Telecom, just to show the global flavor of all this. Bank of America has a similar packet-switched network to support its World Banking Division. We earlier saw that a packet-switched system lets the highly intelligent system decide on the spur of the moment how to route the message, in tiny packets of information, without any predetermined nodes.

In a different engineering wrinkle, Bankers Trust's private network, created in 1982, has some twenty-four-hour trading circuits for direct trading between countries where the business day overlaps. One interesting aspect here is that satellite links are relegated to backup status; Bankers Trust is said to prefer terrestrial to satellite links for avoiding the several seconds delay that is disorienting for traders and may affect their ability to trade in volatile moments.

The story wouldn't be complete without mentioning the VANS, or value-added networks. VANS take the data given them and do something new, or added—for example, authorize credits or validate a credit card's use. The most widely used VAN is the Belgian-based SWIFT (the Society for Worldwide Interbank Financial Telecommunications). With over 2,000 members, SWIFT is technically a message and not an EFT system. However, since it provides the *instructions* to move money's ownership from bank to bank around the planet, its activities are crucial. SWIFT messages instruct a bank to make payment, and the bank then transfers funds from one account to another on its books.

For many purposes SWIFT is considered an EFT system because its messages are accepted by banks as authentic and authoritative, and it has good security. SWIFT II, completed in 1992, offers a netting service for banks trading in ECUs (the European Currency Unit) and the automatic matching of foreign exchange and money market transactions. Around the world, its message volumes have risen most dramatically, from 3.2 million in 1977 to 604 million in 1995.

Electronic Commerce

The term "electronic commerce" is newly minted. Private wires will continue to expand, but electronic commerce may build on the experience of large-value bank flows—the first to take the plunge—and broaden the base dramatically. It portends the inclusion of business firms of only moderate size, and suggests the democratization of the electronic wholesale flows, much as the ATM achieved two decades earlier.

Electronic commerce currently conveys the hand of the Internet, but ACH (Automated Clearing House) technology predates the Internet jump on the bandwagon by quite a bit. The ACH is an automated and paperless payment mechanism used primarily for low-value payments. Originally established by the Federal Reserve Banks, ACHs now are also offered by a few private sellers, such as VISA and Chase. Here is an example of how a government-sponsored (and subsidized) sector could be turned over to private firms, but not very quickly.

In a high-tech age, ACHs prove very useful in a variety of ways. Their security isn't quite up to the level of Fedwire or CHIPS, but their cost is less and they focus on smaller amounts. ACHs speed up clearing for recurrent utility bills and mortgage payments and through direct deposit more rapidly credit Social Security and other government checks. Corporate as well as individual use is expanding, especially for plastic payments. State Treasurers often insist that tax payments be sent this way.

ACH thus becomes a mechanism for clearing all kinds of private electronic payments, such as debit cards for gas stations and supermarkets. It serves the popular commercial base, electronic commerce at a grass roots level, as it were. It is also an important part of the complex electronic government food stamp program EBT (electronic benefits transfer) and the corporate electronic tax paying to be phased in by 1999.

As far back as the early 1980s, ACH technology was indelibly linked with EDI (electronic data interchange) now creeping into the Internet focus as well. ACH was always considered the cheaper and lower-cost medium; the ACH technology continues as a more secure route (at present) for electronic commerce than the open Internet.

If you are a business manager, you may appreciate the convenience of EDI and your banker knows it. With EDI you may instantly track your inventory, payments, and goods shipments. You may pay your suppliers and in turn receive payment from your own customers. EDI allows the traditional banking "bundling" to go hog wild. The money flows are just part of a broader information package useful to a corporation and its customers. One can't say in whose company the payments information thus packaged may travel—invoices, inventories, suppliers, customer orders, you name it. Payment flows are certainly not of a size to match those of their large wholesale brethren wires, but suppliers of EDI services, whether bank or nonbank, are generally sophisticated.

Financial EDI systems come in several varieties: those that clear through banks entirely and those that clear through nonbank VANS such as SWIFT, then spin off the appropriate bank information for bank action at some later date.[6] In the second case it seems unclear, at least in this initial stage of burgeoning EDI technology, just when and how the payment portions of the EDI "bundle" will clear in deposit money. As of early 1997, only limited numbers of banks were prepared to handle it.

The Whole Skein

Fifty years ago the overlap between telephone, banking, and radio and later TV was slim. You could visualize separate spheres of banking and business influence as separate circles with just a little overlap. When people banked, they and their banks might use the telephone, but it was not a primary tool, and your checks were usually shipped out for physical delivery. Clearing houses were bank run; informal arrangements would do the trick since common areas were not abundant.

Now, these separate spheres coalesce in what has been come to be known as the continuum of cyberspace—the threads woven by telephone and telecommunications media, radio and TV, cable, computers, direct broadcast satellite (DBS), and mobile radio and cellular phone. The territory of one area impinges on that of the others and we can think of them all as potential money deliverers—even creators.

Only those adept at engineering can thoroughly fathom the diverse links through which our money flows, and more often than not they can't completely know them, either. Computer hierarchies within the so-called virtual private nets may pick and choose this routing, sometimes on the spur of the moment. Don't ever think that virtual concepts are only in the realm of science fiction, the entertainment media, or quantum mechanics. You may very well be getting those crystal clear sounds in your next trans-Atlantic phone call over virtual lines.

What do these virtual lines have to offer compared with dedicated lines in use day in and day out? It is a simple matter of cost and efficiency.

Dedicated circuits for exclusive use, irrespective of their volume of traffic, can be quite wasteful when usage is sporadic. In the early 1990s, some imaginative engineers figured out ways to fashion virtual private networks (VPNs) that operate on a much more efficient principal.

The VPNs allocate lines dynamically on need, and so there won't be the same links every time (hence the name virtual network). Such a system works more efficiently because sophisticated "intelligent" software lies behind the network switches. Many financial institutions initially worried about quality control and predictability, but VPNs actually have extra reliability compared to discretely leased circuits since they are dynamically switched if line failures occur.

Here we have the Internet principle once again—if the financial information can't get through on one route, the computer switches it to another.

The Internet Overlay

Now let us superimpose yet another overlay, the Internet itself. The Net functions exclusively on virtual lines because packet switching is the nature of its original design. The Net will provide the springboard for new products that its imaginative designers from all countries may introduce that can find market favor. As most everyone knows, the Internet splices on ingenious programs for getting things done and enhances the software and consumer base in potentially very revolutionary ways.

What is most significant for our purposes is that the entry of the Internet into money delivery can cut the familiar banking links. When we have electronic commerce on the Internet, we may also covet a little e-cash to feed our buying appetites on-line. These won't be the big flows, where security is paramount, and banks may enter the process in a central or perhaps marginal way—it all depends on who gets there first and can best establish trust.

In 1994 the White House Office of Science and Technology began to sponsor and provide "seed funding" for a global consortium of private firms—banks, Internet providers, computer and telecommunications companies—to pilot the concept of combining electronic commerce and payments. It's another name for EDI, and the Internet rather than the formal ACH appears to be the chosen mechanism, once security bugs are removed. The CommerceNet included some well-known members of diverse talents such as IBM, the Japanese NTT, Citicorp, Bank of America, AT&T, NYNEX, Mitsubishi, and BBN Planet. There is quite a long membership list, and you can study global opportunities by browsing the World Wide Web at the following address: http://www.commerce.net.

Through this or one of many other private consortia emerging from the cyberspace continuum, the Internet may begin to take on the job of money transfer and become a possible major vehicle for electronic commerce. The banks and their new associates (and also competitors) advertise their wares on the Web, in quite extravagant designs. Now we may choose a virtual bank medium, transfer deposits to it, then move them to somewhere else by the click of a mouse on our home computer. The retail world can slide easily into the process, given some satisfactory security assurances. You and I may deliver electronic money directly, just as we may pass physical money from hand to hand. The mouse or PC becomes our hand, the transfer an ethereal, but no less binding one.

In the Old Executive Office Building of the White House I spent some time with Dr. Michael Nelson, who with Vice President Gore is and has been a prime mover of all this. I asked whether the Internet or its successor will be a major part of electronic commerce. He replied, "Yes, an important part, a prototype that shows that thousands of networks can link together and carry traffic from one part of the globe to another. It is a good model but by no means the only one. Internet will evolve, as will other new technologies, new phone networks and cable networks, huge digital networks that move bits back and forth. We're not quite sure which technology will win out, but there will be faster and faster systems, getting cheaper and cheaper and more reliable and of better quality, as long as we allow for real competition in the marketplace."[7]

Major vendors nowadays ply their trades, and will advertise their tangible wares, with pictures, on the World Wide Web. They also take credit cards. The banks that tried to give American Express a little competition for a very good thing three decades ago didn't realize that by now plastic would be everywhere. Their triumphs, and travails, exemplify an unexpected success story.

4

Plastic Everywhere

While the big money flows careened around the globe, the retail ones phased in with quiet persistence. Their speed has been slower, the money values much less, but this impact is no less profound. Plastic is the electronic medium for consumers, and it has flourished quite unexpectedly. Over three decades plastic has matured; the system has worked —and well. It is an electronic success story.

The term "plastic money" is of course a misnomer. Credit cards provide a line of credit, until eventually repaid in deposit money. In much the same way, the ATM converts regular deposits into cash, given proper signals from the plastics's magnetic strip; the plastic itself doesn't hold value within a memory bank of any sort.

But plastic fooled everyone. It defied logical definitions and became acceptable around the world, even by people who were afraid to take personal checks. The credit card company stands behind the deal and provides guaranteed convertibility into "real" money. Plastic has become a true worldwide money form. But in the beginning there was some queasiness.

Concerns and Reality

Market concerns in the infancy of credit and debit card development ran as follows:

1. Consumers may find novel innovations, for which they feel the proper security may be lacking, prematurely embedded in the payments mechanisms.

2. Consumers may wind up with systems they want, but with fewer options or at higher cost due to private market power.

3. Consumers may lose subsidies such as free float (interest-free loans), perceived as rightful system advantages, and enjoyed under paper-check-paying-systems.

4. Some consumers may be left out of the new payments systems altogether—for example, through private-supplier "cream skimming" that targets the affluent user and leaves poorer and high-cost, higher risk-groups by the wayside .

5. If market power persists somewhere up the line, say by a merger of the two giant credit card systems, other adventurous companies with a good and different product to offer will have trouble entering the market since the user base will already be taken.

6. Or, finally, the government may so fully control the new payments system that private innovation wilts, discouraged by the government's scrambling of normal market incentives.

But what has happened? Concerns 1, 2, and 4 have failed to materialize. Sectors of society have been drawn in, bit by bit, with the entry of the poor just now occurring. Concern 3, the loss of free float, is becoming reality as interest-free grace periods shrink, but an end to that giveaway is perhaps inevitable and not to be decried. With respect to concern 5, the Justice Department worries that the specter of monopoly power may arise again. And, over our heads, is still the threat of undue government intervention in the process, concern 6, as fanned by some recent scandals and risks of exotic varieties.

Let's look at the other side of the picture. Benefits from plastic have been more expansive and certainly more addictive than expected. The credit card may have made profligate spenders out of some, but it has produced died-in-the-wool converts out of most of us. We can't imagine a world without the ubiquitous plastic—it allows us more services and convenience. Our costs of "buying" simple banking services such as cash access slim down when costs are defined to include time and waiting aggravation along with such measurable travel costs as gasoline and shoeleather. Money holders can, and do, shift easily and cheaply from low- and zero-yielding money forms into higher earning assets.

The Changing Money Machine

These results couldn't have been foreseen two decades ago. In distinct phases, people flocked to retail plastic payments forms and few population sectors are excluded. Recently, competition has been keen, almost cutthroat. Merchants take heed, and consumers have generally gotten what they want—and often more than they can digest.

The Siren Song of Plastic

Americans—and the world generally—have entered the seductive domain of plastic money decade by decade. First to be wooed were upscale customers, the big spenders as it were. Given the success and profitability of the venture, the upper middle income types were lured next. Middle America—anyone who might possess a bank account— entered the sacrosanct world of electronic money later, and in the final stages of this electronic sweep we see the entry of the poor, those who depend on the safety net, and receive and spend food stamps.

You might think that your income level first got you your place in the world of plastic and you would be right. Now technology interest, and adeptness, determine your place in the epoch of cybermoney we are entering.

For acceptance into the world of plastic at its start over a generation ago, you were known to want to spend; for retail e-money wooing you will want to surf the Internet or the other realms of cyberspace, where the virtual vendors of the future can reach you. You will mingle with the technically knowledgeable and you must understand the lingo. You are more likely to be young and technically curious than powerful and rich. Yet the analogies are clear, and the issues similar.

Courtship's Start

The saga of the plastic retail transformation begins in about the mid-sixties when American Express, Carte Blanche, and Diners Club developed the "proprietary" (or single-ownership) travel and entertainment (T & E) credit cards. At that time they aimed their sights at the affluent few. The green plastic card, marketed as a status symbol, was conceived as useful for frequent travelers who needed a readily acceptable means of charging for expense account or high-ticket items away from home. If you lived on the well-traveled East and West Coast, your chances of being wooed were heightened—you were deemed likely to spend more.

The vendors' marketing strategy was dual-edged. Money's first criterion—acceptability—was the key. The card purveyors needed card-holders eager to spend and charge. Equally critical were merchants willing to accept the card and accommodate cardholders. To make the system work, both sides of the equation were essential. Thus, the early systems signed up as many suitable cardholders as possible. They paid an annual fee for membership, but were not charged interest on current balances. Holders were expected to be honorable and pay more or less on time in order to retain their privileges.

For the other side of the equation, the accepting merchants, the emphasis was also on "better" classes of vendors. Very upscale merchants were persuaded to agree to accept the card as payment for the ticketed item, say, a fine meal or designer gown. This particular green card was a source of both prestige and convenience for the expense account diner, who might be taking a valued client out to dinner in a strange city. The merchant would enjoy extra business and secure payment, free from worry over whether the check was going to bounce. The diner's credit slip went directly to the local office of the credit card company for almost immediate payment.

In return for an interest charge (the merchant discount, or percentage deduction from face value), AmEx would promptly transfer payment to the merchant's bank account. AmEx later billed the cardholder who in effect received a short-term loan until the account was settled in full. As more merchant establishments joined one or more of the three major T & E systems, each card became still more useful to cardholders.

Quite clearly, synergy was operating between numbers of merchant members and the breadth of the cardholder base. That was not surprising: you can't have a useful card unless there is a satisfactory number of merchants willing to accept it. And merchants won't care to incur the trouble and expense of joining the system unless plenty of cardholders are out there to use it.[1]

Bank Suitors

Next to emerge were the bank credit cards, emboldened by the extraordinary success of the T & E cards. Their inevitable entry, however, was marked by a more egalitarian approach. They found a new niche and sought out the upper middle, and later middle-income, classes and plugged some very gaping market holes.

More limited forms of store credit had been around after World War II, but you could only use your Garfinckle's card at Garfinckle's or a

Bloomingdale's card at Bloomingdale's. The T & E format first introduced the "all-purpose" (or general) credit card that could be used among a group of member merchants and banks were not content to let AmEx and Diners Club reap in the profits unchallenged. Their delay in entering the flourishing business probably reflected both the large scale needed for general-purpose card entry and the recognition of the risk-sharing advantages of joint-operation.

The banks changed the successful AmEx format in joining together. Both bank credit card systems, Visa and MasterCard, started as local joint ventures between member banks. Generally nonprofit, they operated under specific rules and regulations designed to lower costs and unnecessary duplication and help eliminate fraud and misuse.[2]

Bit by bit, they consolidated and linked operations. To achieve greater acceptability, a prime ingredient for any medium of exchange, local and then regional bank card systems merged. They forged stronger national card systems with still broader merchant and cardholder bases, and with acceptability not only in the United States but also abroad. Around the world a new credit-based payments medium based on plastic money was born—a forerunner of electronic money's future. Two competing national bank systems emerged in 1970 to promote the all-purpose cards, National BankAmericard (NBI, with a later name switch to Visa) and Master Charge/Interbank (later MasterCard).

In the Visa joint venture, each card-issuing member bank was a principal (Class A) member. Agent (Class B) system members dealt through their principal (Class A) banks, often their correspondents. MasterCard developed in similar fashion from local to national system. It expanded from its original nucleus, the California Bank Card Association and Marine Midland Bank system. Along the way the necessary payment mechanics, electronic delivery, and interchange developed.

The Fed was conspicuously absent from this process. Systems got to do their own clearing, first on their own books, then with a clearing bank (e.g., Bank of America) that often made temporary loans to members as needed. In the usual tiered process, final settlement might then take place over the books of the Fed through Fedwire if the payee bank did not maintain an account with Bank of America. Visa (with Bank of America and their BASE I and II clearing systems) apparently was doing a good job in its role as mini central bank; MasterCard had equal success with a similar system. The Fed had no particular need to intervene.

Everyone in the business talked about the market synergy between the size of the cardholder base and that of the merchant base. To get things going, you had to boost both, ideally at about the same time. Both cardholders and merchants were critical, and the more of each and the broader the geographic area the better. The credit card companies pushed and promoted wide-scale acceptability, but it took some doing and quite a lot of card promotor risk. Successful early vendors expected to run losses on the plastic operation for quite a few years. And indeed they did.

In the beginning, the credit-worthy cardholder was enticed into the bank card system by mailings and incentives. Scarcely a week passed when some bank member of one system or the other did not deliver entreaties for membership. Free credit was one lure; the new member normally did not pay any annual fee nor incur any interest charge until a free-float (or grace) period, normally three to four weeks, was over. Where, then, was the source of profits that finally accrued? Late payors, of course, did incur interest charges on outstanding revolving credit balances and merchants paid the merchant discounts as a percentage of the gross charge.

The most sophisticated card users, with the best cash flow situation, tended to pay on time. In effect, they got a free ride, piggybacking on the fees of late-paying cardholders and merchants. But they also tended to spend the most, and it's possible that some of the costs—but certainly not all—were transferred back to them in the form of higher prices.

The Way It Works

These systems generally did and still do work as follows. Bank credit cards are offered to depositors or other creditworthy individuals. The bank members of the credit card system agree to provide a line of credit to the cardholder at the member retail establishment. Merchants pay a merchant discount, or percentage of gross, for the privilege of turning the charge draft over to the member bank agent of the bank card company for prompt bank account credit. The merchant's bank then clears or "interchanges" that paper with the cardholder's bank, again for a charge (the interchange fee). Finally, the cardholder's bank collects from the cardholder.

Figure 4.1 below depicts the complicated process. You might call it a form of clearing and settlement, but conducted by private banks without benefit of the normal clearing steps of central bank or clearing house intervention. Still, in both cases, the analogies look a little like plumbing; there are credit "pipelines" and flows in several directions.

Let's say that cardholder Andrea holds a major credit card issued by her bank. It could be any major credit card—Visa, MasterCard, or its newer competitors. Andrea wishes to dine with a client at a fine restaurant and chooses the (fictitious) La Premiere. The price of the meal for two is $100, just to make the math easy. Again, to simplify, let's say the merchant discount—the percentage charge to La Premiere—is set by the

CREDIT CARDS

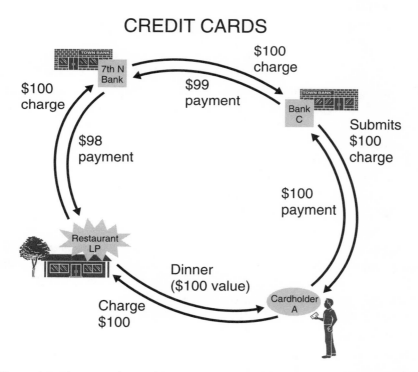

Figure 4.1 Plastic credit cards: how they work. The joint bank credit card of the 1970s portrayed a new and entirely private payments model, a very successful one outside the Federal Reserve. The credit card charge moves from buyer to merchant to merchant bank (7th N Bank) to be cleared through the cardholder's bank. The latter, in this case Bank C, collects the full fee from the buyer/cardholder some days later.

system at 2 percent ($2) for this class of restaurant owner. La Premiere's bank is Seventh National Bank, who accepts the credit card slip for interchange (clearing and settlement) through the system. For purposes of uniformity, this charge too is set by the system, let's say at 1 percent ($1).

Step 1: With her client, Andrea enjoys a dinner for which she is charged $100 by La Premiere. The face value of the bill is $100 after taxes and tip.

Step 2: Andrea signs the credit card slip of $100 and hands it over to the waiter.

Step 3: La Premiere promptly submits the $100 charge to its own bank, Seventh National, which handles the system's credit card business in the area. In the early 1970s the credit card slip was physically submitted; now this and subsequent steps are done electronically.

Step 4: La Premiere receives $98 from Seventh National Bank, or the $100 face value of the meal minus the merchant discount of 2% or $2. La Premiere's cost is therefore $2.

Step 5: Seventh National sends the $100 charge to Andrea's card-issuing bank. That local bank may handle Andrea's other banking business or may have simply persuaded her that it can do a better job—or charge lower fees—than any other available bank card issuer.

Step 6: Andrea's card-issuing bank pays Seventh National $99 or par ($100, the price of the meal) minus the interchange fee of $1. Seventh National's profit is $100 minus $99, or $1.

Step 7: The card-issuing bank submits the full $100 charge to cardholder Andrea (plus an interest charge, if any).

Step 8: Andrea pays $100, plus interest if she fails to pay within the grace or free-float period, to her bank (the card-issuing bank in this case). Her bank's profit is $100 minus $99 actually paid for the credit slip, or $1. To that profit is added Andrea's interest payment if she fails to pay on time. But to that profit we must also subtract cardissuer C's loss of interest on its money between the time it paid the principal merchant bank and the time Andrea actually pays the credit card bill. Also, subtract from that profit any costs of running the system, including the cost of cardholder nonpayment or outright fraud.

Assuming everything goes well, the participants in this complex system get paid. What is Andrea's cost for this convenience, including the usual interest-free loan for a period of days within the grace period? Our analysis may center on questions that economists call demand elasticities. Is a fine restaurant, or upscale department store, sufficiently set apart in buyers' minds that it can raise its prices and still hold the business? In that case, Andrea would be paying for the merchant discount since the restaurant owner would be passing on that cost in the form of higher prices. If the restaurant business is sufficiently competitive, then the vendor will probably have to absorb the cost.

The system seemed fair, yet card users had many specific complaints, especially in the early years. For a decade or so, the bank card rates all generally hovered around the state statutory usury ceilings of 18 percent and during the 1970s, it was almost impossible to find a card that offered an interest payment below that. It could be argued that this was the period of high interest rates for this country as well as high credit card losses. Meanwhile, merchants were often troubled by high merchant discount rates, which retail users believed were embedded in their prices.

This was not an especially auspicious beginning for plastic. But things changed rapidly as the 1980s wore on. Competition developed for both consumer cardholders and merchant accounts. Merchant discounts fell from 5 to 6 percent to 2 or 3 percent, depending on the value and type of business. For cardholders, interest rates dropped sharply below the early 18 percent level. Big users received uniquely tailored rewards such as frequent flyer miles, Sierra Club donations, and free presents. Many annual membership fees were dropped and service became extremely good.

Plastic for the Masses

Competition did its job and the market made its corrections. Entrants sought out other niches. Some banks began to chafe at the rules and requirements of the big credit card system and wanted more control. With the development of ATMs, they were able to compete with the credit cards. They wished to serve their own customers more directly by supplying cash any time anyone was short. Tellers were getting to be expensive; so too were brick and mortar branches.

On-premise ATMs were invented to deliver cash. Placed in strategic places in and around the banks' offices, ATMs were programmed not only to provide cash but also to take deposits and supply other automated services, such as account information. The beneficiaries turned out to be anyone who enjoyed a bank account and this egalitarian touch brought many more people into the electronic age.

In the next step, banks began to splice together their individual ATMs, either through formal joint ventures or informal sharing arrangements. Customers could now get cash any time of the day or night not only from their own bank but also from many other banks and at other handy places, such as airports and supermarkets. Many of these "foreign" ATMs—that is, any ATM not owned by the deposit customer's bank—crossed state lines. Did these terminals and their extended electronic tentacles violate the quite complex and restrictive state branching laws? Congress came to the rescue and made legal what was already occurring *de facto* with the Monetary Control Act of 1980 (MCA 1980).[3]

Deregulation and Expansion

Finally, as if from out of the blue, thrift institutions were going to be able to perform all kinds of bank-like services, such as offering checking accounts. For their quid pro quo, banks now could provide the high interest rates designed to woo back the money lured away by some thrifts and, later, the high-paying New York money market mutual funds.

The spillover from MCA 1980 and its companion Garne St Germaine of 1982 was more than anyone ever bargained for. MCA 1980 put more institutions into the act of providing money, electronic and otherwise. By permitting more varied assets, including higher yielding commercial loans, it helped many institutions. However, that help all too often assumed the form of a temporary band-aid. Many thrift institutions designed to take in savings and make mortgage loans were not yet equipped to look, act, and think like banks. As noted by Professor Larry White, the savings and loans often had neither the expertise nor the supervisory structure, and some were caught red-handed in sweetheart deals or scams.[4]

These problems were not entirely of their own making. The savings and loans were in the horns of a dilemma because the rates on their old outstanding mortgages, carried over from the low-interest days of the 1950s and 1960s, could be as low as 5 percent; however, the rates they had to pay to attract new money were extremely high in the late 1970s and early 1980s when even the prime bank lending rate hit 20 percent. One can easily see the red ink produced by such a squeeze. Something had to be done to rescue them, and fast. That something was deregulation.

Thrift and bank alike could now offer credit cards and ATMs across state lines and state barriers to doing business were lifted. Everyone who had a bank account was almost automatically handed an ATM card, with its privileges. Plastic was no longer non-egalitarian and its geographic limits were boundless. Plastic became a universal medium of exchange.

Masses of Americans were initiated in a frictionless manner into the plastic rites, often at a very early age. What's even more surprising is that parents let their children personally participate almost before they were left alone without sitters. Children enjoyed getting money out of the ATMs and called the then foreboding ATMs "money machines" because they produced money, wads of folding green bills. It was so easy. They still wallow in it all—they had no lifelong preferences or fears to overcome. There is also a moral to the story. Very shortly, the children of that age grew up to spearhead the current new technology, like home banking.

The ATM, increasingly shared, became a necessary part of the banking business. If you were a banker, you had to keep up and join the others to prevent your depositors from fleeing elsewhere. With a joint ATM venture such as NYCE or MOST or PLUS, depositors could not only get cash from their own bank's ATMs but also from those of other member banks. Good deposit customers could get money, and later cash loans, no matter where they might be. A local bank looked more attractive; the cash and credit it produced had wider acceptability around the nation and world.

Inevitably, the electronic systems also looked better, the bigger the scope of the venture or consortium. Mergers were commonplace, and not generally opposed; sharing was expected.[5] With sharing, the systems' marketing attraction soared. So also did the card's recognition everywhere.

Plastic Wound Full Circle

In this manner, ATMs reached down to cut across the population groups and the circle of use closed. All we needed was a bank account and ATM card and our entry into the electronic world was assured.

Nationwide systems, including ATM, T & E, and bank credit cards, now competed head-on. A little belatedly, merchants such as J.C. Penney, Sears, and the oil companies got into the card-issuing business. They had special empathy and a broad consumer base, with terminals already up and running, and they weren't afraid to cut rates. Consumers found that they had considerable choice in their electronic bill of fare.

As the 1980s waned, innovation and cost reductions continued. Merchant discounts plunged further, ranging from as low as 1 to 4 percent, depending on merchant system automation, ticket size, and administrative cost. We also saw a decline in consumer loan rates. Local banks offering cards of the same system plied their wares aggressively, and consumers came to realize that not all MasterCard or VISA cards in their area were the same. They shopped around in response to offers from out-of-town bankers or affinity groups, designed to preserve wildlife species or provide discounts for airline travel.

Eventually, telecommunications (AT&T) and computer companies threw their hats into the ring. By eliminating the yearly fee, AT&T's Universal card quickly jumped to second place.

New consumers were thus pursued. Merchant-based systems offered them very different kinds of electronic payments services and pricing schemes. Emphasis was on signing up mass retailers such as TrailwaysCorp., F.W. Woolworth, or Budget Rent-a-Car—or on tapping previously neglected retail segments, perhaps through the Sears or J.C. Penney retail base. Use of cheaper technologies such as magnetic-tape batch processing could cut costs and, with it, merchant discounts.

The Sears Discover card plunged into competition with Citicorp's CHOICE or its Carte Blanche to serve the family-oriented consumer and Middle-America traveler throughout the country. New, too, were the "no frills" debit card readers positioned strategically in high-volume low-ticket business locations, such as gasoline stations and fast food outlets.

We thought we had it all. But much more was to come.

The Polyglot Nineties

The present decade started off with exuberant variety. Plastic has gradually engulfed most consumers and the debit card pleases people grown tired of running up credit card bills. Grocery stores now let us pay by credit card, ATM (instant cash), or debit card (instant money transfer from checking account). Through electronic benefits transfer (EBT), the welfare net is the latest to be involved.

By mid-decade, plastic had been globalized.[6] Much beyond our wildest early expectations, plastic has become a universal currency form. The mid-1996 Nilson Report showed spending at merchant locations on general purpose cards totaling $1.47 trillion in 1995, and projects further massive growth to $3.26 trillion for the year 2000 and $6.43 trillion by the year 2005. Of 1995's global total, the United States had a 47.5 percent share, Europe 25.8 percent, and Asia/Pacific 18.0 percent.[7]

Card companies make short-term loans and arrange currency conversions dependent on current rates of exchange. Curiously, with all this speed and growth can come the kinds of troubles that afflict payments systems everywhere—the creation of "exposure" between the time the credit is authorized and its obligation dissolved.

The familiar synergy, the perfect fit, may waver and a Catch 22 emerges. If the system guarantees payment up front, it generates short-term credit (call it exposure), much without interest charge. The system cannot refuse to honor the free-float period so long as everyone else does. And the system cannot watch either its cardholder or merchant base shrink. But the guarantee carries a new risk, as plastic payments swell and move to more far-flung places under divergent regulations, currency zones, and understandings.

If the Internet picks up some of the money transfer business, that will inject a whole new wild card into the picture. In contrast to the present credit card arrangements, payment may be instantaneous, which eliminates exposure and involuntary credit extension by the card companies. However, actual delivery of goods (except in the case of intellectual property) may take time. Hence, major risks shift from Internet seller to buyer, who also loses the free float of the credit card arrangement and the system is turned on its head.

The Present Maelstrom

A sudden burst of bank merger activity, along with new creative energy, has emerged in the mid-part of this decade. On the one hand, we begin to see some massive consolidations between a few major banks, for example, Chase/Chemical. Big systems tend to coalesce, too, especially the regionals,[8] and some such as Electronic Payments Systems (owner of the MAC card, the fifteenth biggest domestic card in the world) attract antitrust interest. At the same time, potential suppliers are coming from unexpected places, not only from the large, familiar companies but also from creative Internet splinters.

The big new names often arise from the ranks of the technically brilliant graduate student turned entrepreneur. The market sizzles. Virtual banks piggyback onto the credit card companies to supply "virtual" payments. The familiar credit card spins off an appealing prepaid or stored value "electronic purse." And credit card losses rise again, just as they did a generation earlier when systems first were getting started.[9]

The possibilities are wildly imaginative, as almost any issue of any popular financial publication will reveal. Quicken and Microsoft vie for home banking, either through private bank systems or through the Internet. Visa Cash and MasterCard/Mondex weld a "smart card" onto the familiar plastic. The big computer companies search out the missing market chink, "groupware" or "applets" for an interactive future or "encryption" companies who may serve up the proper locks and keys for market favor. Global competition will mount as others seek to penetrate these markets. It's one big global game of musical chairs and you must grab the chance before it's too late.

Our population is ready to accept some innovations, subject to suitable safeguards, although we don't yet know which ones. My son now bonds with his 8 year-old-son over their newly purchased computer. In quite remarkable baseball games at a simulated Camden Park, they explore its CD-ROM and multimedia capabilities. They give me birthday cards created from their new color printer. My son tests home banking options and the e-money delivery forms, and we talk about the relative virtues of Internet access providers and Web browsers. A generation has passed since it began. Money, home banking, the smart card, the worlds of plastic, the computer, and the banks begin to blur. The world of commerce, payment, and buying merge. Joint ventures become bigger and bigger, embracing telecommunications and cable and computer companies. At hand is the current heavy burst of true electronic money, the tale next told of smart card and computer cybermoney, that can tend to your business while minding your money.

Smart Cards and Cybermoney

It was April 1995, the place was Columbia University, and it was raining very hard, but the hall was packed. There, sponsored by the Columbia Institute for Tele-Information, I first met some pioneers on the E-money frontier.[1]

Encryption expert and mathematician Dr. David Chaum is the founder and CEO of DigiCash. He is friendly and quite hypnotic, eager to guide one through the remarkable possibilities of e-cash. He spoke of digital money creation and encryption in terms never used before in ordinary money jargon.

Lawyer Lee Stein, founder of First Virtual Holdings, casually announced his former life as business manager to rock and movie stars and part owner of the San Diego Padres. He told of partners in the collaborative virtual money venture who work together to permit safe Internet use of credit card numbers from "virtual" offices, scattered in cyberspace from far and wide.

They are a far cry from the bankers I have known. But, of course, my banker friends and central bank employers also weren't much like the early humans who created a money form The bankers of cyberspace fill a real niche. Within twenty-five years after the cashless/checkless society was first conceived, as *The Economist* notes, "millions of people . . . regard themselves as part-time citizens of something they call cyberspace. It is surely not surprising that they should now want to take some spending money when they go there."[2]

But what exactly is electronic money? On wholesale routes, we have for two decades been served by electronic flows, or EFT as it was earlier called. So, in the broadest interpretation, electronic transfer media have been around for a long time. They let us access and deliver our conventional money very fast. With EFT travel, the underlying money, bank deposits, doesn't change—it simply moves around a little differently.

However, consider the eruption since late 1994 of what people call e-money or e-cash, the heavily retail-oriented change. In this current gush we see a fundamental shift, not just in money's delivery, but in its very nature. Its common characteristic is that it is computer-generated and manipulated, and lies apart from other money forms as presently managed by governments. The new cybermoney rests *outside* the usual bank deposit or cash niches. It is not now within the measurable money aggregates, or subject to the same regulatory surveillance and constraints. E-money has a shadowy existence of its own, and may take many forms, some bank offered, some not.

Clearly, e-money has no physical presence so cash of the folding type is excluded. But e-money doesn't resemble any of the other formal money aggregates either. On the contrary, e-money is transferred out *from* official money stock and drawn into new money-like accounts. Your e-value may rest in computer memory on chip embedded in plastic or on a computer hard disk. It may be issued by banks or their credit card systems, as a smart card or electronic wallet, a cash substitute. The issuer may be a nonbank company, which with our help produces cybermoney housed in our or someone else's computer that we can manipulate and use for on-line purchases.

The e-money specifics are very hard to pin down. To begin with, much of what is called e-money really ought to bear another name. A number of e-innovations create ingenious new ways to move around the money we already keep in banks, but those ways don't create a new value form. The following are examples of what we may call e-access media.

Home banking plans let us transfer regular deposits electronically, from our home, over modem and phone lines. They generally use the "closed" electronic banking nets, for reasons of security, as do the *debit cards* that move our bank money to the seller, directly, at the store or point-of-sale.

Electronic bill paying is another variant, again generally executed over the closed banking systems. We start out by cutting checks through popular software. Once set up, it's then easy to graduate to a form of home banking where deposits are moved electronically, and directly, from payor (buyer) to payee (seller). The *electronic check* may move our deposit money over the open Internet. It too does not supply new forms of money, but instead provides a faster means of accessing the deposits we already have in banks.

Some plans *pool credit card numbers* and keep track of accounts for later secure transmittal to the card companies who do the actual billing in the usual way. The credit card numbers then don't have to traverse the open Internet for all the world to see.

Virtual banks and *virtual ATMs and branches* let us transact our regular banking business in cyberspace. A bank's deposits exist, as always, to be moved around, but now the whole rather than only part of the process of storage and access is electronic. The underlying deposits remain in a depository institution, insured, to be accessed in a novel and potentially very fast way.

True E-money

In the case of true e-money, however, we have some value that rests *outside* banks. With the *smart card*, like that unveiled at the 1996 Atlanta Olympics, the "money" is held in plastic memory. For now, its function is to handle the small payments, just like regular cash or coins, and is sometimes called a stored value card or electronic wallet.

Money's resting place may also be a special memory bank within a computer hard drive, issued (also through computer) by a company other than our customary banks—*cybermoney*. Cybermoney rests not in plastic but on computer, PC, or system server or some other exotic information appliance yet to be invented. Cybermoney has no physical manifestation, not even a plastic cover. You manipulate your cybermoney, and the amounts you wish to transfer, through computer. Consider this computer money to represent a kind of e-bill that tends to fuel greater electronic commerce. Of course, the plastic may contain a simple computer-like device, that lets you do both—provide smaller e-coins for vending machines and manufacture the bigger e-bills for the Internet bazaars.

Think of e-cash, then, as secured by a digital "envelope," able to be broken only by those intended to do so. Vendors on the open Internet hope these unique keys will provide safe e-money transmission as well as prevent counterfeiting. Since each number for each e-coin is individually created, every e-coin bears its distinctive brand and can be used only once. The digital signature, also affixed and unique, prevents unauthorized use of the e-coin and can provide a legal analog to the written signature. Digital "wrappers" supplant guards with guns, while digital signatures replace pen and ink.

But can we really "create" our own e-money? (We certainly can't create our own deposits; only banks are capable of that). We merely transfer our assets from one form, conventional money, to another, ethereal money. We manipulate the money and send it along to vendors in the appropriately sized e-coins or e-bills. Meanwhile, others—the e-money issuers—hold the official money backing that we have entrusted to them. They, not we, get to do the money creating, if there is any.

The e-cash we hold within plastic in our hand, or on computer hard drive, is always matched by someone's liabilities—IOUs that they owe to others (in this case, to us). If a bank issues an e-cash card, then its IOU will rest within the bank, but in a special account quite separate from the usual deposit accounts. Of course, there still may be a regulatory presence, even reserve requirements, depending on how a particular central bank judges the circumstances.

On the other hand, the issuer may be a nonbank company—perhaps a giant computer firm or software specialist—and then there need not be any independent bank proximity or overview. If the deposit backing is slim, and links to real banks are uncertain or indefinite, we have a kind of "free" money. Finally, in the case of exchange of intellectual property such as software, we may gravitate to a kind of "e-barter." This extreme and most tenuous of e-moneys is about as far from our familiar money as you can get. But, if it's a type of barter, it has money foundations going back to prehistory.

Bank money vs. E-money

Let us consider the differences between our official bank money and e-money. Start with the easiest comparison to make: cash. People can readily distinguish between cash and e-cash. One is legal tender (i.e., it must be accepted by everyone); one is not blessed with legal tender status. One has a physical presence; one is without physical substance. Cash, when returned to the banking system, is a part of our reserve base; e-money is certainly quite apart from anything either esteemed as a monetary standard or official.

Now, ask the following and more difficult question: How does e-money differ from checkable deposits? Deposits have no tangible presence either—they are merely an accounting entity; moreover, they too can be accessed electronically.

In reply, we see that conventional deposits are expressed as liabilities of state or federally chartered banks, and are a measured part of our money supply—banks may be required to hold reserves against deposits. The things banks can do with our deposits—the loans and investments they can make—are circumscribed by an established system of examinations and regulation. Bank examiners check on how the banks are making use of their deposit liabilities (our entrusted money); they determine whether our money's transformation into interest-earning assets is safe and sound.

In contrast, e-money is computer money. It's not co-mingled with other deposits on a bank balance sheet, nor is it a generally measured part of the money supply. E-money represents a liability (or IOU) of some nonbank firm, or a segregated special account of a bank. Given its newness, the use of this money is as yet not circumscribed in any way by law. Unless there are bank links of some sort, its transformation into suitable loans and investments—as well as the reserves held against it as backing—will depend on the reliability of the e-money purveyor.

Deposits pass freely from holder to holder on the established payment lines. People can trust deposits, pretty much without distinguishing between the original bank of issue, and deposit insurance means that governments stand behind them. For any given type, a deposit is a deposit, nationwide; it also has a worldwide reputation. All conventional money has common stated value within the clearing stream, through which value moves from buyer to seller.

This "commonness" does not characterize the current e-money flurry. There is a remarkable variety of technology forms, digital manner of issue, claims, vendor's reputation, and encryption plans (the security "wrapper"). The digital assurance against counterfeiting, analogous to the watermark on a note, isn't manifest to the naked eye. E-money value may be expressed as various encoded strings of numbers whose exact mathematical composition is unknown, even to its owner.

Also to be worked out are the clearing arrangements, the way the value moves between individual e-money vendors on its trek from me to you. The interface between the systems jumps as the number of e-money issuers rises—so do uncertainties and the risk of glitches. Without common standards, we return to a kind of private note issue or barter. And, since a unique e-money system is a form of intellectual property, we will probably have to contend with patents and pay royalties—a potential irritant and source of legal action and expense.

It is obvious that the range of possibilities is extremely broad.

Electronic Wallets and Smart Cards (Stored-Value Cards)

As useful substitute for cash or small coins, the retail smart card (or electronic purse or wallet) is a direct descendant of the plastic credit card. It also is usually bank- or credit-card linked, even to the extent of sharing space, quite possibly, on our familiar credit card.

The e-cash cards, or wallets, permit us to download money to memory on the card from our bank account. A refitted physical ATM may be the mechanism for transfer—or a virtual ATM housed in cyberspace and accessed by computer on the Internet may do the trick. What is the procedure? Money transfer is from one form—physical cash or bank deposits—to another, the stored-value card (SVC).

Note that we have not created money in any sense. We have simply transformed our existing money into another money media, which we may spend electronically. The issuer of this prepaid money card has the use of our funds until we decide to spend them, the unspent float, just as the issuer of travelers checks holds our money until we cash the checks.

The Gordian knot is severed. We can now spend the stored value without directly accessing a bank account—the value on the card is prepaid. Once in hand, the money can pass from card to card (in some systems, such as Mondex), just as cash can travel from hand to hand without direct bank intervention. The value can also move from card to special "reader" at the merchant's vending machine or store when you want to buy something, say, a bottle of soda or a newspaper.[3]

In its storage function, the "chip card" (as it is often also called) takes the place of the mattress; we stuff our money into the card's memory, not under the mattress. (One important difference: the issuer can make productive use of our funds—the mattress cannot.)

The card's money cargo may be unloaded any time we wish to buy something—if we can find someone (or some appliance, acting on human instructions) willing to accept it. It will also be easy to "charge up" the card again by repeating the process at an ATM or other terminal, including eventually home PCs and virtual ATMs in cyberspace.

The "money," be it of bank or nonbank origin, can meanwhile migrate from holder to holder. The issuer—whether government, bank, or nonbank—knows it has x amount of money-like liabilities out there, but may not know who holds them at any given time. This uncertainty about money's whereabouts worries officials at the F.B.I. and Treasury in cases of potential money laundering or tax evasion, and the general anonymity of e-cash and its potential ease of transfer causes many gray hairs to sprout.

For e-cash holders, however, its great convenience may outweigh such worries. For one thing, processing is self-contained. Heavy, jangling coins are replaced; the owner need not fumble around for suitable small coins in dark or inconvenient places. In prototype, the smart coins or cards do all—and more. They contain chips of great sophistication that can make change and keep track of expenditures; they may do other useful things, too. The holder may track the value of an investment portfolio, update health records, convert foreign exchange, or pay tolls at toll booths, provided the toll booths are so structured. With a "pull down" mini-computer/processor, the holder need merely call up the appropriate directory to learn of the transfer and recording of money balances or whatever transaction is made.

Think of the range of information potentially available from that chip-in-a-card. The holder may compute the value of his portfolio while waiting for lunch at the club. He pays for lunch with the card, by subtracting its value from the card's money pool. However, a quick look at his investment portfolio is not reassuring—a catastrophe has occurred. The stock market has just crashed; its value is down dramatically. Distraught, he is hit by an approaching car. At the hospital, our hapless victim is in very good informational shape. The card spews forth all the necessary medical information; no time is wasted obtaining blood type, insurance forms, allergies, previous diseases and immunities, and the like.

The following scenario is more attractive and broad-based. You may convert dollars into francs or lire electronically on your next trip to Paris or Rome. You may attach the card to your windshield and the appropriate amount will be deducted from the card's value as you breeze on past a toll booth. Your e-purse may function in parking meters, vending machines, even slot machines. All this is more than

SMART CARD'S MONEY TRAVELS

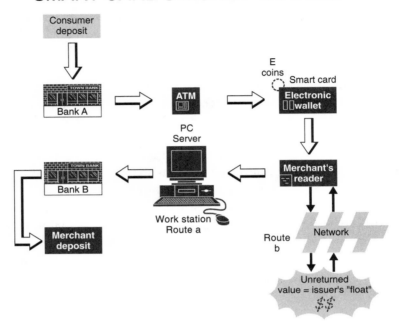

Figure 5.1 Smart card's money travels. Money's journey in a smart card (or electronic wallet) e-mode takes it from bank deposit to smart-card memory. There, it can sit until used to buy something. Selling merchants can return the value to their banks, hence move the funds back into official money within the regulated banking system (Route a). Or, a merchant can hold the issuer's value (Route b) or find someone outside the banking system willing to accept it. In that case, the $ values can move around outside the banking system quite freely, based on faith in the integrity of the issuer.

hypothetical possibility. New Zealand and Finland have been pioneers in using prepaid value cards. The Dulles, Virginia, "Fast-Toll" is performing well. MasterCard and Mondex test the smart card—replete with money conversion possibilities—in their home countries and Australia. In Denmark, a consortium of banking, utility, and transport companies has announced a card that would replace coins and small bills. In France, the smart cards for pay telephones are now in general use. The government of Singapore has authorized a system that would communicate with cars and make appropriate charges from their smart cards at chosen points on a road. The Belgian Proton delivers e-cash in ten countries as of early 1997, through Belgium's Banksys consortium.

Nuts and Bolts: Prepaid Cards and E-cash

But how does e-cash get from my bank to me and you? It helps first to note that the prepaid value stored on a smart card (or electronic purse) resembles ordinary cash in function although not in physical appearance.[4]

Conventional Cash

When you need a little cash, you withdraw it from your bank, either by using a teller or an ATM, which supplies some folding bills. A cash withdrawal reduces the bank's assets (vault cash) and its liabilities (deposits) by an equal amount. The bank's reserves also go down since the cash it holds constitutes, for the bank, legal reserves. Meanwhile, you have switched assets: your deposits at the bank are exchanged for currency, which is legal tender and backed fully by the Federal Reserve.

E-cash

Now suppose that you choose to swap your deposits for e-cash, prepaid on an electronic purse. You plan on driving very far and will need an ample supply of this virtual cash to feed both yourself and toll booths. In preparation, you download e-cash to card memory from your deposit account. Look at what happens in Figure 5.1. Bank deposits move from your Bank A, through the ATM, to your electronic wallet in the form of e-coins: deposits are down, but your prepaid e-cash is up by exactly the same sum. Unlike the cash example, you don't have legal tender. In its place, you have value that is backed by its private issuer, not by the government.

After you download the deposits from your bank account to fill your electronic purse, the bank's liabilities change: its deposits are down, but its special "nondeposit" (e-cash) liability account goes up by an equivalent amount. As you see it, your deposits are replaced by e-cash embedded in your prepaid electronic purse. How does the bank view this transaction? Your bank no longer has that original deposit as a liability but has instead the equivalent of your stored value that it can use—the "prepaid card" liability, or "vault," perhaps it's called. Any value that hasn't been returned to a bank, because the owner is too lazy or penny-pinching to spend it, represents a kind of float that the issuer can use. (Whether or not the bank issuer has to hold any reserves against its new e-card liabilities will, of course, depend on the regulator.)

Assume you now decide to withdraw some purchasing power and partially empty your electronic purse. The merchant or employee who collects the proceeds from the vending machine does not gain any cold cash. Instead, he collects the value of the sale of sandwiches or soda, say, in a special card reader or terminal that can "read" all the transactions. Once the card reader accepts the card as valid, the issuer owes the e-value to the merchant. When the merchant finally deposits the e-cash proceeds in the bank, say Bank B, the prepaid e-funds flow back and become an official part of the money supply once again.

The cycle is completed—shadowy e-money converts into real official money. However, there is the matter of clearing to resolve if several e-money issuing banks or credit card companies are involved. If a bank receives more prepaid e-value from merchants than it issued, it will need to make up the difference from other banks. Hence, prepaid systems will also require a mechanism for final settlement.

If banks join with some computer companies or other nonbanks, basically the same mechanisms will apply but with an extra step in the process. Nonbank issuers hold some prepaid e-card liabilities on their balance sheets, adding complexity to the process but not altering the rather troubling matter of backing and guarantees. Whether these cards are accepted in the end by merchants may depend on such assurances, along with the presence of a proven track record.

Cybermoney and the Internet

More freely flowing may be the larger e-bills of nonbank computer or Internet money, roaming quite outside the credit card or banking system. I call it cybermoney, since its characteristics seem conducive to gathering up the bounties of cyberspace.

Let us consider what happens when e-money is issued by nonbanks. Imagine that it flows on nonbank computer networks, such as the Internet. This process works a little differently from the electronic purse example previously described. Nonbank cybermoney may pay for goods that beckon from the virtual malls of cyberspace in a manner shown in Figure 5.2.

With the flick of a mouse, a consumer withdraws funds from her

CYBERMONEY'S PEREGRINATIONS

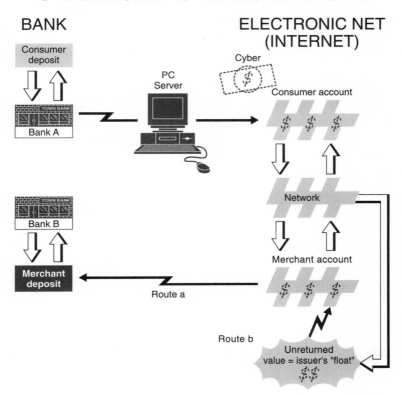

Figure 5.2 The peregrinations of computer cybermoney. Cybermoney dispenses with physical trappings entirely; even the plastic cover becomes unnecessary. Via the computer, cybermoney may travel directly from on-line buyer to merchant and the merchant's regulated bank account (Route a). Or, cybermoney may meander for a time back and forth from the issuer's account. This bypath can generate investible funds for the issuer and network (Route b).

checking account in Bank A and purchases e-value (again, let's call it cybermoney) on a network account. In the process, the network operator from somewhere in cyberspace credits the stored value chip on the consumer's computer, provided specifically for this purpose. Or, the e-bills of cybermoney may rest within memory on a hand-held personal communicator or on a far-distant computer server, perhaps run by the issuer. The e-issuer now owns the holder's original bank deposits, which

Smart Cards and Cybermoney

are also matched exactly by what the issuer owes the consumer.

In the next step, the consumer sees something in the cyberspace mall that strikes her fancy and executes the transaction, again with the touch of a button. Purchase and payment are simultaneously executed. The merchant is paid in cybermoney and the consumer's e-account is appropriately drawn down .

What is the merchant going to do with the e-bills just received? There are several possibilities, each with a different impact on the banking system. First, the merchant can decide through the computer to return the cybermoney value to the merchant's checking account, at his Bank B. In that case the flows are returned to the banking system. The merchant could also retain the value on the network to make payment to his suppliers, through the paths of electronic commerce.

If the merchant wishes the nonphysical funds to circulate *outside* the conventional money system, the side effects can be interesting. The value that is *not* returned to the banking system represents: (1) float the network operator can invest, as shown at the bottom of Figure 5.2, and (2) a withdrawal of the medium of exchange from the banking system and its safety net. If a lot of merchants decide to bypass banks, the banking system quite obviously would retain a shrinking slab of the money pie; the central bank's ability to know the whereabouts of the cyber-money that circulates around the world would also lessen.

Plastic vs. Cybermoney

In certain respects this cybermoney for the Internet bears some resemblance to the bank-linked electronic purse discussed earlier. Each gives us a means of making electronic payments quite independent of any formal bank accounts. In both systems, value must be securely moved from the bank account to the e-money form and safely maintained while the transactions are executed. Also, in each scenario, the time of eventual and safe return to the banking system at some future date is quite nonspecified. That is of course a matter of personal choice, and bears on how protected from loss the holder feels.

Consumers and merchants might feel more protected if the e-value were a liability of the familiar credit card or banking system. On the other hand, perhaps the cybermoney issuer is a big firm whose name is on the tip of everyone's tongue and at the base of most people's computers (or telephones). That kind of familiarity inspires respect, too, especially if the vendor guarantees users against loss or comes to pay some market-determined rate of interest to account holders. On the other hand, would-be smaller entrants may object on the grounds that the massive company has a "deep pocket" or can afford inducements (or threats) they cannot possibly match.

Central banks may worry, too. When nonbank computer systems handle payments independently, transfers among merchants and consumers may slosh around over the open Internet, unrestrained and unknown. The funds may stay there, circling in cyberspace indefinitely. Cybermoney flows may pull funds out of the banking system permanently; in the most lucrative scenario, even without any fee income, they also may generate a large volume of investible float in the hands of the nonbanks, escaping scrutiny or even normal disclosure requirements.

Cybermoney Fears

Without hyperbole, there is cause for guarded concern. The question is what any rootless "money" will be worth prior to redemption in real money, whether it will trade at par (full value) or at nonpar discount—or for only certain types of Internet services. (Owners of the wildcat bank notes that circulated prior to the National Banking Acts of 1863–64 had this same "nonpar" clearing problem, as did many in this century just before the creation of the Federal Reserve.)

The matter of who is backing the money (and in what) is critical, in the market's assessment of its reliability. Unless the backing is firm and the issuer well trusted, nonbank e-cash may succeed in one and only one limited money sense—acceptability in the Net's bazaars.

On the other hand, it seems doubtful whether money will be accepted for very long—at least for legitimate purposes—if it does not at the same time satisfy the requirement of serving as a reliable store of value. Overissue of money can also be a problem, as everyone knows. When the supply of money is increased too fast, its value erodes and prices rise. Banking history is filled with stories of how hapless owners, under these circumstances, had to carry around bags of practically worthless cash. The flight from rapidly eroding value is swift. If issuers wish to remain in business, they cannot make e-loans through "printing" unbacked e-money for very long.

The essential ingredient for providing a good and enduring store of value is convertibility into "real" and stable money that has lasting value. In theory that could require a dollar of real cash in the "real" economy for every electronic money dollar in the "phantom" economy. Presumably banks will be brought in to provide that kind of reassurance, but they may become the tail wagging the dog if bought or created by a powerful company explicitly for this purpose.

Even a "safe" compromise such as the promise of a liquid and gilt-edge security outlet may prove unworkable. Without some supervision, the established reserve holder's urge to do something a little more rewarding, say a little virtual lending on the side, may prove irresistible.

The original e-money creators down the line may also try a little virtual money creating of their own. Specifically, cybermoney issuers may attempt to lend out their own e-money float (their unclaimed e-money liabilities owed to card holders). Under these circumstances, it will be difficult for an unsuspecting user of cybermoney to know exactly where and in what form the reserves backup may exist at any given time. Unmeasured and unrecorded, even their existence may be unknown.

The big name and trusted company currently has the advantage in disseminating cybermoney technology. People trust a bank or credit card company because of its proven track record. I am reminded that IBM's name gave credence to the PC revolution of the early 1980s. However, IBM's leadership in making PCc (which were very good, but also expensive) was later to be usurped by the unknown, but equally competent and much cheaper, clones. Once the technology becomes entrenched, perhaps a generation hence, who would issue your e-money and what could back it?

"Free" Money

Just as with the early goldsmith, the temptation to move away from a fully backed digital money to what we call the "free-money" mode may prove irresistible. People will want real (not virtual) credit from any banker with whom one leaves deposits. It will make no difference whether the banker's address is cyberspace or a bank building replete with brick and mortar branches. There is a final stage in which full e-dollar convertibility, replete with 100 percent real money backing, ceases to be a condition for e-money. As in the case of the early goldsmith—or the early banks in this country prior to establishment of the Comptroller of the Currency—the nonbank "banker" of cyberspace must make the determination of the prudent ratio of real money backing to "freecash." I define freecash as money without formal and legally enforced reserves backing.

Freecash or free money can arise in yet another hidden way—a kind of fraud. If issuers say they are providing backing but do not have to establish how, in what form, or when—with no legal remedy if they fail to keep promises—this also constitutes "free" or rootless cash by my definition.

The nonbank firms in either case may get to create some money. At best, the base will not be official reserves of a central bank but bank deposits, the new "reserve" base in a virtual money world. That does not seem so strange. Many banks (called respondents) hold reserves, officially, with other banks, their big city correspondents. Perhaps computer issuers will maintain their reserves with the bank respondents, who hold their reserves one layer up with the big city correspondent who keeps reserves at the central bank.

Perhaps they will hold reserves with one another—a prospect that may cause central banks to fret. Imagine a world in which a smaller digital money firm, Micro B, holds reserves in a much bigger and more powerful central digital money firm, Macro A. Micro B's reserves (the assets it uses to redeem customer balances) then consist of liabilities of nonbank Macro A, perhaps a very well-respected computer software company. For a bank presence we substitute a nonbank one. It's even conceivable that the nonbank may make loans through the issue of cybermoney, its own liabilities, to the borrower.

First, however, the world must get around to accepting the integrity and redemption promises of Macro A; people must trust it not to overissue or debase the currency. Gold and silver coins used to be debased by kings of the realm when they added lead, and people wound up not trusting the kings very much, but usually they didn't have any other options. Holders had their own tricks too; regularly they used to shave off a little gold from the coins and pass them around in the hope that no one would notice. We once could detect counterfeit bills by feel. Now, we must rely on something we cannot feel—encryption technology—to prevent digital forgery, at either an ATM or other terminal that provides the computer money or the Internet that delivers it.

Someone will need to find a way to make home computers trustworthy as well as tamper-proof. Perhaps the original issuer could catch any attempted fraud and reject the transaction. Perhaps the seller could check the history of a money balance before accepting it. However, after the e-money—whether bank e-cash or nonbank cybermoney—moves around a bit, one cannot count on the original issuer to be able to detect its whereabouts, let alone any fraud. The central bank issuer of the physical cash obviously can't track it either.

Reserve Whereabouts

What is the progression? A central bank's cash and base money, and other forms of legal tender, are backed by the government. A commercial bank's deposit money, contained on a ledger, has central bank money as backing and a means of convertibility. Bank money has behind it an established scheme of government regulation including examinations and reserve requirements. When private nonbanks create money, our money system depends on the judgment of those e-wizards who inherit the mantle of note issuer and moneylender.

The foes of central banks may argue that the market will do a better job than a central bank of regulating the supply and flow of money and credit since central banks have often been thought to be swayed by politics. The merits of universal money have been ably debated by leading scholars. The plans that don't make it will wither on the vine and customers will be sadder, poorer, yet wiser. Others say the e-money system may be shaping up over national lines by function in the manner of Middle Ages guilds. A global and unified e-currency may be coming.[5] At the other extreme, we may face a system splintered and anarchistic like the Internet. Cybermoney may be used mainly for the transfer of electronic intellectual property, as a kind of electronic barter.

"Unregulated offshore and personal currency schemes will not win out. People will always want the judgment, the trust of banks," declares Kawika Daguio of the American Banker Association. "They won't rely on nonregulated vendors of value. Here you have two of the most critical areas of society, money and security. The governments will have to step in to supervise and regulate cybermoney issues."[6]

The Other End of the Spectrum: Government E-money

And, indeed, governments are already thinking about their possible future intervention while denying any immediate plans to thwart the market's untamed innovative impulses. In its Report to the European Monetary Institute, the Working Group on EU Payment Systems concludes that only credit institutions (or schemes appropriately regulated) should be allowed to issue electronic purses. "EU central banks should continue to monitor developments in the field of prepaid cards, possibly in co-operation with other central banks outside the EU. . . . In some cases they may wish to discourage some initiatives in order to protect the integrity of the retail payment system" is the shared view.

In contrast, former Federal Reserve Board Vice Chairman Alan Blinder does not favor intervention in direct e-cash issue at this time since he believes the market to be self-policing and does not wish to quash innovation. He suggests "patience and study rather than regulatory restrictions," but states, "we do believe, however, that certain rules need to be clarified and future developments should be monitored closely."[7]

Eventually, some governments may come to issue e-money directly, as a peculiarly ethereal form of cash. A few European central banks believe this would be a definite possibility in case e-money arrangements did not work properly. Finland's scheme already is a single one, now government-sponsored, as is New Zealand's. Dr. David Chaum, DigiCash's CEO, suggests banks should take responsibility for the issue of digicash.

In this country, an early prototype of a state-sponsored type of e-cash is called electronic benefits transfer (EBT). EBT is efficient, helps eliminate fraud, and is said to increase the dignity of welfare recipients; however, its privacy implications are troubling, as is the government's massive role in the process. The way EBT works offers a counterpart to the free or rootless e-money story at the other end of the e-money spectrum. Neither extreme is an ideal to be coveted; both have radically different dangers.

A Government E-money Prototype

Already operational in a number of states, with federal backing, EBT is expected to take the place of food stamps everywhere by 1999, probably earlier. Many versions of government EBT money currently exist, but in the hypothetical scenario I have devised, the government, in this case a state, does the following:[8]

1. Selects the winning contractor, who may be bank or nonbank processor.
2. Provides an instant cardholder base—the food stamp recipients EBT is designed to serve.

3. Maintains and "fills" the electronic accounts of EBT recipients, the former food stamp people.

4. Gives merchants (through the winning contractor) free terminals, an instant cardholder base, and a vehicle with which to piggy-back other credit/debit card transactions that have since flourished in supermarkets. The winning contractor takes on the necessary interface and training and electronic delivery chores.

EBT: Mechanics, Again

With fifty states to implement EBT, there are and will be many models, but let us pose one hypothetical process, as shown in Figure 5.3.

AN ELECTRONIC BENEFITS NET

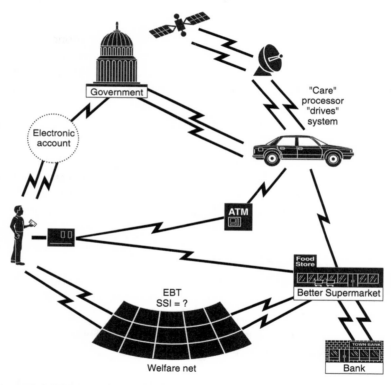

Figure 5.3 EBT: An electronic safety net. The state governments provide electronic benefits transfer (EBT). The holder's food stamp values may be downloaded onto a special plastic card that functions like a smart card charged up with prepaid value.

The Changing Money Machine

Step 1: The EBT holder, Andrew, gets a $100 electronic food stamp credit from his state government, under block grants from the U.S. Treasury and Department of Agriculture. This amount, $100, goes into an "electronic vault" at a special commercial bank account, divided into smaller accounts for EBT recipients, shown on the left-hand side of the diagram. Andrew downloads the money from the electronic bank account, at the appropriate time, to memory on his EBT card.

Step 2: The EBT recipient, Andrew, holds a plastic EBT card issued by his state, that now says he has a $100 EBT credit. That $100 value is stored in memory on his card, which can also record how and where Andrew spends the $100. The contractor who wins the bid—the bank, processor or financial services firm—may also keep track of what happens to that $100.

Where and what is the money in this case? The unspent store of value is recorded in memory on Andrew's EBT card, as magnetized filings of iron oxide or newer optical memory. Andrew holds the "money" thus in memory on the card, but it is limited purpose money because it can only be spent for food, or other purposes proscribed by the government donor. It does not have general acceptability and can be used only at participating stores and only for certain kinds of goods.

Step 3: Andrew buys $100 worth of groceries from a willing merchant B, the Better Supermarket. His EBT card goes into Better Supermarket's terminal, which has been provided especially for this purpose by the contractor (Bank C's processor affiliate, Care Processor). Better Supermarket's terminal deducts the $100 from Andrew's EBT card value and credits Better Supermarket's account.

Andrew gets the groceries, Better Supermarket enjoys the business, and C's Care Processor affiliate handles the transfer of "funds," all electronically.

Step 4: Andrew's EBT account is drained of the $100, through deductions (decrements) from the card's chip through Care Processor, which does the bank-like work of funds transfer. Better Supermarket or its bank gets the $100, again handled through Care Processor.

Consider another scenario. Andrew wants both groceries and money, $50 of each, say.

Step 5: Andrew spends $50 at Better Supermarket, following the process just noted. To get the $50 in cash, he may go to Better Supermarket's ATM, which is part of the approved ATM system for the state EBT plan. He gets cash, just as in any ATM, by inserting his EBT card.

Smart Cards and Cybermoney

Step 6: There is a difference from the ordinary ATM model, however. The $50 Andrew receives is "driven" from the state government's electronic account through Bank C's Care Processor plus the ATM system it hooks into. In some systems, Andrew may be able to get his $50 directly from the merchant; once again Care Processor will do the "driving" (i.e., money transfer) and keep track of everything.

Obviously, the consortium expands. Banks are not alone in this one EBT scenario; also very prominent are state governments and the winning contractor, not necessarily a bank. And, if EBT clients do not have bank accounts, the government by default (aided by the winning contractor) becomes the banker for the very poor. Who is, or is not, a bank is much blurred.

Who Is Your Banker, Now?

Fortunately, our money system will almost certainly be mixed in free democracies. That is, in practice we likely will see some stew of all these ingredients: a great stir of private innovation, banks as creators or as partners, with governments looking over everyone's shoulder, discretely. Your banker can come from anywhere, and from any firm of good reputation, or, most likely, from some combination thereof.

To illustrate, let's say you buy something substantial and of value—a printer from San Francisco or Japan or chemicals from Germany—and the seller needs his money fast. You want neither the bother nor the high cost of going the big money route (CHIPS), but the cash-equivalent electronic wallet route won't do either, because of limited value capacity and/or security—just now.

What then? You are the payor since you owe the money. Your payment instructions must flow through to the payee, the seller of the item you covet. The question is, in what and through whom? Just rearrange the central hub a bit to figure out who really runs things in a system. There are many possibilities.

1. You may be dealing with a bank subject to banking regulations and clearing requirements, assuming suitable arrangements have been made to provide the computer and security expertise. (Think Barclays Bank, First U.S.A., S.A. Banksys N.V., Deutsche Bank, and so forth).

2. The "banker" could be an arm of the computer company who runs the system, either bought for this purpose or created as a bank-like

subsidiary to perform the banking functions including the taking of deposits from customers. (Take any large computer company with whom you've had dealings and consider its owned or affiliated bank).

3. The "banker" could be a nonbank processor that now does a goodly amount of this "driving" (i.e., processing) of electronic money, and maintains links with a bank or ACH.

4. It could be a new type of entity altogether, designed especially to process this kind of computer money and its services. Perhaps this new-age entity provides for links to a traditional bank, perhaps not.

5. The government with its designated bank agent may be "banker" as in the case of EBT, discussed earlier.

6. Finally, the "money" so generated may travel to another network, a Japanese or European or Kenyan or Indonesian net, before reaching settlement in "real" money at its final destination, or several legs in the journey thereafter. We then have a global banker, in fact, if not in name or law. Recall that these legs in the journey, however convoluted, need not take very long—perhaps a fraction of a second.

Along the way, interface with other computer networks is likely. The cardholder may start out with plastic payment, then see the money commuted in subsequent permutations in the chain into e-cash or cybermoney. Or, she may begin with local or national Internet providers, or any one of their foreign counterparts, as a means of accessing the money transfer lanes of the earth.

Once set on its trek, who knows what land the e-money may cross at any given point. In realms of money and commerce, the digital money packets negotiate the unmarked web of cyberspace, as electromagnetic waves that circle out and on. Engineers and bankers may have a different view of how to put the money whole together and we will examine that synthesis next.

6

Money's Synthesis

A modern alchemy succeeds where the old failed. The ancients of the Middle Ages were never able to change lead into gold, but the medium of electronics turns magnetized particles (bits) into money-like value. Money seems for a time to be conjured out of nothingness, to be returned to nothingness either quickly or at an indeterminate moment.

However, it isn't the e-money holder sitting at a PC, altering the stream of e-cash values digitally, who creates the money. From his or her point of view, all that happens is the exchange of one form of value for another newer form. Nor do we know, at this time, whether people will even want to do—and pay in this manner for—much significant business on the Internet. We don't yet have a do-it-yourself money form, although a lot of people are trying to create a demand for one.

Under these circumstances, what then is money? I can repeat all the old standards found in any textbook—they continue to make perfectly good sense. Money must still be defined as a form of value generally acceptable in payment for goods and services. This general acceptability is an immutable requirement, or we degenerate into a kind of e-barter or rootless value of some indefinite sort. Although electronic money does not always meet the next test, a true money form must also serve as a unit of account and a medium for storing value effectively. When the merchant sells a diamond over the Internet or the home shopping channel that merchant wants some lasting value in return.

But what exactly is it when the e-money sits in memory in a plastic e-purse or smart card, or travels through cyberspace? This question has bothered me for many years, and scientists have helped to provide some plausible answers. The following is a distillation of our discussions.[1]

Money at Rest

When at rest, as seen in the previous chapter, e-money sits in computer memory just as cash may jangle in our wallets or deposits may rest in bank accounts. E-money has its counterpart as liabilities (IOUs) of the nonbank issuer, in the same way that cash is a central bank liability and deposits are owed to us by banks to whom we entrust our money.

We access our e-money by a computer processor, we access our deposits by checks (or electronic wire), and we access our cash by transferring it personally or by truck or plane. The latter two cases are easy enough to understand. But what specifically happens when we hold and move around e-money?

The classic old computer system works like a Morse code: in basic machine language one way is a zero (or off signal), one way a one (or on signal) and so forth down a whole string of current ons and offs (or 1s and 0s). The assembly language of the computer interprets this basic machine language and an advanced software package will make it all comprehensible for you.

The most common permanent storage is magnetic—tapes, or hard or floppy disks, although optical storage is rapidly supplanting them. On any type of magnetic storage, the principle is the same. The tape or storage medium is full of minute magnetic regions, each with a north pole and a south pole, that normally face every which way. Let's say you bring a magnet directly on top of the little magnets and reorient them with the north pole facing up. Are these tiny magnets, which certainly are not elementary particles, bigger than molecules? Yes, typically they are iron filings, collections of molecules, deposited on tape or disk as in a smart card. Applying a strong field lines them up—it magnetizes them. When a section of the tape or disk is magnetized, that represents a 1.[2]

When you want to record something, you apply an electric current to make an electromagnet, sometimes on (1), sometimes off (0), and that generates a sequential string of 0s and 1s to provide your storage and tell you how much money is in the memory. Later if you (or a merchant) want to read it, the computer reader engages in the following logic processes. When it sees these ons and offs (or 1s and 0s), the reader says, Aha, a blip—I see it's a one. If the reader doesn't see any blip, it thinks, Oh, it's a zero, and so on for all the little particles—for however long the stored message takes.

Suppose we use a disk instead of a tape. The disk, floppy or hard, is also covered with little magnetic regions, and has the advantage of allowing you to get from one part to another without having to pull it all through. With random access memory (RAM), your computer's head can get right to it. Other still more advanced forms of memory, such as magnetic optical memory all work under similar principles. DVD technology (digital video disk or digital versatile disk) is the newest form of optical storage. Whether familiar CD or DVD, the optical storage still uses 1s and 0s under the same basic principle, but does this by etching little marks in the disk. Light is reflected off these marks in different ways, for a 1 or 0, which the computer can understand to record our money values.

The security had better be pretty good (with several layers of backups in case of emergencies) or someone could erase or make changes by running a strong magnet over portions of the disk. And of course the software at both ends must be "honest" since you or computer pirates have the ability to fiddle with it. When the "money" sits in memory on the bank's computer, this surveillance is more complete. When I instruct a bank to take $100 from my account in its computer memory and redirect my money to yours, I can be pretty certain it will, and equally certain that the $100 will come out of my account without fail.

However, the question still persists about how this process occurs. How does this message get from me to you if, for example, I'm in Washington and you're in Tokyo? Now we are talking about payments, or money transfer messages in motion. The analogy is to physical check delivery, or the manual handing over of $100 bills to a merchant, or quarters to a soft-drink machine.

Money in Motion

We easily understand the concept of instructions to transfer money when they exist as writing on pieces of paper—i.e., checks. Assuming you sell me something, my check directs the transfer of deposits from me to you. When the paper completes its journey, my deposit account is debited and yours is credited in that final act of settlement, several days or even weeks down the road. But if the pieces of paper on their trucks and airplanes do not direct the money transfer, what does?

Suppose we look at satellite transfers. Let's describe this with an analogy. Say you want to send a message to someone on the other side of a pond. You make waves in the water by moving a paddle up and down so that the wave propagates across the surface of the pond. You take the paddle, oscillate it (move it up and down) for a period of time, then stop for a while, then oscillate again, stop again, and so forth, and the person at the other end of the pond observes the bobbing up and down of a buoy sitting near him on the water. With this procedure, a 1 would correspond to an oscillation, and a 0 would mean no oscillation. The observer interprets your signal according to the presence or lack of wave oscillations.

The water wave analogy is a good depiction of how electromagnetic (EM) waves are used to transmit information, such as money messages, over telecommunications lines. I want to send a message from Washington, say, to put money into your bank account in Tokyo while simultaneously taking money out of my account. (This can be a message over Fedwire or BOJ-net or the Internet, because, whichever we choose, we are dealing in EM waves for most of the trip.)

We start with the beginning point, the Fedwire transmitter that creates the electromagnetic wave by jiggling electrons up and down (reversing the current back and forth a few times). The wave travels up into space and bounces off the satellite and down to the receiver in Tokyo. Electrons in the Tokyo receiver move up and down in response to the incoming EM wave, just as the buoy in our water wave analogy moves up and down in response to the incoming water wave. The oscillating electrons create a current that can be measured in the form of signals that someone in the Tokyo bank can read and act on. These signals show the message that's coming in on the screen and also permit the interpretation of that message—to credit your account in Tokyo while my account is being debited in Washington at the other end.

And, they can do this very fast. All electromagnetic waves—electric, radio, microwave, or infrared—propagate at the speed of light, unless passing through water, or other media that offer resistance. Given this information, it seems that neither fiber-optic threads nor satellite get my money from Washington, D.C., to Tokyo instantaneously. In the case of fiber optics, the glass threads themselves provide some minuscule resistance, while the satellite route into geosync orbit and back covers sufficient mileage to cause some disturbing echoes. Therefore, e-money flows are not quite instantaneous under even the most ideal circumstances and of course human indecision or delay must also be dealt with. When you want to turn over money swiftly, you can certainly do so. But how do you create it, in this day and age? Therein lies a complex, yet interesting, tale that deserves to be answered before we continue.

Money's Creation

The basic physical laws of conservation of matter and energy assert, quite firmly, that the elementary particles making up the magnetized clumps of iron oxide, or the stream of money payments, cannot be created out of nothingness. (An exception is the virtual photon, which we discuss in a later chapter). The money *value*, as contrasted with the building blocks of its *physical composition*, is not so constrained. Money can replicate itself, especially when it is computer generated. Bankers can exercise a sleight of hand, and one that is also quite legal.

Of course, this characteristic of money always existed. When Federal Reserve Banks make loans or buy securities (all assets), they pay the borrower or the seller through creating a new deposit (a liability). The member bank borrower's deposit account at its Fed Bank goes up; or the seller of government securities gets a check or its electronic equivalent drawn on the newly created Fed balance. Reserves are legally defined as deposits at a Federal Reserve Bank (plus any cash in bank vault). Thus, a check drawn on the Federal Reserve confers reserves status. In that act a new reserve deposit becomes created. When spent, the reserves flow from bank to bank, and when they receive these new reserves, the receiving banks can also make new loans and create new money.

For the banking system as a whole the potential deposit creation can be many times the original reserves manufactured by the central bank. Overall money creation of the conventional sort is limited by the banks' available reserves relative to their required reserves (the reserve ratio). The banker also wants to be sure, in the manner of the early goldsmith, that she has sufficient cash reserves on hand to meet any likely depositor demands. Otherwise, she may satisfy the reserve requirements but fail to satisfy her depositors, and the net effect will be the same—disaster.

If reserve requirements do not exist, as with the newest money forms, then the restraint against overissuing the money will be in the form of issuer prudence rather than the force of any law. Judgment and deposit backing promises are the name of the game. Money creation is free and the nature of its motion, fluid. The Internet e-money can be as nonconstrained and anonymous as the mysteries of cyberspace itself.

Bankers' Money

Given all the bizarre possibilities, what really is modern money, if we allow ourselves to think as bankers, or economists? In the electronic age, anything that deserves the title of money still rests on a reserve base, however attenuated. The present e-money creators promise not to do away with reserves, at least at present. But we have more and more layers, superimposed, with conversion times that may range from instantaneous to the thoroughly indefinite.

Each layer converts into another money layer, generally but not necessarily the one just above: deposits into reserves or central bank money, e-money into nonbank liabilities of the creator, then into bank deposit money, and so on. Stuck somewhere down the redemption chain of x numbers of layers, pyramid fashion, may be the newly minted e-liabilities of a great variety of nonbank issuers (Chapter 5).

But very near the reserve top or "money base" will be the bank deposits—liabilities of banks or financial institutions that are creating money that central banks think is safe and liquid enough to fall within the official "money" category. I call that type our "conventional money."

To this familiar money brew, now add the two-decade-old electronic money transfers (EFT, or e-flows) and the new e-money just beginning to percolate. Electronic transfers are of course not strictly electronic money; as a kind of money flow, they combine both the underlying bank money and its escalated rate of possible turnover. The electronic flows are a far cry from their paper counterparts, the bank debits of old, and they stretch to the limit what can become a medium of exchange around the planet. Money-like value is in motion and continuously available for purchase of goods and services throughout the day. The flow represents all money—whether in physical form or as memory on computer or plastic—times the rate of its continuous use.

The Coming Together

Let's try to put it all together, old and new. The Federal Reserve dollar note depicts a pyramid with the all-seeing eye of our central bank at the top. The pyramid of the ancient Egyptians has always been thought capable of unique skills, some of them mystical. The money types also mold themselves into pyramid-like form as we move from the smaller packet of central bank reserves, or modern electronic gold, to a nebulous and rather large cloud of electronic money-like value that is used to transact business in the active capital markets around the world.

My rough grouping of money types—many of them overlapping in "mixed" form—is shown in Figure 6.1.[3] The powerful and mystique-surrounded reserves (R) go at the top; they consist of all the banks'

THE MONEY SYNTHESIS

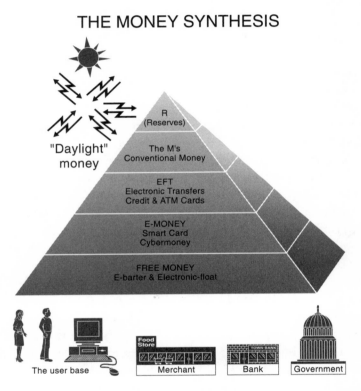

Figure 6.1 Today's money: the synthesis. Reserves perch atop the money pyramid. Conventional money (the measured M's) is next to be shown. The e-transfers, or EFT as earlier known, follow. One level below is the newest kind of e-money: the smart card and computer cybermoney forms slowly taking shape. Free money, by definition without specific formal backing, and e-barter collect at the base of the pyramid. (Adapted from Solomon, 1991, Figure 1–1, with permission of Kluwer Academic Publishers.)

holdings of cash plus the deposit balances of a central bank. These reserves form the basis for the money system. But notice the many forms of money they can support.

First is *conventional money* or M money, as defined officially by the central bank. This includes the public's deposits, savings and money market accounts and other components of official money aggregates, the various M's, M1, M2, and M3; these range from the narrowest to the broadest conventional M money. The transactions money (M1) is backed by the reserve base (R), as are the broader money forms, whether or not formal reserve ratios are applied.

The Fed's conventional and published M's are discrete, point-in-time concepts, and they are measured at the end of each business day. For the new e-money they can act as reserves themselves. Often they appear as settlement balances for the electronic money flows, including those on most retail nets (Visa or MasterCard). Either directly, or at one or more levels removed, the conventional M's support the e-money, just as central bank reserves support the conventional M's.

Electronic *daylight money* is shot out from the reserve base, shown in the left of the figure in a daylight/nighttime sequence. When funds are insufficient, it is created as "intraday" overdrafts, a type of daylight electronic credit for which the Federal Reserve now charges a small amount. In theory, the overdrafts can give rise to matching bank customer credits and short-lived daylight money. The Federal Reserve debits the payor bank's account at the same time that the funds move over Fedwire (on "real time gross settlement"). For those banks in a debit position over their cap, an overdraft can be created.

These transitory intraday Fed reserve credits must inevitably self-destruct when the overdrafts are drawn down at the end of day, only to arise again like the sun the next morning (on business days).

Our payments system is fairly unique in providing this particular daylight money, but transitory exposure surrounds payments systems and their players just about everywhere. This occurs because debits from a payor's account are not always made at the same time as credits are delivered. Central banks and systems attempt to reduce the exposure (or float, if you will) that can extend overnight or a day or more, depending on system arrangements.

The other groups in Figure 6.1 represent *electronic flows or money* in somewhat more durable form since their expected life span can theoretically extend beyond the transitory. Banks have driven the wholesale e-flows and (with credit card companies, perhaps) may issue most retail e-cash, too, after making suitable arrangements to nonbank inventors of encryption and other technology.

Nonbanks could also create some e-money, in which case they will be responsible for making good on claims to merchants or holders. Cyber-money consists of any one of several different types, but essentially it represents value that someone can spend, value that someone will accept, and most important value that moves outside the typical banking channels.

Bank-linked E-money

If a particular e-money flow retains regular (say, end-of-day) settlement links via conventional banking modes, it can be construed to still fit within the conventional money system, at least at settlement time. Links with conventional money forms have not been erased, just moved down a notch. We call such electronic money *bank-linked e-money flows* (see Figure 6.1). It becomes deposit (balance sheet) money when it's finally settled, but *prior* to settlement or while in motion it's e-money flows with firm bank links.

For example, money may flow on retail electronic nets such as a debit card or automated clearing house (ACH) for transfer to the merchant owner, say, of the fast-food franchise or the gasoline station. What is being transferred is the conventional bank deposit, and settlement is over Fedwire. In this case, the electronic money retains a very firm bank link. To take another example, the money-like values flowing on CHIPS are gross electronic flows that move a lot of markets during the day. But they are netted out (or settled) at the end of day in reserves over the Fed's books. In these cases of bank-linked e-money flows, the links with conventional money forms have not been severed but merely altered through the additional superimposed layer.

Any money flowing on these bank-linked electronic nets is traceable, although often with a lag; debit/credit card companies and the trade press provide yearly data and comparative estimates (e.g., VISA and *The Nilson Report*). At least for now, customers make the transfer from conventional money holdings. Even though it is segregated in a special account, any bank-offered e-cash (such as the electronic purse) retains a bank link unless a rigid wall is erected to separate them. For the moment, there is at least some backing, albeit attenuated and at one or more levels removed, in conventional reserves.

Thus far, most computer money issuers have chosen to align themselves with banks in this fashion. They generally require that customers hold deposits in segregated accounts in a designated bank, which downloads the matching amounts to the holder's computer memory as desired. But that scenario need not necessarily apply in the future, especially when we consider nonbank cybermoney.

Nonbank Cybermoney

The nebulous *cybermoney* that may move on the Internet or private nets of the future may defy identification and tracing. Mixed within it may even be a little "free money" (without much formal backing, either bank or nonbank) or some mysterious *electronic "barter" flows* about which we know still less.

Corporate barter flows move commingled to other parts of the nation and the world on the present secure private electronic nets. Smaller retail barter values will certainly flow on the Internet when electronic commerce gains its security and foothold there. At times, these flows may clear through other electronic money credits to other nets, or in goods or claims to goods (barter modes). Informal commodity standards (oil, airline ticket credits and debits) may exist for some; these may provide for an eventual "net" monetary settlement at some future time in order to retain a satisfactory unit of account and workability.

Whatever the present arrangements, we generally see layers resembling those in the correspondent banking network. The layers I've found are like skins on an onion—the farther you get into the e-realm, the more layers, and you peel them off bit by bit.

In gross, the proprietary electronic flows tend also to be far removed from the real economy or from productive economic activity. More than 80 percent of the dollar value of CHIPS represent foreign exchange transactions, and on Fedwire about two-thirds of the value is associated with securities and interbank payments. "The relationship between gross flows and economic activity is so gross as to be meaningless," Federal Reserve Board Director of Research Dr. Edward Ettin observes.[4]

E-value Clouds

Up there, the value used as payment for goods and services is also frequently commingled with other information flows. The messages to transfer money often move on dedicated private wire to payees, perhaps through the intermediary of SWIFT, or spun off as financial flows from an EDI package. As we will discuss in more detail in Chapter 10, there are many clearing houses and their rules are generally not standardized. Flows are settled in no particular proscribed way: perhaps deposit money, automated clearing houses, Fed funds, electronic claims to goods (barter), even other information flows. They may not be settled at all in the conventional manner through banks. Clients may keep their money value as "deposits" in a money market mutual fund and move it around by computer when they want to invest in one longer-term asset or another. Book entries may move liabilities from one account to another within the one umbrella mutual fund organization.

The varied means of access and the potentially high rate of turnover —plus ease and speed of use—can contribute to the volatility of financial asset prices. Such money "buys" financial assets at wholesale, futures, and options of financial assets and commodities; it hedges private traders and investors against risk, and flows around the world on private wires, carved out, unseen, in little digital packets.

This cloud-like money can move silently to and from satellites 22,000 miles up in space, through corporations and banks in solo, on their private lines, or as part of broader joint ventures composed of many partners. True, you do eventually have to pay in "real" bank money. But that eventuality may be stretched out, depending on how the final payments netting occurs—whether through bank-linked money or special clearing depositories or electronic barter strategies of many ingenious types.

Electronic barter flows may serve the needs of different firms as buyers and sellers interact in payment with one another (interfirm flows). Or they may cross oceans within the corporate infrastructure so that they may place buy-and-sell orders with speed or distribute products and parts electronically within the infrastructure (intrafirm flows).

As you get farther away from the reserve base and the money that passes through banks, it becomes harder to track "money." This is especially true with bundling a lot of different corporate information or settlement in some kind of commodity account (e.g., oil or futures). The value of an aggregate-flows gross becomes supported by a dwindling reserve and money base relative to the expanded electronic blob as a whole.

A Realistic Mix

That is a futuristic scenario, one I find quite uncomfortable, and one not likely to entirely take over our historic money forms and institutions.

Some new money purveyors argue that unless digital money forms totally supplant conventional ones, our money system will remain clumsy and inefficient. I disagree. At least for as far as we can see, both should coexist in the most exquisitely complex fit. Table 6.1 compares the official and electronic-enlarged M's as I see them. Table 6.2 describes a

Table 6.1 Official and Electronic-enlarged M's

Money Base: Reserves (R)	Electronic Base: Money (M)
M1 = Transactions money	M1* = M1 + smart card + other electronic cash substitutes
M2 = Near money (small) + M1	M2* = M2 + retail small dollar electronic flows (M1*)
M3 = Broad money (large) + M2	M3* = M3 + wholesale large dollar flows (M2*)
	M_E = All residual M* with no official M money counterpart

Note: Official money is backed by reserves, e-money usually by official M money. M1 (on the left) represents our transactions money; to that, we add e-cash substitutes (right) for M1*. An enhanced M2 format may add the retail flows (such as any small Internet payments that may arise) to yield M2*. An electronic-expanded (M3*) version of M3 might also encompass the wholesale large dollar flows.

Table 6.2. The Fit: Electronic Money and Conventional M's

The M's	Daylight Money	Smart Card	Bank-linked e-cash	Nonbank Cyber-money	E-float and e-barter
M1		x	x		
M2		x	x		
M3		x	x	x	
ME	x	x	x	x	x

Note: The Xs in this matrix indicate the kinds of conventional money most likely to match or back the new money forms. Since they are expected to be backed in full by bank money, smart cards should mesh well with official M's. Bank-linked e-cash in most present systems also has an M backing.

However, "daylight money" based on a temporary overdraft is of an evanescent nature. Nonbank cybermoney can remain outside the official money system in its computer travels, and hence has shadowy contact. E-float is a kind of Cinderella uncleared overhang or exposure, while e-barter can proceed without bank help. M_E comprises all this residual e-money without a conventional M counterpart.

plausible match between these two concepts, which almost couldn't be more different.

Money Under Pressure

This money flow concept is rooted firmly in classical theory. The concept of "effective money"—money times its rate of use—was developed in 1939 in Professor Gottfried Haberler's *Prosperity and Depression* and caught my eye on my latest rereading of this great classic. Dr. Paul Henderson, then of the New York Fed, talked of money flows on a visit to the Department of Justice in about 1982; and it made a memorable impression.[5]

Effective money, or money flow, includes all the money stock multiplied by the number of times that money turns over in payment for goods and services. Money-like value is in motion and continuously available for the purchase of goods and services throughout the day. In our modern setting, the flow represents all money—whether manifest in physical form or on computer memory—times its rate of continuous use.

Money flow is somewhat like the water flow you get from a faucet or a stream. When it comes from the faucet, water is under pressure, and the greater the pressure, the greater the amount of water available for use. In a similar manner, money flow consists of two parts: the underlying money times the rate at which it can turn over and be respent during the day. The greater the pressure, or speed, at which the underlying money moves, the greater the spendable credits within the day. For money, the water pressure translates into velocity. Or, to put it somewhat differently, spendable money credits during the day depend not only on the size of the underlying money base but also on how fast it can turn over within an imaginary money pipeline—that is, on money's effective rate of use.

As the money courses around the world, now greatly under pressure also, the ethereal money nets (once standards mesh) "speak" privately to one another. Traffic rises, and the links and interconnections grow and multiply to provide a "mixed" and particularly fluid kind of money, depending on where they move. Continuous money flows seem the proper name for this mixed conventional and electronic money. On electronic nets it may be difficult, indeed downright impossible, to separate

Money's Synthesis

97

the underlying money from its rate of use, or velocity. The two parts blur and combine just like bank debits in the paper era.

The blurring intensifies as we move from familiar wholesale nets to new ones. Already operational (Mondex) is direct plastic-to-plastic smart card contact and money transfer, without any need for terminals. The virtual ATM of cyberspace may also do the job. The interface could be a terminal at a merchant location or a hand-held personal communicator or home PC.

The "money" pressed forward over many electronic nets—large and small dollar, wholesale and retail—scatters into a variety of money permutations. It just depends on user needs and wishes, technology adeptness, and pocketbook. Choices also increase. The user tradeoff between reliability, cost, and quality determines the money user's decision to select one electronic money form over another, as first analyzed by Linda Moore.[6] Given the speed of money transfers, and the equal speed of information flow, suppliers can also grow by leaps and bounds.

Money's Future

The rapid rise in computer literacy provides the spur to computer money innovation of many kinds and from many lands. The Internet's vast untapped bazaars await, and now that the World Wide Web is commonplace, it is easy to get hooked on its pictures and wares. The notion of computer-generated cybermoney with which to pay no longer seems quite so strange but, given security problems and their wide publicity, its acceptance is still distant. On the other hand, in some form or other, smart cards will probably eventually find a niche.

As the cost of forging telecommunications links across oceans drops dramatically, nonofficial money forms grow more cost effective. Their rising cost advantage suggests the future growth of the presently most uncontrollable money form of all—the e-money flows already outside the familiar central bank M's. At the same time, interdependence between the world's money systems is heightened. This may provoke both collaboration and some competitive conflicts for supercontrol of electronic systems and their interconnected links.

Given the seamless electronic web of international money and capital flows, we are perhaps all one global joint venture. It's not surprising that monetary policymakers change their control venue from money growth to targets attuned to markets, as we next observe.

The Changing Money Machine

Part **III**

The Role of Government

Money Control Layers

The first Alvin Hansen symposium, in April 1995, was one of those rare times when great economists almost couldn't think of much to disagree about. The Harvard University hall was packed; Professors John Taylor and Robert Solow and their discussants and Economics Department hosts were assembled to discuss the proper monetary policy, and whether the Fed should control the federal (Fed) funds rate by rules or by discretion.

Professor Taylor offered rules for Fed funds targeting based on the gap between real GDP and its normal or "natural" full employment level (potential GDP). He found that they worked well to match the actual Fed funds rate, except for a little shortfall in 1992–94. Everyone thought policy was just about right in April 1995 when the Fed was plotting a "soft landing." What was left to debate?

Do you let a pilot fly his best to manage planes or interest rates, as Nobel Laureate Robert Solow put it, or do you give him some rules to help him do it, as Professor Taylor was proposing? Another Nobel Laureate, Paul Samuelson, noted from the audience that even pilots don't have rules but merely feedback guidelines.[1] Conspicuously absent from this discussion was any talk about money control, or even reserves control.

What is that intangible thing—money—that someone is supposed to control? The Federal Reserve quite publicly acknowledges its own difficulties in this area. However, it is less generally known that Fed

Chairman Volcker had pulled away from money targeting as far back as 1982 when retail bank electronic forms first began to proliferate.

Links Unglued

The links between money control and policy became unglued, if they were ever even firmly in place, almost before monetarism was given a chance. The Monetary Control Act of 1980 and the Garn St Germaine Act of 1982 allowed for many new money forms, such as bank money market accounts for consumers, that could be accessed electronically. The idea was to give bank customers the same advantages as investors in the pooled money market funds—that is, higher yields even on small amounts. It was also decided that banks should not have to hold any reserves against these market accounts. Banks would then be on a level playing ground with the big-city money market mutual funds.

The banks, and their customers, were the intended beneficiaries. But the central bank was the loser. Since the new accounts bore no reserve requirements, they were beyond its scope of direct control. Moreover, people began to shift their money back and forth, often electronically, and it became difficult to pinpoint narrow money, which received the brunt of the withdrawals and shifts.

As a result, beginning about mid-1982, the Federal Open Market Committee (FOMC) shifted its focus from narrow transactions money (M1) toward the broader money aggregates (M2 and M3). It began to correct for deviations from money growth targets more slowly, in recognition of this money account blurring. Chairman Volcker announced that the policy switch was being made for "technical" reasons and everyone knew, or should have known, what the problem was—the Fed's inability to do much else.

Governor Henry Wallich described that 1982 policy change from money growth to an eclectic market targets mix, at the 1984 annual meeting of the Midwest Finance Association. He rushed out of the room to catch a plane to Germany toward the end of the session and asked me to defend his position before a throng of quite hostile monetarist nonbelievers. The Governor's candid paper made a deep impression.[2] Professor Robert Rausch, a member of the critics' "Shadow Open Market" Committee, accused the Fed of duplicity in its attempts to control money growth; the Fed was never really trying, he said.

Indeed, it soon became obvious that the Fed could not control money growth, at least in the short-run. The uncertainties were too great. Normal links from policy levers to money supply were jarred, and some were apparently severed altogether. There was nothing to do but switch policy gears.

Control Levers

Several factors have produced disruption in the policy/money chain. The recession that occurred at about that time reduced the income (GDP) velocity of money, as would normally happen. However, the new jolts relate also—and possibly primarily—to deregulation and technology, and, especially in more open countries, to the greater capital flows that follow in the wake of both.[3]

The familiar linkages, from policy to money, work as follows. A central bank, through open-market operations or loans to member banks at its discount window, can create (or destroy) its member bank reserves. How may this sleight of hand be executed? The Federal Reserve Bank of New York creates reserves by buying government securities, and paying for purchases by issuing its own new deposit accounts to the seller. An asset is bought, and a matching liability (of reserve deposits) is created. Just as most other central banks do, the Federal Reserve defines its member bank deposits and cash in vault as legal reserves. The newly created deposits are thus newly created reserves.

When any central bank produces new reserves in this manner, its member banks can make loans and create new deposit money in multiple amounts. Just how much will depend on the average reserve requirements against deposits (in reciprocal form, the "money multiplier"). If the reserve requirement is high enough, say, 100 percent, the banks can't indulge in any extra new loan and money creating; if it is low enough, say 0 percent, the sky is the expansion limit, subject to individual bank prudence.

Under these circumstances, the money control dilemma involves the following consideration. Some post-deregulation money forms (e.g., money market deposit accounts) do not have any reserve requirements, which puts these types of money creation beyond the reach of general credit control. Moreover, many more gaps are yet to come. Unless formally defined by central banks as transactions accounts, the newest money forms such as e-cash or cybermoney won't bear any reserve requirements either, and we won't even know how big or where they are.

If deposits become an endangered species, then central banks may need to figure out other ways of reestablishing control. Professor James Tobin has suggested reserve requirements against assets (minus capital liabilities) of all banks.[4] Many central banks impose "differential" reserve requirements depending on the category of deposits direction and use. This strategy can work when the lender is a bank or regulated depository institution, but the emergence of e-money raises questions about how any central bank is going to be able to know exactly what is going on within the balance sheets of nonregulated private entities, let alone impose reserve requirements of this nature against them. Another suggestion has been to limit e-money issue to regulated banks, possibly to the Treasury in the manner of its normal currency issue. But that responsibility may make the government a hated data collector, and could thwart technology.

Under the present regulations, central bankers face another predicament. The path to the most efficient and competitive payments mode suggests that experimentation by users based on cost and quality is the best—and perhaps the only—way to go. But if consumers unpredictably shift from one money form (demand deposits with one reserve ratio) to another money (MMDA's or smart card e-cash, which have no reserve ratio), a central bank's links between money and reserve base are seriously disturbed.

This problem of unpredictability has of course been important, in the gradual Federal Reserve downgrading of money—first the narrow transactions money M1, then the broader aggregates—and significant elsewhere as well. According to Andrew D. Crockett, of the Bank of England, "In most countries that have used monetary aggregates as a guide to policy, previously stable relationships have tended to break down." Professor Charles A.E. Goodhart of the London School of Economics talks of the rising central bank independence from governments and the resurgence of policy "discretion" (generally freed from rigid money growth rules) that accompanies it.[5] Publicly announced monetary aggregates still continue to be important as intermediate targets in Germany especially, and to a lesser degree in France, Italy, and Spain, but the United Kingdom abandoned monetary targets even in lip service in 1987. Other countries—including the United States—that go through the formalities of money growth announcements follow a more discretionary policy in private based on specific market needs of the day.

The greater freedom generally granted central banks is not surprising. Deregulation, or "financial liberalization" as it is known abroad, undoubtedly plays a part. Greater mobility of capital makes it more difficult to control monetary aggregates. In many countries, the volatility of exchange rates is a contributing factor, since inflows and outflows of funds can have temporarily significant effects on the monetary base. The weakening of the traditional relationships between money and nominal GDP poses a difficult question for policymakers.

Last but certainly not least is the matter of technology and the ease of money transfer. It can never be known whether people will prefer to hold cash, which *is* reserves, or money market accounts or private computer money, which require zero reserves. Very likely they will choose something in between, the garden variety demand deposits or a mix of all, then vary their holdings. A central banker can never be sure.

This fuzziness in what amounts to uncertain personal behavior clouds the "multiplier" relationships, or the extent to which additional injections of reserves into the system will actually be translated into money creation by banks. Those who still favor money targeting hope to be able to work out the new relationships, once the technology settles down. However, that may take a very long time.

In summary, a central bank's leverage over money creation shrivels because (1) it is not clear what money is in the world of exotic new technologies; (2) the use of different accounts shifts unpredictably, given the electronic ease of transfer; (3) much money is not subject to reserve requirements (e.g., MMDAs or e-cash); or (4) network architecture is such that EFT and e-money systems can move funds undetected outside the formal banking system in unlimited multiples. When exchange rates are also primary targets, the conflicting goals enhance the pre-existing difficulties in money targeting.

More Links: Money and the Economy

Still another set of linkages switches the focus to all the good things one may wish for the economy, such as stable prices, international financial harmony, exchange rate stability, sustained economic growth, and so forth. Traditionally, with varied instruments plucked from a well-stocked toolbox, all central banks hope to achieve the "apple pie and motherhood" goals of price stability and economic growth, plus international financial tranquility.

Implementation presents a problem, however, especially if exchange rate stability is also a primary goal. Given practical realities, the Federal Reserve first aims at reserves or other operating targets, while also paying lip service to the now downgraded money targets. For example, the Fed hopes to achieve price stability and economic growth through altering the cost of money for investing and spending. Higher rates (or "tighter" money) make it more expensive for people to borrow and hence cool the economy if upward price pressures loom. Lower rates (or "easier" money) make borrowing cheaper; ideally, consumption and new investment are encouraged, which stimulate growth, when recessionary clouds portend.

The vehicle for this fine-tuning is the Fed funds rate—the price bankers pay for swapping reserves (deposits at a Fed bank) from those who have reserves above the required levels to those whose reserves are below the minimum. Since the Fed can create its own deposits merely by buying open market securities and paying for them with newly minted deposits, it can also regulate the supply of Fed funds (i.e., reserves). But when you have control over the supply of reserves, you will also have a pretty good shot at regulating the price (or interest rate) at which the free reserves (or Fed funds) are traded.

In 1994–95 eight successive increases in the Fed funds rate averted a feared price inflation by raising borrowing charges. A soft landing finally occurred, and, in retrospect, even most former critics now agree the Chairman's preemptive strike against inflation worked out well. From late January through the balance of 1996, any hint of price inflation was cooled and the Fed funds rate remained stable.

Arguably, price stability can be won by various policy means. The chosen route to attaining it instinctively depends on one's monetary theory or "religion" and most basic of political and economic convictions. Monetarist theory analyzes the relationships between money growth and all the positive elements identified in the economy: stable prices and real growth of incomes. The present discretionary theory has its theoretical base in Austrian and Keynesian theory and its practical roots in old-line central banking.[6]

The classic monetarist model of Milton Friedman emphasizes the links between money, permanent income, and prices with interest rates seen as being of minor importance. Money growth is then the major determinant of short-run changes in nominal and real income. Both Professor Friedman and the rational expectations theorists, including another Nobel Laureate, Robert Lucas, wish to limit a central bank to following some pre-established money growth rules. To do otherwise is to scramble the normal market incentives and fool rational market agents, they believe.

A discretionary market model, such as what we now have in practice, stresses the great importance of interest rates for charging or cooling a spending or investment fever in the macroeconomy. Most current models also take expectations into consideration and heed the rational expectations theorists' cry for openness and an absence of jerky or large policy shifts. Policy stability seems to be a current common aim, especially since it appears that funds that go into capital markets are very sensitive to changes in interest rate perceptions. On the other hand, if policymakers are less certain about what it is they are targeting, does this make policy instruments more vapid at the same time they are more open? For example, Chairman Greenspan's testimony to Congress in February 1996, interpreted to suggest that the Fed would put a hold on further policy easing, triggered irrational waves of U.S. bond market selloffs, plus some dollar weakness as well.[7]

Velocity, or Money's Use

Talk of money's velocity also has its special fashion cycles, tailored to the realities of the day. From the time of the 1951 Fed–Treasury "accord" until about the 1970s, our policy was largely market based, and velocity wasn't often stressed. "Leaning against the wind" was how Chairman William McChesney Martin described his pragmatic approach.

The monetarists had their day in the sun in the years 1978–82 when Paul Volcker came to the Fed with the express desire of rolling back double-digit inflation. Since then, the Federal Reserve has once again followed the market's course. Given drastic change, and the political mood, perhaps it had no other choice.

This switch seems in keeping with the times—a little bit of official money growth goes a longer way. Given our present transactions volumes and innovation, one neither expects, nor wants, official money stock to rise at rates that formerly would have seemed appropriate. Credit cards reduce public cash-holding habits, while ATMs permit cheaper and faster access to interest-earning accounts as well as to cash when needed. The payment of market rates of interest induces customers to economize on narrow transactions money, which bears little or no yield. It's easy to take advantage of any higher market yields electronically. Indeed, much money moves out from the banking system altogether. At the same time, an underground economy interested in moonlighting and/or tax evasion increases its stash of hidden currency, which adds to the uncertainties concerning money's whereabouts.

The years ahead will see continued sweeping changes in money demand and use, and portend an erosion in the ability of central banks to control money. Paper check writing may decline, relatively. Merchant point-of-sale (POS) devices, along with ATM use at grocery stores and malls, may reduce our physical money needs. Payors will send greater proportions of money payments directly via bank wire systems or the Internet. People may initiate money transfers on line from home computers or smart card terminals via satellite. Users may economize on zero or low-yield transactions money balances and take advantage of cheaper, faster, more efficient payments opportunities. Except for cash, narrow transactions money may become an endangered species.

The velocity of official money under these circumstances can rise toward infinity, while the public's demand for official zero-yield money could shrink to nothingness. I don't really expect that dire scenario (for central banks) to materialize, however. Something will continue to "turn over" as official money, although we are not quite sure what it may be. If central banks are still around, and I am also very confident about that, the velocity of what serves as official money—whether national currency or an international electronic unit of value—will matter.

It still makes a big difference whether money holders stuff any remaining cold cash inside a mattress, dig holes in the ground for their precious gold, leave smart card balances intact on their card, or zap funds around the world many times a day.

It also matters whether we look at the discrete *income* velocity of money or its continuous throughout-day *transactions* velocity. The Fed's three V's corresponds to the three M's. The GDP velocity of M3, for example, shows us how many times average M3 money stock went into GDP for the quarter. Thus far, GDP velocity of M1 and M2 (V1 and V2)—despite some very erratic shifts, especially in the early 1980s—seems to be back on historical track, as compared with 1960. V3, even more jagged since 1960 and especially in the past decade, is maybe two-thirds higher than in 1960—not a great amount. On the other hand, transactions velocity (or money's continuous use for all transactions) has moved up sharply. That result is not surprising given the rising transactions on Fedwire, CHIPS, and other electronic nets coming on-line.

Transactions velocity includes the throughout-day electronic flows, which serve a powerful buying—and potential capital market jarring—function. Continuous transactions flows are not all documented, and much escapes measurement altogether. The startling two trillion-plus dollars daily on Fedwire and CHIPS is well known. At least another trillion also flows daily on wires of other central banks. The Bank for International Settlements data show (for 1995) the daily over-the-counter derivatives flows alone at close to $1 trillion dollars, far exceeding earlier expectations.[8] Daily turnover of the exchange-traded interest rate and futures contracts appears to be even higher.

For the world's big clearing banks with much wholesale and international business, the rate of deposits turnover may be as great as 100 or 1,000 times a day for transactions money flows. Potentially, this money may turn over within fractions of a second. Needless to say, each time the money turns over, it's used to purchase something. That money flow ($M \times V$), the underlying official money times its rate of use, buys financial assets. It circulates around the world and moves capital markets, causing them to rise and fall. It sets us wondering about the appropriate concepts, and monetary theory, for a contemporary age.

A Money Flows Theory

The concept of money flows arises quite naturally under the circumstances. It combines all money of whatever type, along with the velocity of each, and it covers all transactions, which occur at many multiples of the official reserve base. Money can be considered a *discrete* and netted MV-based concept relative to final GDP in a series of snapshot cameos captured at end-of-day intervals. Or we may observe the whole *flow of money continuum*, or "effective money" $M \times V$ for the purchase of all transactions (including financial assets) throughout the day.

One may think of money flows as continuous in time, used and usable throughout the day and around the world, in capital markets as in real goods markets. In concept, money flows represent the full value of payments transactions throughout the day, year, or other time period, specified in terms of dollar or other currency.

Many years ago, a student commented that money flows, and central banks' attempts to control them, reminded him of leaky pipes and plumbing problems. I thought about that for a while and then decided he had a point—indeed, some of the terminology is similar: we talk of excess liquidity and of draining or pumping reserves into the system. Perhaps the flows of water and money do have something in common. When you heat fluids beyond some critical level, the characteristics of the system change quite abruptly. Perhaps this physical fluids phenomenon tells us something about what the fast money flows may do to financial systems, when money velocity is "heated up" beyond some critical level, at particularly turbulent times for markets.[9]

The only economic lab experiment we have on the subject, the 1978–82 money control "experiment," tended to support the hypothesis that a narrow focus on money growth was accompanied by greater gyrations in *both* interest rates and short-term money growth. Both money and interest rates behaved better when the Fed abandoned money targeting in rigid form after 1982 when it decoupled or cut the links between rigid money growth and interest targets. Another, related, argument holds that money control was set in motion just as deregulation was occurring. The deregulation caused previously held beliefs and estimates of behavioral relationships (or elasticities) to change. In either case, control was doomed unless the Fed could understand the demand for the different aggregates.

Since then the Fed has tended to move rather cautiously, and usually in small steps, when altering the Fed funds rate. It recognizes, intuitively or otherwise, that any given policy change seems capable of producing a sharper market impact. Amid the money churning, a central bank must seek to avoid destabilizing the markets without possessing the ammunition often available to those who would speculate against its currency or debt issue. Any central bank's tools for doing this have unfortunately been blunted since there now exist layer upon layer through which any money control mechanisms must filter, some tangible (e.g., cash), some accounting in nature, some electronic based. All move, potentially, within the financial economy in one interconnected but murky mass.

The effective money multiplier (i.e., the relationship between money base and money) stretches like a rubber band as we back away from conventional M's into the realm of space-age money. From a modest 2.4 for M1 money, the M3 money multiplier rose, in 1995, to 9.7. In contrast, the gross "money flows" multiplier, if one can think in those terms, soared to over 1,300 when transactions (both electronic and check based) are considered. It is not surprising that under these circumstances a central bank might have difficulties in official money control.

"Effective money," which buys goods and services of all types, consists of conventional money plus electronic money times the continuous rate of use of the whole lot. From the fusion, we derive the combined money flows concept. As we move away from conventional money to the money possibilities of the future, the fusion of the old M and V becomes the true effective cojoined medium of exchange. When money exists as credits on an electronic net—one isn't quite certain where this would be at any given nanosecond—it becomes difficult if not impossible to separate out the underlying M and its turnover, or velocity V. At the extreme, there is only one giant MV blob—money flow in its entirety.

Effective Money and Jagged Control Chains

The electronic value flows, and bundled financial units, portend to be the most troublesome from a control viewpoint since no one knows how big they are. Sometimes we know something about the size of the settlement balances, sometimes not. The gross flows may settle net in the money base directly—in Fed funds or reserves (CHIPS, the ACH's). Or, and perhaps more typically, the clearing may proceed as links in a jagged chain: first, netted out on the system's books, then transferred some time later to designated clearing banks, then to credits, say, on CHIPS, and finally to reserves net settlement.

Credit cards as well as securities settlement take this link-chain clearing and settlement route. For some other flows—especially the new types that are Internet linked—there may be fund conversion delays of all sorts, some by payor choice. In some other cases, we see a kind of game of musical chairs.[10] Payees often ask why, when funds can move so fast, do they have to wait so long to get their money. Again, the refrain that often recurs: funds move fast, settlement is not all that fast. The sand in the gears is something a lot of people including the official money guardians would like to flush out.

The meandering deposit settlement modes all reflect an attenuation of control links; money gets to be settled in other money, rather far removed from Federal Reserve control. The other barter-like electronic settlement modes still farther up the line—through the Internet or some other open system—can also warn of a severing of the links between base reserves and money in any predictable policy-related sense.

There is an irony in this situation. The raw new images conjure up some uncomfortable old ones—those that predated and hastened the development of the Fed system. Prior to 1913, the reserve pyramiding within the banking system was thought to contribute to the recurrent panics of the time. Money tended to be layered on a deficient reserve and gold base. Big city banks held reserves of cash and gold; smaller respondent banks held reserves in the form of central reserve city deposits, at one or more layers removed. In case of recurrent bank panics, the big city correspondents often did not have enough reserves of gold to satisfy their own cash-starved customers as well as those of the dependent country respondents.

This unhappy scene could also be replayed with cybermoney or prepaid cards, which, while related to deposits, are able to be transferred in split seconds into cash (assuming the physical cash exists on hand). If the central bank directly issues e-money to bank customers, this problem may be avoided. In the event that cash is insufficient, it can be generated by the central bank. The modern tool of open market operations goes far toward removing the threat of the reserve shortfall that existed in a pre-Federal Reserve environment. It is easier to manufacture Fed funds as reserve backing than to create gold out of thin air.

Still, a concern exists. The pre-Fed pyramiding pales in the face of what is arising in the electronic age. The specter of digital cash served up by virtual entities, their nonbank liabilities potentially a settlement media, causes central bankers to shudder, whether or not they admit it publicly. To get around that particular nightmare, some have suggested that central banks retain sole responsibility for issuing digital cash. On the other hand, many—but not all—central bankers turn away from the thought of inhibiting innovation in a nascent industry, or taking on its function.[11]

The Future: Back to the Past?

In the hypothetical extreme, there may be no M or monetary base, merely continuous turnover in the money flows total. The money multiplier for the value sector then shifts up to infinity. (If settlement lags get longer, we may also approach this baseless money system.) But of course this proposition becomes nonsense, and then central bank liabilities may cease to function as a money base or standard. By necessity, a new payments standard is substituted for that particular value segment, based on commodities or "promises" of private bank-like high-tech entities.

Call it electronic barter, if you wish. In this scenario, credits are provided based on the full faith and credit (or power) of the issuers of digital money. Instead of gold or dollars, there may be oil or financial futures or cybermoney as quasi-monetary backing for that sector of society's new money. Instead of required reserves there will be the buyer's general reputation and reliability or stores of commodities, real or intangible, present or future.

The electronic issuer—which holds the commodity credits and settles transactions—may be self-regulated and subject to marketplace review. The new system may well be (Pareto) optimal for society, given its awesome power and efficiencies. Buyers will reject the risk prone and the unsound. The electronic commodity barter that users want may be well tailored to the needs of corporate users, hunched in front of their "groupware"—or of those shopper/Net browsers who may wish to use home terminals for many purposes, including buying tires as well as phantom intellectual property.

Business suppliers of this free-spirited medium of exchange may act judiciously, in the manner of the successful Renaissance goldsmith who knew how much reserves to keep on hand to meet any cash outflows—an early type of what later came to be known as fractional reserve banking. They may meet and pass the tests of the marketplace with carefully burnished reputations. Such suppliers may function wisely in the manner of the correspondent banker who holds reserves for others and makes loans to client (respondent) banks as a lender of last resort. Or the nonbank suppliers may enter the banking system through purchase or charter of a specially constructed bank and voluntarily endure regulation. Some nonbank creators seek out the embedded experience of banks quite eagerly, although not necessarily the most highly regulated ones.

Given all the possibilities, the future attenuation of Fed control over money may not be a problem. Other, more effective means of control may be and have been substituted. There may be decades in which to make the proper adjustments and necessary fine-tuning. But we cannot be sure since we cannot know who or what will hold the power. We shudder to think of aggressors seizing that payments power along with any misbegotten oil or national resource treasure or chokepoint monopoly control within the electronic system. To prevent the reins of power from falling into the hands of a high-tech robber baron, antitrust surveillance has mounted. Regulation of e-creatures may be in the cards, as a matter of public protection.

The Alice in Wonderland Paradox

Control implications are, however, less dramatic. Given the altered dynamics of EFT, it comes as no surprise that central banks have shifted policy strategy in the past decade. First, the new money forms and flows stretch—it seems almost sometimes to infinity—the links between reserve base and what can serve as a medium of exchange. Given the attenuated links between what central banks try to control and what they have to control it with, short-term money control becomes difficult and often downright impossible.

Second, the fast flows of electronic money alter the feedback mechanisms. The *stability* parameters of money control systems change. We enter an Alice-in-Wonderland world, given money flows speeds. When central banks try too hard to control money, they easily can make things worse. Not only do money growth aggregates become more erratic, but so too may interest rates. The present and most eclectic mix of targets has the advantage of defusing (decoupling) any money and interest-rate chain reaction in the event of instability. With flexible targets, the unhappy spectacle of money and interest rate volatility feeding back on one another becomes a less likely prospect.[12]

Lip service has been generally paid to rules, but a most cautionary form of good old-fashioned discretion wins out in the end. Changes in Fed funds rates have been gradual, policy shifts quite subtle, and the targets market oriented. The present policy is by no means new. Successful central bankers have always had to function, in varying degrees, according to the feel of the market. A backing away from money growth rules was inevitable. The money flows continuum has been both higher and less predictable and the degree of money pyramiding atop a small real reserve base is unprecedented. Indeed, the banking and deposit link may be gone altogether for some electronic money forms. With discretion, the Fed has adapted to the reality of new money forms and flows and so have most other central banks. They have done so to keep a grip on internal macropolicy and financial markets and most have succeeded.

The Role of Government

114

More tentative has been the honing of the systems that manipulate and deliver the money, and sometimes their alleged grip on would-be competitors is not to the liking of the Antitrust Division. After a hiatus, the Department of Justice is back into the money business, locking legal horns, however, with a very new breed of money entrepreneur.

Markets and the Law

There once was a very young attorney general at the Justice Department who was admired by his staff for getting things done. He liked to play touch football and he also had friends and relatives in high places. His name was Robert Kennedy and his brother was the president. One day in 1961 (as the story was told around Justice), the distinguished economist and Harvard professor John Kenneth Galbraith said to Bobby and the president, "I don't understand. Tell me if I'm missing something. The prime lending rate for big city banks always moves up at precisely the same time. The banks act in unison. Now is this purest of pure competition or collusion? Why doesn't someone find out?"

And so Justice got into matters of banking. It also entered into alliances with bank regulators. As the Justice Department and its regulatory counterparts wrestle with necessarily untested concepts, the worlds of Bill Gates and payments systems are thrown together. The trek from Bobby Kennedy and the *Philadelphia Bank* case to high-tech payments markets is an interesting one, with useful lessons for navigating the impending rapids.

From Camelot to the Internet

From those early years of Camelot, the antitrust interest in banking has waxed and waned. You might say that it's in a full-moon phase once again. Then and now, it begins and ends with cascading merger waves. A surge of bank mergers in the 1950s, mild compared with the present-day levels, would energize Congress into enacting new legislation, the Bank Merger Act of 1960. This act required the three government banking agencies to apply competitive standards in evaluating bank mergers and the Attorney General would henceforth give his or her views regarding the probable competitive effects of each and every merger. A new generation of banking experts seeking practical legal experience was born within the Department and many of the trial attorneys were eager to bring cases.

In the Supreme Court's landmark decision in *Philadelphia National Bank* (1963), the Court held that commercial banks produce services that are unique, that "enjoy cost advantage or . . . subtle consumer preferences which sufficiently insulate them from effective competition from other sources so as to constitute a separate line of commerce." Within the next thirty years, that narrow definition would change in ways beyond belief.[1]

At the same time, the Justice Department began to inquire into pricing patterns and restrictive practices in the banking industry, culminating in the Minneapolis bank price-fixing cases (1964). That interest has also enjoyed a renaissance in the current electronic money environment. Justice instituted cases—in retrospect some significant, some not—and by the publicity received got banks to reconsider their modes of operation in light of antitrust standards. EFT suddenly became an unheralded force that would reshape markets and how one ought to look at them. Through a process of self-regulation and negotiation, and of course the powerful thrust of technology, greater competition was seen as the norm—cozy relationships between bankers, as sometimes alleged, became an unacceptable way of doing business.

Antitrust had been enforced at least as enthusiastically, if not more so, by Republican administrations than Democrats. I remember a rousing talk in the Department's Great Hall by then Attorney General John Mitchell at the beginning of the Nixon administration, on the evils of bank concentration. However, enforcement zeal in the form of challenges litigated to a conclusion was not a characteristic of the later Reagan and Bush administrations. Antitrust's Economic Policy Office analysis was thorough, but the Department's conclusions now typically supported negotiating settlements to eliminate particularly egregious restraints.

The Role of Government

In the 1980s, the antitrust presence in banking matters shrank, which gave young engineers and computer people a freer hand in the markets just gearing up. New entry into software and slices of the EFT markets by innovative computer entrepreneurs was spectacular, and freely allowed the market to test new ideas.

The current regulatory pendulum seems to be swinging back. Some of the young, but no longer small, computer firms and innovative EFT systems are beginning to swallow others up. A few computer software companies have established overwhelming market shares of their own, in operating systems (Microsoft) or financial software (Quicken). Rightly or wrongly, the thought of potential robber barons lurking in their midst worries some suppliers and competitors, frankly frightened by the invisible hand of those perceived as more powerful. In response, the Assistant Attorney General for Antitrust has reentered the fray. The Department's Sherman Act monopolization powers are dusted off and reapplied, as adjunct to its anti-merger powers.

The Fed, Antitrust, and the other regulators and academia are working together once again to sort things out, in their own, appropriate new way. The Comptroller of the Currency assembled many of us to revisit the issues in November 1995 along with the talented younger people now handling these issues in (or against) government. Largely organized by Professor Bernard Shull on leave from Hunter College, the Conference was comprehensive. It was sparked both by a bittersweet college reunion atmosphere and a desire to find out what was really going on. The specter of Bill Gates and the Internet was evoked—unusual at a banking conference—and there was a little of the old fire-eating antitrust zeal from the past, albeit muted. Many faces were familiar, but the regulatory and antitrust thinking had adapted to the times.[2]

The issues are transformed, but clouded. Whether you talk to government or privately employed experts, any unease about the newest wave of massive bank mergers is softened by the changed political and regulatory climate. Consultants to bankers argue that banking markets ought to include electronic suppliers from afar, just as their predecessors used to argue a generation ago that the thrifts should be included. So what is new? In bank merger cases, defendants always carved out the broadest possible markets so as to make their market shares as minuscule as possible, while the government trial attorneys tended to think the opposite way.

Regulators of all stripes thus have different views of relevant markets, usually broader than *Philadelphia Bank* but not yet covering the whole swath of cyberspace. But some continue to be perplexed, especially when it involves carving out appropriate markets in which to delineate competitive clogs, if any. Given data deficiencies, plus rampant banking changes just about everywhere, it is not easy to analyze the competitive effects of bank mergers. At the Comptroller's Conference, when he discussed using the "cluster" approach to analyzing bank mergers, Federal Reserve Board Vice Chairman Alan Blinder said, "I thought when I took on this job that there has to be a better way. Now I'm not so sure."[3]

Whether to Merge or to Share

Faced with the electronic unknown, banks scramble to acquire other banks in order to achieve efficiencies. Although data on the efficiencies of large-scale mergers are ambiguous, the latest wave of bank mergers has gone largely unchallenged. Nationwide concentration has increased considerably, but the U.S. banking system still remains by far the least concentrated in the world.[4] Regulators don't usually bring formal merger cases to litigated conclusions and have generally required that those seeking to acquire others divest branches so as to prevent ill effects in certain markets.

There has been some renewed interest in the theory of linked oligopoly, which analyzes the possible tacit understandings that may arise as a matter of mutual forbearance when the same leaders meet head-on, over and over, in many markets. In the absence of specific evidence of harm, however, the mergers that encompass linkages between many markets have gone unchallenged. Nonbank suppliers may stand in the wings, ready to push for business.

What is different now is the focus on how the electronic systems, including banks and nonbanks, may develop. Will we have systems controlled by the powerful few, such as software giants or large regional systems? The regulators (including Antitrust) are concerned that someone now, or in the future, could control the new technology chokepoints (PC-operating systems or financial software or regional card systems), then leverage their position to control the newly developing electronic banking commerce. But, points of view differ.

The Innovators: One View

Suppose you are a bank or high-tech firm hoping to get into the business of electronic commerce and e-money. It's an expensive proposition, risky and complex, and you will need a lot of expertise as well as cash. How do you go about making your way into the minds and hearts of consumers as Visa and MasterCard did some twenty years ago?

Look at the point of view of the private players, the people of innovating ranks who must bear the expense of their innovation, often substantial, along with the risk of failure. They must also consider the law and how courts will view their often novel strategies. Most of all, they must develop and market a product which the public will want and accept, at a price that people can afford but will still produce profits. Keeping all these considerations in mind, some of them conflicting, your optimum approach once technology and financing are in hand may take several directions:

1. First is the joint venture or consortium route. This is the tried and true way, from our plastic card past, although much broader in both business partners and geography. When you fashion the bits and pieces of an EFT system together into a non-exclusive system, open to all wishing to participate, you normally don't get into antitrust trouble. Usually, it can be argued that efficiency demands the venture's broad scope. Quite often, you must be part of a network in cyberspace in order to ply your trade.

The White House sponsored CommerceNet, with informal links over the broad web of cyberspace, and it dwarfs any banking markets the Antitrust Division of my day had ever struggled with. In this particular collaboration, IBM hooks up with AT&T and MasterCard and BBN, the Internet provider, as well as other key telecommunications people and banks around the world. Quicken has responded to overtures by banks as a route to the electronic commerce of the e-money age, and now announces that it may strive to do your banking business for you over the Internet, provided encryption partners can supply the necessary security. The range of those who wish to get together, quite voluntarily, is breathtaking; equally compelling is the need for collaboration in many cases.

2. A more hazardous course of action is the formal merger. You buy (or otherwise acquire) whatever you may need in the business, as one

swift route to synergy—provided that no one objects. This may be critical if the goal is to beat out the competition. Microsoft is said to buy budding companies and patents important in the emerging technology. Electronic Payments Systems (which runs the MAC system) seeks to expand its operations through combination, as have many other regional ATM systems. IBM wishes to gain a quick and well-positioned fix into "groupware," the missing middle link between software and the mainframe.

The merger can be voluntary, as the proposed Microsoft/Quicken combination was before Microsoft threw up its hands when threatened with antitrust action. Or, it can require more persuasion as happened with IBM/ Lotus. The objective is to get the synergistic link for a calculable and bearable cost both direct (payment to the stockholders of the acquired company) and indirect (the avoidance of possible antitrust retribution).

The Regulators: Another View

The government has priorities, too, but they do not necessarily reflect the private sector wants. It seeks to encourage the fastest pace of innovation, in order to make markets fluid and responsive and consumers happy at the lowest cost. However, regulators want to avoid any clogs on competition. and won't tolerate anyone's getting an iron vise as the gatekeeper for critical chokepoints in a "bottleneck" system—such as an area's sole ATM—that everyone needs to use and access.

What exactly is the government supposed to be looking at? Any infringement of the antitrust laws, Clayton Section 7 (the merger statutes) or Sherman Act Sections 1 and 2 (contracts in restraint of trade or monopolization) is clearly in its ball park. To avoid such possible violations, you first have to identify some markets, both product and geographic, in which to do your analysis of any bad market factors or, in the jargon, "anticompetitive effects."

Second, and in the same vein, the government thinks about how the public may fare in a period of uncertain system standards. Like a many-headed creature, each regulatory brain—the Fed, other regulatory agencies, as well as Justice—will want to guarantee that markets and entry can develop free from restraints, and that no one secures monopoly power, thus defeating the normal market forces. Again in the jargon, the object is to avoid "market failure."

The following tightrope must be walked: Government wants the

Microsofts of the world to nurture their staff's creative imagination and come up with the best technology solutions. At the same time it wants to assure that all players in (or otherwise likely to be in) the market remain free to do their own thing, too, unconstrained either by coercion or more subtle constraints. Since government interference can both help and hurt, it must operate in a delicately balanced equilibrium that's shifting all the time.

A Moving Market Equilibrium

The change in market equilibrium comes swiftly when a whole new technology sweeps into view. Bankers must work with the high-tech communications/computer throng if they wish to retain or expand their position. The servants of government, whether the Fed or the Antitrust Division, sometimes must review, and perhaps help redefine, the operating regulations and standards. The time-honored rules of the game cannot be assumed to apply to the new banking procedures being brought on-line. Just look at the complex credit card system described in Chapter 4, or the ATM/debit card modes discussed in Chapter 9.

The money world has never been the same since the birth of plastic money. Credit cards ushered in a different money "thing," offered by private joint ventures put together in a moving money environment. System members initially set the standards, and, quite naturally, they attempted to enhance or at least preserve their place in the sun. That wasn't easy when the major innovators were no longer limited to players in financial markets but included vital contributions from the merchant and computer fields. Some of these new players have talked as though the banks may now become obsolescent as a necessary intermediary in transfer of money value between buyer and seller. Whether that is likely or merely an argument for greater deregulation of the banking functions of all players, we will discuss later. As a minimum, the old rules and standards of the banking game will need major rethinking, given the role of greatly different networks.

Yesterday's Legal Standards: An Anachronism

Former Assistant Attorney General Don Baker believes that today's network opportunities all too often will be unnecessarily impeded by yesterday's legal rules. Legal uncertainty can thwart new and uncertain business opportunities. An old, vague, and broad statutory concept—outlawing "every contract, combination . . . or conspiracy in restraint of trade"—can discourage useful development if it is unthinkingly applied to membership and access policies of the electronic joint venture.

Three factors are working to place innovators in a vise. First, antitrust courts and government enforcers have generally failed to perceive the importance to market forces of nurturing *competing* networks. Second, they have focused too much on competitive handicaps faced by individual firms, who would rather force their way into the going systems crafted by others rather than construct and operate their own. The third key error, Baker believes, is the historic tendency to treat all joint ventures—and joint venture networks—with hostility. Joint ventures all too often have been summarily condemned to the status of cartels or boycott—or, less pejoratively, to that of public utilities—when instead they constitute the framework for doing business productively and without necessary harm to the free market of which they are, or can be, a part.[5]

The network concept has always been an area of great difficulty in antitrust and it now becomes even more troublesome. The traditional nineteenth-century financial network was a securities or commodities exchange, a physical location at which traders and brokers agreed to consummate transactions during certain hours in certain ways. The location might have been a coffee house, a street corner (as in the old Curb Exchange, now the American Stock Exchange), or just a big room.

Let's look at what happens in the information age. The modern network need not be tied to a particular physical location—and indeed it usually is not. It functions over distance-insensitive electronic links and its facilities include the computer software and hardware scattered around the markets it serves. Its rules are those hurriedly hammered out by members over spans, relatively short in time, but hugely distant in space and geography. Moreover, wherever government helped to fashion the rules, the results were not always successful. Although the Division did a pretty good job of fostering competition between card issuers *within* systems (look at all the places you can obtain a credit card, the different terms you are offered), the matter of *intersystem* competition may fall short of the ideal. The story of the credit card antitrust disputes is illuminating.[6]

The Bank Credit Card Debate: "Duality"

Happily, the first decade of national bank card development was one of considerable competition between the nascent developers. A major bank card issuer was either a MasterCharge (now MasterCard) bank or a BankAmericard (now Visa) bank. In the mid-1970s, however, a series of events led to what is referred to as duality, an environment in which most major banks quickly became members of both national bank card organizations and issued both cards, usually on similar terms. In 1974, Visa sought a business review clearance from the Antitrust Division for a bylaw that would prohibit dual membership for both card-issuing banks and agent banks. Justice was especially concerned that the proposed bylaw might effectively "freeze out" potential new systems. MasterCharge sat on the sidelines. After agonizing over the issue for almost a year, the Division declined to grant the requested clearance. The basis for its ruling was insufficient information to make a satisfactory determination.

In response, Visa completely reversed its position and removed all restrictions on dual membership. Almost immediately, banks rushed to join both systems at an astonishing rate, in part to protect their existing merchant accounts. As a result, the two nationwide joint ventures now have overlapping memberships throughout the United States, and competition in the bank credit card area is between card-issuing banks, not between networks.

Now most banks offer consumer cardholders both Visa and MasterCard plastic and provide merchants with customer authorization and clearance on both transactions. Most member banks offer the merchant a "blended" processing option. The merchant discount (i.e., the cost to the merchant of the card services) became the same for both MasterCard and Visa transactions, even though their interchange fee has never been identical in recent years. Competition between those that issue cards at retail is fairly high these days, but the level of competition between individual systems and their joint ventures is still low.

ATM Debates: A Similar Story

Early on, scholars worried about whether a joint venture could become so broad in scope that no competitive alternatives would be viable. If competing systems are killed off, or merged at an early stage, then you may be doomed forever to a monolithic supplier. In that situation, the one supplier would require regulation to repress any monopoly pricing tendencies. Universal access to the dominant system might be mandated for all comers on a bottleneck theory that users had no other place to turn.

Again, a change in government policy from strict to lenient was evident. In the early years of EFT development, the Justice Department was rather tough on overly broad ventures. In 1977, it denied a business review clearance request by the Nebraska Electronic Funds Transfer System (NETS) because it thought the venture was too broad. NETS was proposing to set up a statewide ATM and POS network among all Nebraska financial institutions. The government denial was based on the premise that beyond some size needed for an efficient banking network, it is preferable to encourage competitive network alternatives rather than universal access to any, and all, would-be participants.

Justice made its presence known in other ways. Wayne Boucher (who was the staff director for the NCEFT) commends Justice for its stand against compulsory state sharing statutes, because they were thought likely to inhibit the growth of many capable competing systems. Justice section chief in charge of banking, Ken Anderson, was said to have proclaimed at the NCEFT meetings, "You guys had better not get together to mandate sharing. And don't recommend state legislation to that effect either. You'll get into deep antitrust trouble."[7]

In the beginning, ATM networks grew rapidly in the 1980s, then regional network mergers began and along with them the coalitions. Look closely and you soon begin to see one dominant regional system emerging in each area: MAC and PULSE are the examples in the legal cases we soon discuss.

From Strict to Lenient and Back Again

Why did it happen? Systems mergers both formal and de facto took place in a variety of ways during the mid-1980s. The Justice Department is reported to have investigated some of them, but did not formally object to any. Systems efficiencies surely were partly at play, since a larger scope enhances card acceptance over broader areas, which is useful for any medium of exchange. The policy for banks was consistent with the generally permissive approach to mergers during the Reagan Administration. Emphasis was placed on what the Justice Department called the "economies of ubiquity." Mergers between competing systems were seen in terms of data processing markets, an approach that put so many firms into the market that the greatly reduced market shares were practically guaranteed to remove any possible antitrust objections.

I asked the Fed's Dr. Steve Rhoades how the saga appeared from his perspective. The Board's special interest in bank mergers, he said, began in 1970 with the Bank Holding Company Act that put the Fed in charge of regulation and activities in that area. The Board took a generally conservative position at the beginning because of considerable uncertainty about the implications for bank competition and aggregate financial concentration. Since 1980 the Fed became more liberal in connection with bank merger policy, partly reflecting changes on the Board as well as newer findings in economics suggestive of fairly easy entry possibilities (contestibility theory). No one of the systems then in process of formation was thought capable of exercising monopoly power.

The situation today appears somewhat different. Joint ventures may not now be forming so much as merging. There is considerable rethinking of the broad concept of data processing as the proper market in which to analyze proposals. In at least one matter before the Board, the market was split up into three different services, terminal driving (processing), switching (in effect, clearing), and access.[8] Apparently, the Board, like Justice, is sensitive to the question of what large ATM systems (such as Pennsylvania's MAC) might be able to do to competitors if restrictive rules are applied on members' activities.

Justice Reentry in Full Force

Ongoing investigations are always under wraps of course, but it's important to know what publicly is being said and done in the field. I asked the Civil Procedures Unit for the Antitrust Division's cases, press conferences, and speeches on banking and computers for the past three years. Quite properly, I was told to narrow the search to the "most relevant" material, unless two spare file cabinets were available to house it all. The fax was duly redrafted, and two large boxes of material were sent on the very afternoon of the week-long federal furlough. They show the extent of the antitrust interest.

Among the highlights was the proposed Microsoft/Intuit merger, which would have brought Quicken, the leader in personal finance software, under Microsoft's control. Quicken's 1994 market share was almost 70 percent and the company could boast of more than 7 million users, the elite of the well-endowed computer comfortable. With Microsoft's "Money," the number two personal finance competitor, the merged company would soak up more than 90 percent of the market. It came as no surprise, therefore, that in April 1995 the Antitrust Division filed a civil antitrust complaint to block the $2 billion deal. "Allowing Microsoft to buy a dominant position in this highly concentrated market would likely result in higher prices for consumers who want to buy personal finance software and would cause those buyers to miss out on the huge benefits from innovation," said Anne Bingaman, Assistant Attorney General for Antitrust. "Moreover, Microsoft's control of that market will give it a cornerstone asset that could be used with its existing dominant position in operating systems for personal computers to seize control of the markets of the future, including PC-based home banking." That's known in the trade as leveraging a position in one market to achieve dominance in another, in this case the one of electronic home banking just starting to materialize.

According to the Justice Press Release that accompanied the complaint, both Microsoft and Intuit recognized that their combination would enable them to eliminate the substantial competition between them in the personal finance/checkbook software market and the emerging market for home banking. Their complaint quotes Intuit's chairman, Scott Cook, as saying to his board of directors that the acquisition would eliminate "a bloody share war" and allow for "enriched terms of trade." The complaint also states that a Microsoft executive concluded: "As a combination we would be dominant."[9] Such language is not helpful when you are a defendant. The merger was rather promptly abandoned, and Intuit has gone on to move into home banking on its own in alliance with many different banks. A lively rivalry has developed between the two major companies who wished to get together, but were thwarted. The Antitrust Division's role was significant.

Networks and a Market Maze

The Antitrust Division looks at complex markets when it makes such determinations. Each situation involves intricate analysis because of the many different interacting layers in the "productive process." The big broad system stands atop this new pyramid, a kind of market-driven oligopoly or utility that serves many smaller systems, institutions, and customers down the line. Level 1 consists of any giant global system network, whether Visa or MasterCard or, for that matter, the Internet itself.

Each will sell (or, in the case of the Net, give away) a basic system service to the wholesale "seller" just below (Level 2), perhaps another interconnected system (PULSE or NYCE or MAC), that handles important regional card arrangements. Next down the line, Level 3 may provide the "gateway access" or switching (clearing) services, and in effect permit the electronic bits and pieces to "talk" to one another and communicate and process the necessary information; we may call these the processing and other wholesale services.

Thus enriched, the wholesale services flow down to the retail institutions, through another layer (Level 4), once again through a smaller clearing "switch" and processor, who keeps track of the accounts. Banks who take care of the merchant charge slips are thus served, and they provide cash (ATM) or credit (VISA and MasterCard) to all the millions of card-holding consumers at the final retail Level 5.

The problem for regulators is to make sure that the efficiencies of the electronic media don't get siphoned off within the many layers on their way down to you and me, in the event that someone manages to grab off some "monopoly" profits in ingenious ways. The following techniques, some not altogether hypothetical, may cause problems for the competition-minded regulators or for Justice.

First, if systems mandate costly rules or practices that are not strictly required by the nature of the business, prices downstream in the intermediate markets may be higher than necessary. (Note that sellers competing downstream for our ordinary banking business may be members of the same EFT system upstream.)

For example, the system, given market power, may levy higher than competitive charges on downstream members, and tacit rules may be developed that will make entry by lower cost firms difficult. The joint venture format, through exchange of some information, may attempt to monitor retail pricing arrangements. In the unlikely event that joint venture contracts specify pricing or other terms downstream at retail, the specter of horizontal (or vertical) collusion and Sherman Act violation is raised.

Another danger is that any Level 1 joint ventures (adopted, say, for clearing purposes) will be broader than necessary. The shared system may encompass financial markets able to be served elsewhere. Ideally, the electronic system may resemble a new technology clearinghouse, suitably updated from paper clearing modes, and just one of many retail competitors. But that may not happen if an octopus-type joint venture, through restrictive contracts or other coercive techniques, pulls the levers on how its members may conduct their other retail banking operations.

Third, entry down the line may be impeded. The EPS complaint that we will discuss in the next chapter focused on this problem, especially on the system's processing restrictions. If Level 1 sellers require their members to limit their purchases of certain services, as, for example, processing, to the system or its members, then that will make it very difficult for outsiders seeking to enter into the business.

That anticompetitive result is fairly obvious. But there are other ways by which similar anticompetitive results can be more subtly achieved. Technical specifications imposed by a joint venture may be structured to make outsider entry more difficult. These specifications may in fact have the effect of impeding entry even if that was not their intention. System requirements about standards, mandatory terminal sharing, or magnetic stripe specifications, for example, may increase new system entry barriers. They may also impose unnecessary direct added costs on retail banking consumers.

A current battle is waging over standards and the common interface, which will permit all the systems to "talk" to one another. But antitrust focus is set quite carefully on any spillover restraints and clauses. The problem is to be sure the standards are not unilaterally forced down the throats of others by some one seller with monopoly power and that cooperation where necessary does not invade the retail marketplace. If the credit card story of the last twenty years has made anything clear, it is that the presence of a unified electronic system need not preclude a happy retail solution down the line.

A Coda

From all indications, the Antitrust Division means to tend to such matters. I recently returned to the Justice Department to speak with Rebecca Dick, now Deputy Direction of Operations, a former colleague and one much admired. The Antitrust Division is actively monitoring EFT systems, and the EPS (Electronic Payments System) settlement is very important. Its MAC system, from New Jersey and Philadelphia, is the largest ATM net in the country, and EPS had rules in place that made it very difficult for other ATM networks or processors to enter and compete with them. The evidence was dramatic.

In the historical spin from Camelot to the Internet, the banking options of the future can be freed from their brick and mortar limitations. We follow markets mired seemingly in quicksand. On the other hand, the local commercial banks still serve the vast majority of households and small businesses. The entrenchment of any national "virtual" banking has a very long way to go.

Quite abruptly, the dynamics seem to change again. MicrosoftNet turns out not to be the giant behemoth that would drive out the on-line companies. On the contrary, keen competition for all comes directly from the Internet. Vendor plans change—often abruptly.

The players in the money game search out other suitable partners in a kind of ritual mating dance. Sometimes the unions are very happy and very successful—sometimes they are not so lucky. Once consummated, these alliances can get to be uneasy, even rancorous. In an unhappy family situation, partners may be rivals on other business fronts, and spend their days in system squabbles and lawsuits, as our money odyssey continues.

9

Partners and Rivals

Former Assistant Attorney Don Baker is a leader on the law of EFT and has written the definitive volumes on the subject. In the Antitrust Division's quiescent period of the 1980s, he provided the antitrust guidance to private systems who were groping for the proper answers. When we both first came to Justice in the 1960s, the offices offered a view of some shifting political winds. Demonstrators stood outside to protest the Vietnam War; financial innovators knocked at our doors. It was a different era, both for politics and for banks. The EFT systems were about to be born.

About three decades later, in the winter of 1995, Don and I reminisced in his offices. Don commented that in those early days we were probably ahead of the market, "and John Reed and I began giving speeches and it was only later that things developed. In that early period we tended to think of EFT networks as competing, separate brands. But then in the eighties some people began to think of EFT networks like railroad yards, where you are dealing with monopoly and compulsory access."[1]

Where an existing system is effectively the only game in town, access may be an essential element of the problem. What also must be dealt with is the matter of internal strife between participants. Some will argue that to compete with networks and be attractive to card issuers, they will have to exercise control over charges and keep them competitive. so that card issuers will not turn elsewhere. A band of dissidents takes another approach: let's view this as running a toll bridge and keep the tolls as high as possible to truckers, retail consumers, and anyone else who will pay.

Togetherness, a Way of Life

So what is new? Payments have always worked in joint and interdependent fashion. However, in the old days the partners were usually banks—people of the same fraternity and with a common orientation. When they disagreed, they tended to keep their differences to themselves. Ever present in the background were the central banks maintaining equilibrium and prepared to do the clearing outright or through exercising their quasi-governmental power.

Take the matter of getting money's ownership switched. As one may well imagine, the plain mechanics—or financial gears that do the clearing (switching)—are very different, depending on whether we choose physical or electronic methods. It could also matter whether the switching is done by banks or for banks and their customers by computer-communications megacompanies where financial transactions are a profit-making activity.

For paper, many years—even centuries—passed in which all the arrangements could evolve in orderly fashion. There was perspective, and, most of all, time to hone the techniques. The old paper-based systems had a few joint ventures of the formal sort, like the bank-run clearinghouses, but the links between banks were often informal and part of the tradition of correspondent banking. Privately, the paper payments rules were fine-tuned and clearly understood. Banks did things for one another because it was in their mutual self-interest. They had the option to clear through local clearing houses where they existed, or through the bigger correspondent or central banks on whom they might depend. The proper choice was a matter of market preferences, the area served, the necessary clearing speed, and cost—all the usual business decisions. Peace and harmony did not always reign between clearinghouse members, but usually things could be worked out informally.

To make matters even easier, the old bank/customer relationship tended to be pretty much one-on-one. That basic fact simplifies decision making and adds stability. The banks provide loans and services to the customer; the customer duly supplies the basic "core" deposits and interest fees (or service charges) in return. Offsetting this may be some implicit credits for interest-free deposits or other fee-based business.

Of course electronic payments also deliver through systems. What is new is where and how. Participants may now stretch from outside the banking community. Some partners, brought together by the needs of technology, were never beholden to the central bank nor to the old ways of doing things. They may seek to craft their own rules from scratch and often have different viewpoints.

Too often some unpleasant surprises develop. The entangled system members may have reasonable differences about issues they consider greatly important, sometimes diverging to the point of open conflict. It is, if anything, more complicated when the computer and telecommunications people enter the business.

Internal strife is compounded by two concurrent factors. First, plastic is rapidly evolving from credit card to ATM and now the more exotic retail money forms, such as e-money and the electronic purse. Second, the EFT fraternity is ballooning from the classic banking fraternity to the encryption, telecommunications, and computer specialists. These people may have a very different business perspective. The rules change, market equilibrium is upset, and in the extreme you get bitterness and even lawsuits. Let's look at how the ATM (or debit card) system generally works and then examine the kinds of frictions it has spawned.

ATM Systems: Nuts and Bolts

An ATM system is called a debit system since we get cash, not credit, from the plastic card, and our bank account is debited for the proper amount. Assume that the ATM is located at the merchant's store, say, a supermarket. The customer has just bought groceries and needs cash. The process is shown in Figure 9.1. The consumer has an ATM card from the bank where he maintains his deposit account. This allows him, within agreed limits, not only to avoid a trip to the bank to get cash but also an automatic method of paying for purchases at the supermarket. The ATM card, and the system configuration of hardware and software, provide an alternative to the live teller for the purpose of obtaining cash and it is very convenient to be able to do this at the supermarket.

The cardholder uses his ATM card at the supermarket's ATM terminal and sends a set of instructions to his bank for the necessary cash. He does so by punching the proper commands into the ATM.

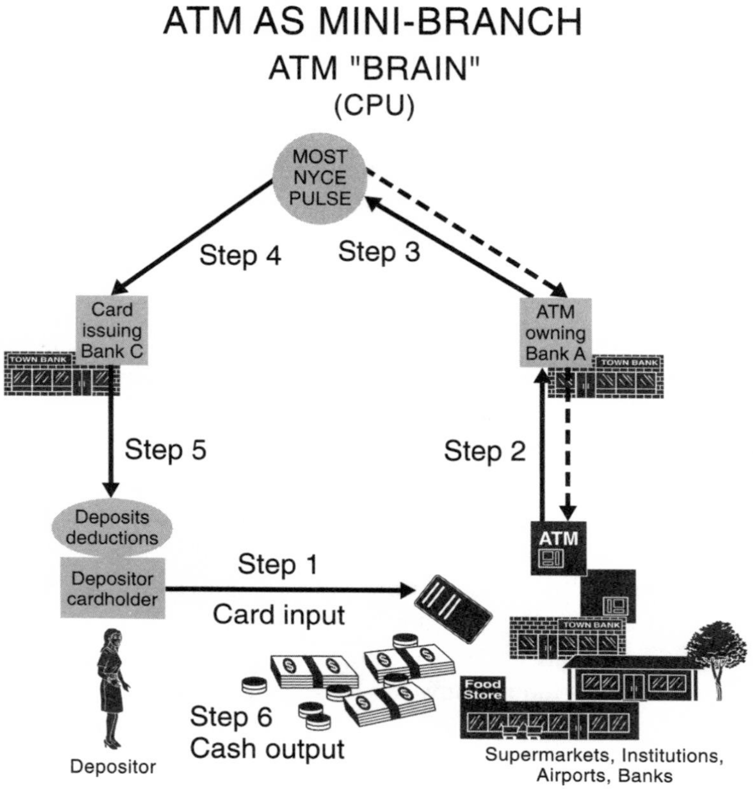

ATM AS MINI-BRANCH
ATM "BRAIN"
(CPU)

Figure 9.1 ATM flows and money delivery paths. When the ATM card holder inserts her card into the machine, computer instructions are sent along though merchant or bank to the system ATM brain or CPU. The CPU, in turn, sends signals in two directions. First, the ATM holder's bank is instructed to deduct the amount of the cash payment from her deposit account. Second, a message is sent through the ATM-owning bank and on-site ATM to provide the desired cash for the customer, shown duly flowing out.

The electronic message flows from the merchant's ATM (and his bank) to the CPU (or central processing unit). The CPU is a sort of electronic central clearinghouse. From CPU, the message is transferred to the grocery buyer's bank. When it arrives, a processor logs the transaction through a computer and deducts the cardholder's deposit account. The system CPU, at the same time and in pursuit of its clearing function, sends a confirmation message back in the reverse direction. That reverse message instructs the ATM in the supermarket to produce the desired cash.

The customer retrieves both the card and the cash from the ATM—there is no need for human messengers to run around from bank to bank, to take slips requesting cash and retrieving it; there is no need for the formal clearinghouse either. The faceless, but very efficient, central switch does the job for everybody.

It is a good system, although often quite expensive for the consumer. It also breeds interdependence. Technology has not obliterated this basic fact of payments systems glue, whether old-time physical or modern intangible. Behind the scenes, electronic system members usually manage to resolve some questions or conflicts that may arise. Other questions, however, may remain unresolved.[2] Let's look at some that can cause trouble.

Pricing Questions

How may system services be best priced upstream, by the all-encompassing joint venture or consortium? We must consider many prices.

The first is the interchange fee, a form of internal reimbursement from one member to another when one receives important and costly services from the other. The interchange fee also passes between members in a credit card system—in this case from the merchant's bank to the cardholder's bank providing the collection services. It will likely evolve to the more exotic money forms, say digital cash offered by one bank or encryption company and then be received by another. "Money" passes from buyer's bank to seller's bank through the nonbank digital clearing mechanism, and there will be an interchange fee perhaps going by another name.

Switching and some other minor system fees go directly to the system, to cover system services performed for all. Here, the switching function is the computer equivalent of the bank clearinghouse.

The card-issuing bank works out a satisfactory pricing arrangement with its retail customer, usually as part of a broader banking relationship. No charge is normally made when the customer uses an ATM owned by her own bank because in that case the ATM is the low-cost substitute for the live teller; the customer deposits provide the implicit payment for her ability to get cash when needed, as in a paper-based system. However, when the customer uses an ATM owned by another bank, the practice is for the ATM-owning (deploying) bank to charge a "foreign" fee. This charge, fixed in advance and uniform for all foreign (i.e., non "on-us") ATMs, will cover all or part of the interchange fee compensation paid by the card issuer to the ATM owner.

The final factor is the arrangement between the merchant and the merchant's bank, when an ATM is placed in, say, a grocery store or airport. Who will bear the cost of terminal deployment in such a setting has been a hotly debated topic within the payments arena.

The presence of in-house ATMs can help sell groceries or lubricate slot machines. But the merchant's bank may consider the deposits and other banking business generated by the merchant in deciding who should pay for terminal deployment. In a similar manner, negotiations between the card issuer and the ATM-deploying bank will normally include the whole banking relationship; a broad ATM net may attract more business and generate more core deposits for the card-issuing bank.

The payor and payee banks in the paper based system recognized this fact of interdependence. Indeed, payee banks normally charge little or nothing for preparing deposited paper for collection. The expectation is that other banks will return the favor. Of course, in a paper-based system, if payee banks see their customer base becoming unbalanced, they will seek to attract deposits against which the system costs can be defrayed by minimum balances or fees. In fact, banks usually strive to enhance deposit base in order to enhance their available loan funds.

For card-issuing banks, the pricing of the whole structure of fees for electronic services may be seen as a mode of interbank competition for deposits. But non-bank ATM deployers do not normally have depositor needs to worry about in their quest for profits. They are mainly concerned about how many people use the machines they set up in other people's places of business.

Shared Costs and Responsibilities

What is the proper sharing of internal costs between joint venture partners when they collaborate to provide important money services to the public? The system divides into cardholder base and terminal base, often provided by someone other than the cardissuer (see Figure 9.1 above). (In fact, the terminals are frequently utilized by more than one competing system.) As we have just seen, an interchange fee is paid by the card-issuing bank of deposit to a "foreign" ATM owner (i.e., an owner other than the card issuer). The interchange fee represents the net price for both services performed and services received. Given this dual role, joint venture partners can have very different views of what is proper compensation.

In on-line point of sale (POS) transactions, the interchange fees could flow in either direction: the merchant gains access to the customer's funds immediately, but the card-issuing bank hopes to secure the merchant's deposit business. Of course, if the government is prepared to shoulder the POS cost, including staff training as in EBT, that reduces strife and expands the system—perhaps at the expense of access to alternatives.

The matter of shared responsibilities must also to be resolved. Again, the more lopsided the system balance, the greater the potential for internal strains and dissension. And, obviously, the greater the system options for joint venture members, the more the potential for internal strife. If a card issuer has the choice of shifting from regional system A into regional system B or into either national systems 1 and 2 or computer systems X and Y, it will be more feisty than if it were stuck irrevocably to the only switching/clearing game in town. This point well illustrates the benefits of competition; it is indeed helpful to certain system consumers, but not necessarily to system harmony.

The Benefits, Shared

On the other hand, what are the relative nonprice (collateral) benefits for participants and how does one best measure them in the interests of system harmony? Are rules the best way of distributing all the benefits you can't quite measure?

Proper hammering out of rules considers the ancillary business generated by a well-functioning ATM net, or the loss of business if you don't go along with other innovators. For the biggest banks, bank prestige is normally a plus, along with the perceived ability to forge nationwide banking links to span the (former) statewide branching barriers. Many now stress card individuality and product advantages, including bonus points or special screening of suspicious card charges.

Thousands of small, community banks must keep apace with the times in order to satisfy customer depositors. If the electronic purse proves to be a successful addition to credit and debit cards, they'll all want to market that as well. Banks must look at the bottom line in terms of all the intangibles because, in the end, they translate into more core deposits and a bigger share of the financial services pie.

Retail customers appreciate a money access medium that enables them to get cash in a variety of far-flung places. The bank's logo at the top of the card is a reminder of the issuer bank who supplies the many options, but the so-called "foreign" terminals, run and financed by others, are very helpful in broadening card acceptability and getting the proper customer image across. Merchants and their banks also gain from the extra business generated by the presence of ATMs to spew out cash quickly in the middle of the night to hungry or thirsty patrons.

A Broken System Symmetry

What happens when the system lacks balance? Does the era of rugged individualism by a few who want to do their own thing or those with different profit orientation take something stabilizing away from payments modes as we comfortably know them?

Economic choice is of course a good thing. System members will wish to be free to focus their system business emphasis heavily on one side or the other, card-issuing or ATM deployment, depending on their optimal business strategy. However, system imbalance of this sort can breed internal conflict.

An ideal picture of system symmetry is not the way the electronic world works much of the time. Consider the position of a firm that is primarily an ATM deployer, but has little or no ATM card base. Its managers would very much like to enjoy the cash inflow of a higher interchange fee that will of course be paid by the card-issuer banks of the system. If they pay what the ATM deployer asks in order to provide their cardholder with this convenience, however, they may see their own profit dwindle sharply. What to do? Some members may threaten to leave the system rather than agree to higher interchange costs. Fewer members in the system, however, means fewer card issuers and fewer cards, and hence less incentive for terminal deployment in handy places. That can easily reduce the value of the regional card further to card-issuing banks and their customers alike.

Higher interchange costs could force the embattled card issuers to raise foreign fees for use of the "not on-us" ATMs. However, instead of paying the higher foreign fees, cardholders may just revert to the ATMs owned by their own bank where possible, a sorry scenario for the system. The absence of substitution possibilities means that the success of each contributor to the final product (money dispensing or card services) uniquely depends on the actions of all other members. Everyone must play ball together; each member usually recognizes this unique interdependence.

Sometimes this recognition is slow to filter down. By analogy, it was hard for the interdependent baseball players and team owners to get together in that sport's fateful 1994 season. Where private solutions are not possible, the sparring parties may call on the courts or the Antitrust Division to resolve conflict. If the Division turns away, the private bar or state attorneys general may utilize the antitrust law triple-damage provisions to take up the resolution slack—the legal precedents are limited. However, *NaBanco v. Visa* (1984), a private suit, challenged the interchange fee set by Visa in the credit card arena. Another private arbitration, *First Texas v. Financial Interchange (PULSE)* was also important in the ATM environment.[3]

The PULSE Arbitration as Example

PULSE is a nonprofit joint venture, founded in 1981 by seven Texas bank-holding companies to provide a link between the automated teller machines of its system members. At the time of the case, PULSE served over 1,800 member banks and was one of the nation's five largest regional networks. First Texas Savings Association was an S&L member of the PULSE system since 1983 when it requested entry for itself and its then competing ATM network, MoneyMaker. PULSE members had some misgivings, but eventually acceded in the face of threatened suit. In an area where prior cases were few, if any, the law concerning compulsory access in these cases is difficult. Entry was arranged without any legal test.[4]

The 1987–88 dispute arose when First Texas objected to a proposed cut in interchange fees. First Texas' displeasure was understandable since its focus was on putting out ATMs, not building up a cardholder base, and First Texas therefore had more to lose than gain. It asked for a legal resolution and agreed to binding arbitration as the cheaper and faster alternative to court action. Implementation of the new lower interchange fee was delayed, pending the outcome of the test.

The Arguments

In its legal brief to the arbitrator, First Texas disputed the network's right to set interchange fees for all system members. When PULSE attempted to lower such fees to meet the competition it perceived from the national networks, First Texas charged that the PULSE board was acting as a buyers cartel. In seeking the fee cut, PULSE was, the brief claimed, exercising market power in product and geographic markets for ATM switching and cash dispensing in the state.

First Texas had proposed what it called a free market pricing plan. The idea was that each money machine owner could decide the charge for use of its terminals by system cardholders. PULSE objected strenuously on grounds of cost, customer inconvenience, and uncertainty. PULSE also contended that First Texas' allegation that PULSE held market power was circular. It was true that, with the addition of First Texas' MoneyMaker, PULSE was switching 95 percent of all interprocessor ATM transactions in Texas. But if First Texas hadn't forcibly insisted on MoneyMaker's entry into PULSE in the first place, PULSE would have had strong competition from MoneyMaker. PULSE also noted that the national ATM switching systems such as CIRRUS and PLUS generally charged lower interchange fees on switched transactions and argued that they would capture much of PULSE's existing business. Some important PULSE members threatened to drop their PULSE membership in favor of the lower cost national systems if the proposed interchange cuts were not implemented.

Banks that founded PULSE and were card issuers had a focus based on their own view. However, First Texas' motives, it was alleged, were affected by its lopsided way of doing business. In March 1988, First Texas operated 862 ATMs. Only 180 were on the premises of a financial institution—most were placed in 7-Eleven stores. First Texas' ATMs, including its 7-Eleven money machines, made up one-third of all PULSE transactions. However, its cardholders' usage wasn't very significant and constituted less than 5 percent of all PULSE-switched transactions.

Based on low use per terminal, the strategy wasn't very efficient either. Of course, consumers liked having ATMs in convenience stores for their use at odd hours; their personal consumer welfare was enhanced, at least at that particular time and place. Whether this fact served consumer welfare generally was the ultimate question in the arbitration proceedings. Consumer welfare is a subjective concept based on personal preferences and not easily quantified.

The Opinion

Professor Thomas E. Kauper's opinion, of August 19, 1988, started from the premise that

. . . PULSE is not what it once was. Changes in its membership have brought an imbalance between buyers and sellers. . . . A greater degree of care is required than before. . . . Claimant's case is of necessity built largely on economic theory. It cannot establish precisely what would occur under the "free market" approach.[5]

Professor Kauper determined that PULSE was the dominant ATM-switching network in Texas. In addition, he concluded that ATMs are themselves a relevant, if fragile, retail market for antitrust purposes. He then conducted a rule-of-reason analysis of the PULSE interchange-fee arrangement. He found that a uniform fee was permissible under the antitrust laws, but only if a method could be provided for ATM deployers to individually set the surcharges and rebates for use of their ATMs.

PULSE accordingly was directed to reinstate the interim fee schedule, and was prohibited from making any further changes in its interchange fees until (1) it adopted a policy permitting the imposition of surcharges and the granting of rebates by ATM owners to test the market for unsatisfied demand, and (2) the level of any interchange fee is determined in accordance with appropriate cost-based procedures.

PULSE was not required to scrap its existing system. The ATM owner would be free to set the fee for its ATM usage. If the owner sets such a surcharge, the consumer is informed of per transaction cost by computer message at the money machine. If the consumer decides the transaction is worth the cost, he instructs the money machine to execute the transaction. The customer is billed by his own bank, who issued the card, through his regular end-of-month bank statement.

The Impact

Subsequent events have made it impossible to test the practical effects of the Kauper decision. First, the "troubled bank" status of claimant First Texas would lead to its arranged merger with the California-based Gibraltar Financial, which also later underwent transformation. Some leading members of PULSE (e.g., MCorp and First Federal) were merged by regulators after the PULSE decision.

PULSE itself continues to flourish in good health. In accordance with Professor Kauper's order, PULSE agreed to institute the variable pricing approach on request for any terminal deployers; however, there have been few takers.

Meanwhile, the legal spotlight moved elsewhere. The issue of what

ATM deployers could charge at casinos when customers ran out of cash was the new focus. In March 1989, Valley Bank of Nevada filed suit in the U.S. District Court of Southern Nevada against both PLUS and Visa, with which PLUS has strong ties. (PLUS is a national ATM system that for some reason has never done as well as the regional systems in capturing the ATM market.) Valley Bank charged conspiracy to fix prices. Valley's plan was to charge customers of other banks in the PLUS system whatever the market would bear for their use of a Valley ATM. However, the PLUS national network (of which Valley Bank was a member) prohibited its members from charging customers of other members an individually set fee posted on the ATM site. Valley argued that the PLUS 50 cent interchange fee was inadequate for covering Valley's ATM costs. But PLUS system management was adamant.

In mid-1989, Nevada passed an act making it illegal for any electronic system, such as PLUS, to prevent ATM discretionary (variable) pricing by any member within the state. Valley National promptly proceeded to charge a flat $1 rate in merchant establishments, such as hotels, airports, and casinos; PLUS and Visa then sought an expedited court review of this legislation. Once again, the present pricing mode for electronic services was on the line and once again the practical results were ambiguous.[6]

In December 1995, the issue of free market pricing arose when some nonbank ATM deployers clashed head-on with VISA and the bank members of PLUS. ATM deployers, including nonbank processors, wished to charge what the market would bear, for example, at race tracks and casinos or convenience stores, but the founding members objected. There was no litigation or arbitration and the matter was settled internally. Variable pricing was allowed to proceed, within the PLUS system, and "foreign" ATM charges were duly raised in April 1996 by those that chose to take this course. On this spin of the merry-go-round, the ATM deployers had their way.[7]

Justice and the EPS

Legal recourse was, however, sought in the case of Electronic Payments Systems (EPS), and its resolution constituted a significant step forward in the establishment of a body of case law applicable to the new business.

EPS, Inc., is the operator of the MAC ATM network, originally started by Philadelphia National Bank, itself of antitrust defendant fame. Justice stepped forward to challenge EPS practices in an April 1994 suit (under Sherman Act Sections 1 and 2) that alleged that in order to be a member of MAC's crucial ATM network, banks were compelled to purchase data-processing services from EPS. This was the first "tying" case brought by the United States in more than ten years and the first Justice antitrust enforcement action in the EFT sector in seventeen years.[8]

Significantly, the complaint recognized that ATM networks may enjoy substantial market power on a regional basis, based on their efficiencies of networking. The problem was to prevent that power from being "tied" or leveraged into other markets, where the possibilities of plenty of other competition existed. Data processing was alleged to be an example of just such a market.

EPS had rules that prohibited any member bank from seeking data processing, or the ATM switching of its transactions, by anyone other than its MAC proprietary network that was owned by only a small group of the member banks. In short, EPS was tying data processing to the sale of access to the MAC network of ATM terminals. It was also a monopolization case because Justice argued that the tie made it difficult for any likely new entrant to gain a foothold. The power came from the fact that MAC had roughly a 90 percent market share in Pennsylvania and a strong position in adjacent mid-Atlantic states (as a result, in part, of prior mergers that had gone unchallenged). The complaint alleged that MAC also used its control over ATM processing to prevent network-member banks from connecting with competing networks.

The Antitrust Division defined two relevant markets. The first was a market of "regional branded ATM access" based on the needs of banks to provide their depositors "ubiquitous access to their accounts." Because no other service constitutes a reasonably close substitute for regional ATM network access, the complaint declared that regional ATM networks constitute a product market. It is by far a narrower market than previously defined either by Justice or the Federal Reserve, and hence is indicative of a more activist regulatory stance.

The Division's second market was ATM processing, which involved "providing the data processing services and telecommunications facilities" in offering regional ATM access. This market is also narrower than previously contended by the government, since it is limited to the ATMs, and more likely will result in a finding of monopolization in regions where one ATM is dominant.

The consent decree, which settled the case in October 1994, required MAC to open its network to independent ATM processors on a nondiscriminatory basis. MAC was permitted to offer volume discounts for processing, but they were to be cost justified on a nondiscriminatory basis. Moreover, MAC was required to sell its network services "at prices that will not vary with the processor selected" and to provide a more open environment for third-party processors.[9]

Other Recent Controversies

Problem areas for resolution in banking, such as whether a particular merger is anticompetitive, have always been plentiful; so too are allegations of Sherman Act violations such as price collusion or restrictive deals. But the PULSE and EPS problems were different. The older, run-of-the-mill situations mostly reflected disputes or difficulties between market participants who were *outside* the organizational structure. What is unusual in the present milieu is the conflict *within*—that is, in the intramural confines of the legally configured joint venture.

Still more important is the basic nature of the dispute that involves the manner of pricing and, in the case of EPS, restraints on member dealings, which have an impact on the nature of the money services for others in these pioneering new schemes. To the extent that government authorities are unwilling to exercise their statutory powers, the private bar must steer the resolution through arbitration (PULSE) or the appropriate private action, at private expense. With regulators now appearing more willing to pick up the ball and perceived as an important force to be reckoned with, this may result in more speedy resolution. It is also useful that Justice is making its policy position clearer and is coordinating its competition-minded efforts with its counterparts abroad.[10]

A couple of illustrations provide the flavor of that remarkable shift. A little less than a decade earlier, Visa, which owns PLUS, the biggest national ATM network, and MasterCard, which enjoys partial consolidation with the second biggest national ATM network, CIRRUS, sought to establish a joint venture together, ENTREE, that would offer point-of-sale (POS, the original name for on-line electronic banking). The industry's concern was whether anyone else would enter the nascent on-line business, if faced with that powerful behemoth.

Justice in this case choose to sit on the sidelines, but the state attorneys general jumped in to fill the void. They argued that the extreme concentration of the new venture proposed by Visa and MasterCard would stifle new entry in point-of-sale and, implicitly, the future on-line electronic money transfer business as well. A May 1990 settlement between the Visa/PLUS and MasterCard/CIRRUS coalition and the attorneys general of fourteen states produced a kind of "split-the-baby" decision.

The settlement did help to clarify the outer expansion limits. The two sponsors agreed to abandon their proposed and comprehensive debit-card joint venture, and the dreaded threat of one monopoly electronic banking system was removed. However, neither MasterCard nor Visa was required to divest their individual ownership in PLUS nor CIRRUS, the two leading ATM systems. Hence, the partial de facto consolidations between credit card and national ATM systems were allowed to stand. Two national systems might remain, but they would not be terribly competitive ones, given their already close relationships.[11]

In a twist of irony, the latest wave of technology may actually unwind these consolidations. When you scan the consortia members prepared to do battle for controling the computer-based operations in the future, you'll see that in the Visa/PLUS and MasterCard/CIRRUS camp are Microsoft and Netscape, respectively. In their charges for critical technology, the MasterCard camp had accused the Visa camp and especially its cohort Microsoft of generating baseless fees. However, the new joint standards announced in the spring of 1996 tentatively yielded to MasterCard/Netscape concerns, and there is hope that on other narrower matters competition between the rival factions lustily continues.[12]

Antitrust quarrels are seen abroad as well. A very important one was also amicably settled following European Union antitrust anxiety. In June 1996, Visa International's European members reportedly dropped proposals to prevent Visa banks from issuing rival credit cards. EU Competition Commissioner Karel Van Miert's warning was the instrument of the duality's European demise, which was hailed as a major victory for member banks. The family quarrel was settled, without the legal bills and hassle of the olden age in which our story started.[13]

In the Age of Internet

The latest wild card of course is the Internet itself. What will happen when, and if, these systems move to the Net's open delivery grounds? Is the Internet paradoxically to become the dreaded quasi-monopoly that captures for itself the scale efficiencies of a grand cyberspace net of nets? If so, its open nature then becomes an advantage.

The Net has not had the profit motive to depend on for either construction or guardianship; when financing was required, the government (National Science Foundation) put up the money. Government sponsorship now takes the form of encouraging private people from many countries and disciplines to get together under nurturing circumstances. Academia still also has a huge stake in protecting its integrity since young graduate students both develop the Net and know how to safeguard it.

Private retail wares and virtual banks are overlaid, as any stroll on the Web will show, and the shakedown from one technology to another feverishly continues. It is reminiscent of the PC wars, when the innocent Altair yielded to Apple, then to IBM and its clones, while operating systems moved from Sun's daunting Unix for the scientifically rigorous to DOS to Windows for the masses.

In mid-1996, Sun Microsystems began to popularize its Java-based interactive operating environment that it hopes to run on pagers, telephones, and other inexpensive information appliances. On the Net, Java hops over operating systems altogether and provides a next-generation threat to Windows. To help the computer illiterate, Sun's JavaBeans builds new types of software from reusable components, as if from a child's Tinker Toy set; undoubtedly it is also directed toward those markets of the future now growing up.[14]

In our present rough and tumble environment, and for some customers, geographic barriers tumble with the emergence of the Internet ready to produce retail services, including, potentially, our banking. Perhaps you can see your loan officer and arrange the terms of your loan interactively through the medium of cyberspace. Regional, national, and international systems can co-exist and aggressively vie for your business. Banks need no longer be the vendors; that function may be performed by the encryption, telecommunications, cable TV, or computer people. The global village puts a different spin on markets and on the many ways we may perceive the universal money that is to be.

Part IV

Universal Money and World Capital Markets

10

Money of the Global Village

Information and trading messages gyrate on financial wires as well as the Internet and it is getting easier to involve more people plus a host of markets, given the many varied e-money trading possibilities. There may, however, be a dark side.

Consider the activities of those who manage to speculate against a currency, say, the dollar or pound sterling, and drive it down. Often in cooperative tandem, the central banks try to stem the downward slide, but the speculators sometimes have more short-term staying power. In September 1992, the Bank of England's attempts to support the pound sterling transferred some billions to the hedge funds traders—not a pretty spectacle. In February 1996, the speculators are said to have reaped a similar advantage from the Bank of Japan's attempts to prop up the dollar in the wake of a decline in U.S. bond markets.

Informally, global banks say that only a relatively small portion of their foreign exchange trading is for real trade and capital transfers. For the rest, banks take positions of their own or for customers. The degree of speculative activity cannot be documented. However, the Federal Reserve Bank of New York reports that overall currency trading has risen sharply, to the trillion dollar level, while growth has been most spectacular for those dollar transactions that are computer traded.[1]

The worldwide computer network links and the speed of message travel have been growing exponentially. They set in motion the twin engines of rising capital markets opportunities and exotic risks.

The Mesh of Cyberspace

Network theory tells us how the mathematics works, to proliferate both opportunities and perils. Well before the popular Internet explosion, I was first introduced to network theory by Tokyo University's distinguished Professor Yasuhiko Oishi. The occasion was the Institute for Posts and Telecommunications Policy's 1990 First International Conference on *Networks and Society*.

The range of papers was as great as the home geography that separated us. Professor Christian von Weisacker's keynote speech outlined some key concepts underlying networks.[2] Computers and communications networks make possible the global market for securities since more and more people can be reached with relatively little additional cost. They can buy and sell at any instant at almost any time of the day.

The networks' distributive efficiencies are immense, with escalating numbers of nodes, or links, between people. Think of these nodes as information switching centers. The Internet is an example of the mother of all networks with many connecting nets in many cities and countries, all hooked to even more people sitting at their own PCs or servers. Let's say a single node of a network connects n individuals. A node of nodes may connect n nodes. Such a network with one secondary node connects n^2 people. A third-order node may combine n second-order nodes and hence connect n^3 users, and so on.

But, while the number of people connected thus rises *exponentially* with the number of nodes, the cost of connecting the nodes (or networks) rises only in *proportion* to the number of nodes through which the connection passes. As the systems mature, they can reach vast numbers of people in ever-rising numbers with relatively small additional cost.

The benefits of all the global interlinking of information and markets have been enormous. Everywhere, the flow of capital has risen dramatically, into third world countries, nations of the former Soviet empire, Latin America, Asia, and Africa. Investors enjoy a broader investment base and better information on which to make their decisions. Issuers see distinct opportunities for lowering their cost of capital by placing securities with foreign investors. Capital can flow almost instantaneously to its desired destination. Money market funds "bundle" individuals' savings and recycle them for special overseas funds.

Governor Eddie George of the Bank of England reiterates this theme of advantageous explosive growth and myriad markets interaction, spiced always with a note of caution.[3] The economic benefits are substantial, but he believes they have a less appealing aspect. The interdependence of financial intermediaries they generate is potentially a powerful means of widely communicating problems around the world. In the literature, "contagion" is the word sometimes used and it doesn't refer to measles. The Governor's warning turned out to be a premonition of sorts.

The Barings Decimation

An example was the Barings' Bank disaster of February 1995. How could a twenty-eight-year-old trader, Nicholas Leeson, sufficiently manage to escape home office scrutiny to immolate the venerable investment firm that had financed the Louisiana Purchase? Apparently, it was because of lack of information, greed, and not knowing when to cut one's losses. Nick Leeson dealt in futures contracts, derivatives that were based on the Nikkei 225—an index of Japanese stocks—in both Singapore and Osaka. In the beginning, this was arbitrage both standard and fairly low-risk, and it takes advantage of small price differences between the two markets.

Later in 1994 Leeson began selling futures options in a fancier derivative known as a straddle, a far riskier (but potentially more profitable) bet that the Nikkei would stay within a certain range. Unfortunately, the Nikkei plunged more than 1,000 points after the Kobe earthquake in January, sinking Barings deeply into red ink. Then the gambling instinct took over more completely. Instead of cutting his losses, Leeson purchased large amounts of a Nikkei futures contract expiring March 10, thereby doubling his bet. He also "shorted" futures on Japanese interest rates and government bonds, selling contracts that Barings did not own.

By the time the British authorities began the sale of its assets, the losses at Barings reportedly had grown to $1.24 billion. To the good fortune of all, losses were mostly self-contained and no general ("systemic") contagion developed. In common with other derivatives exchanges, both the Osaka Securities Exchange and the Singapore International Monetary Exchange (Simex) operate clearing funds, financed by contributions from members. In the wake of the crisis, Simex and the Osaka exchange promised that these funds would meet any contract losses to individual counterparties expecting to be paid through Barings. This assurance helped calm the markets, and counterparty losses appear to have been minor.

"In the grand scale of things, Barings is not that big," said a senior U.S. official, according to the *Washington Post*. But at a reception at the Federal Reserve that evening, Chairman Alan Greenspan said he was amazed at the size of the Barings losses over such a short period. "How on earth could you lose that much money that quickly?," the *Post* quotes Greenspan as musing. Contrasting today's computer-driven financial technology with that of twenty-five years ago, the Chairman joked, "The productivity of losing money is really extraordinary. Twenty-five years ago, you could not lose that much money that quickly. You could not write the slips fast enough."[4]

The Lessons

Fortunately, private exchanges and sometimes central banks have been quick to respond to stem any perils including the dreaded scenario of financial meltdown. But individual banks won't always be so protected—only systems. The lesson has been learned that banks who get into trouble of their own doing may be allowed to fail.

The Economist considers that "Amid the howls of outrage, it may seem strange to say that Barings' fate was one of the best things to happen to the world's financial system of late." Before Baring's death, the City assumed that the British government would never let a prestigious bank fail. When it did, its action "had a wonderfully sobering effect."[5] Banks and securities firms everywhere reviewed their internal controls to ensure that they were tougher than Barings'; they looked afresh at the creditworthiness of the firms they traded with. Not unnoticed was the lesson that Barings broke the most elementary rule by leaving the actions of rogue trader Nick Leeson unpoliced by any independent "middle office."

Often the blame—and the shock—spread further. Look at the threat of systemic risk, the risk that one bank's failure could spread to other banks throughout the system, sometimes called Herstatt risk. Herstatt, a relatively small German bank very active in foreign exchange dealings, was ordered into liquidation in July 1974 by the German banking supervisory authorities. The suspension of its payments took place *after* the closing of the interbank funds transfer systems in Germany. All of Herstatt's Deutsche Mark obligations for the day were fully paid, but its U.S. dollar obligations (given the time zone differences) were not. Herstatt had not yet completed the payment to its counterparties (those to whom payment was due, its payees) in U.S. dollars and a number of those who weren't yet paid faced the prospect of losses.

Although the bank was much smaller than Barings, Herstatt's failure caused great disruption to the interbank funds transfer system in the United States. CHIPS was particularly hard hit. The Bank for International Settlements reports that it was only with great difficulty that normal interbank flows were re-established. In the end creditors received partial compensation, but this episode illustrated how uncertainty regarding the size, distribution, and resolution of exposures (or unpaid funds, float of a sort) might lead to a broader financial crisis.

In the case of the Barings failure, not too much damage was done except to the grand old institution. In the case of Herstatt, with its counterparty and time zone risks, a lot of people in many countries were very frightened for a time.

Markets Without Borders

These examples illustrate how markets and market players are intertwined. I've visited quite a number and often thought that central bankers are of the same fraternity. The marble-constructed Bank of Japan looks like the Federal Reserve Board, or the Bank of France or of England or Switzerland, all solidly impressive. The unfailing willingness to share information and ideas contributes to this similarity. Like their imposing edifices, central bankers are cut of the same fabric—one feels both comfortable and chatty with these unique workers. They worry about the central bank's independence and perceived interference by Treasury or the government, and empathize with the problems of the day, political and otherwise. The scene can be replayed in Washington, Zurich, or the Far East, with not much change.

The Markets Grid

The payments structure evolves to reflect these closer ties and tightened arrangements. Frankel and Marquardt were the first to describe the international payments changes reflecting EFT links.[6] Shortly after World War II, a small number of core banks were the main providers of large-value payment services; their major focus was transfer, clearing, and settlement services in their home country currencies. Central banks usually weren't involved until you got to the clearing and/or settlement of transactions in the local currency. Correspondent banking devices were the chief way in which members of each currency's core group provided payments services to others.

Much of this classic postwar structure still stands and settlement both of money and securities generally continues to be layered, in the correspondent banking manner. The core banks are still dominant, working often together within systems. However, foreign currency trading grew rapidly after major currencies were allowed to float, as we saw earlier. International capital and money markets expanded almost as rapidly. Major financial firms from a number of countries increased their scale of banking activities in each other's countries. The success of the big electronic wires for the transfer of money was very important.

Now, composites like the European Currency Unit (ECU) provide an alternative to national currencies. Figure 10.1, from Frankel and Marquardt, shows the new structure of the international payment mechanism. The yen and German mark along with the European Currency Unit have joined the ranks of key currencies, each ringed by their large value payment mechanism. The central focal point has also shifted; it is now a common core group of settling banks, and no longer the U.S. dollar.

"Cross-border" payments have more than one country and often more than one currency involved. They are handled by a system that still looks very much like correspondent banking. Systems don't connect directly, and there is little netting between them. Nor do nonresident banks generally participate directly in domestic interbank funds transfer since nonresidents don't normally hold accounts with the national central bank. Instead, payments in any particular currency tend to be executed in a roundabout way via banks located in the country of issue. These within-country banks, in turn, typically make use of their own branches or subsidiaries or correspondent banks abroad to execute the cross-border transactions.

The simplest system works somewhat as follows. Assume that X, a bank located in London, wishes to pay U.S. dollars to Y, a bank in Germany. Let's also suppose that both X and Y hold accounts at the same correspondent bank in New York. X may then order (usually electroni-

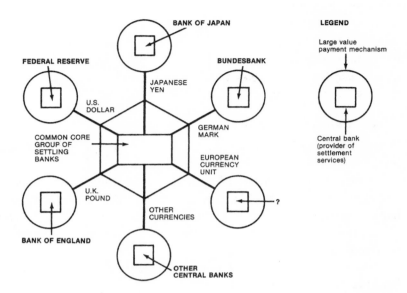

Figure 10.1 New structure of the international payments mechanisms. At the heart of the present structure are the common core group of settling banks in the major currencies, which in turn deal with their central banks. Banks have also expanded their scale of activities in each other's currencies. Within the European Monetary Union (EMU) is foreshadowed the development in 1999 of a single transnational currency and clearing group, based on the Euro. (With permission from Frankel and Marquardt, Federal Reserve Board of Governors, from *Electronic Funds Transfers*.)

cally) the New York correspondent bank to transfer funds from its account to that of Y.

Let's look at a rather more complicated arrangement. In Tokyo, the Chase Manhattan Bank operates a dollar clearing arrangement primarily to serve Japanese and Asian interbank markets. Operating during the Tokyo business day before U.S. markets open, correspondent customers of Chase move dollar payments by sending and receiving payment orders that result in credits and debits to customer accounts at Chase's Tokyo branch throughout the day. Once Chase posts a payment to an account, the payment is final, Chase stands behind it, and the customer may withdraw funds.

Instead of an overarching global settlement system, the linkages between the various domestic systems occur primarily—but not necessarily—through correspondent banking relationships. These links also transmit the intermarket shocks—and risks—about which there is much to learn. A central bank official who has thought at length about the questions is Dr. Y. Oritani of the Bank of Japan. His suggestions include the possibility of greater direct central banking links.[7]

Toward Currency Unification

In our example, a central bank network (such as Fedwire or BOJ-Net) is linked with both its own banks and their overseas office as well as the other international networks. A financial institution's in-house network will connect its overseas branches with each other and with its central bank or private wire (CHIPS). When it lacks overseas offices of its own, the bank will deal with banks overseas in the currency zones in which it transacts business.

Other future possibilities now arise. They range from the central banking-dominated to the kind of individualistic payments mode one associates with Internet delivery schemes—and of course everything in between. The central banks may link up through their individual wires, and then radiate out to bank and other commercial users. A global network of central banks—or, more dramatically, their unification—could facilitate funds transfer over national borders, and it could do so with on-the-spot real-time finality. The direct international link could also facilitate a quick extension of credit whenever central banks might wish to play the role of lender of last resort.

Such cooperation could also be important as a first step toward creation of a global central bank that issues unified money. But, in that arrangement, nations might lose their freedom to choose independent policies of macroeconomic stability, and worry about their economic sovereignty.

Now we're back to that same old question, without really knowing it. The globe-spanning private systems and the Internet provide an integrated currency, even if it is a virtual one (Figure 10.2). While an Internet-based link for wholesale payments seems implausible, unless security is radically overhauled, the Net may move some smaller values. Buyers could arrange on-line for deliveries of Thai silk or wood carvings or leather goods from anywhere. In theory, they'll be able to pay with a stroke or two as well. This is perhaps the unregulated way to create a global "money" of a sort. People are more ready for it now than they

GLOBAL MONEY

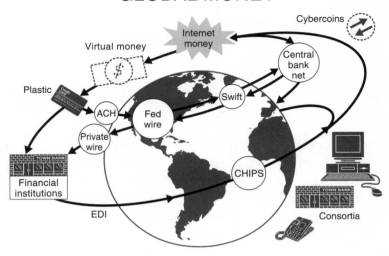

Figure 10.2 Integrated global money. Global money in concept exists now, whether or not we recognize the fact. Moving over country borders, one familiar money form transforms seamlessly into another form, through universal wholesale networks with currency exchange values arranged. Some new retail e-cash money forms can also handle and exchange a multi-currency basket of monies, as, for example, the credit cards, Mondex, and Digicash.

were fifty years ago. The "seamless web of 24-hour trading", to use the apt term of the Federal Reserve Board's Dr. Thomas Simpson, may then extend unencumbered to all the virtual malls of the world.[8]

Global Capital Markets, a Seamless Web

Capital markets are similar to money movements in most ways. They too have tiered transfer arrangements, with special depositories acting in the role of correspondent bank. When it comes to settlement at the end of the chain, Fedwire handles much of the cash and the securities transfers. To me, however, the capital markets settlement arrangements appear more diffuse and varied, the clearing and settlement schedules more asynchronous, and the problems less well understood. The lags between transfer and payment—creating exposure or risk of many varieties—also seem to be greater. It is a system badly in need of change, and now in process of careful adaptation by the experts from many countries.

The traders could be watching the blue-and-white earth from satellite in swiftly passing time zones, night and day, along with their asset-transfer instructions. But they are not; the traders are safely positioned on the earth. Only the money and the "virtual" securities transfers take the higher route. Yet the image, or allegory, sticks. Dr. Simpson's example shows quite dramatically how the globe, or our concept of it, has shrunk.

The U.S. securities market pulls together the complex web of money, securities, and derivatives trading. In that deep global market, there is nearly "seamless" around-the-clock trading. The market opens each day in the Far East (Tokyo) while it is evening (of the previous day) on the East Coast of the United States. A number of securities dealers—most with trading operations also in London and New York—stand ready to buy or sell the more popular issues at posted bid or offered prices. When trades are completed, prices are transmitted around the globe within moments over on-line financial news services.

During this time period (daytime in Tokyo, nighttime in the United States) there is a special evening session for trading futures contracts in Treasury bonds on the Chicago Board of Trade; the availability of the futures market complements the cash market by enabling dealers and investors to adjust the overall positions and exposures to price movements. In addition, during this period buyers and sellers in Japan can hedge the foreign exchange risk associated with dollar-denominated securities in the foreign exchange market. Some of the dealers in Treasury securities also serve as dealers in foreign exchange.

As trading in U.S. securities winds down in Tokyo, it is opening up in London, and a different team at each securities firm takes over. Future contracts on Treasury bonds on the LIFFE (London International Financial Futures Exchange) complement trading in the cash market in this time zone. From London the baton is passed to New York (and the Chicago Board of Trade futures pits) as daylight breaks.

Meanwhile, where are the Treasury securities all this time? They are held in nonphysical form, specifically, in book entry (electronically) on the books of the Federal Reserve System. Ownership is transferred and payment is made the next business day in the United States. A trade made, for example, on Tuesday in Tokyo—Monday night in New York—would settle on Wednesday in New York, about a day and a half later. The settlement medium would be federal funds, balances on the books of the Federal Reserve Banks. These balances are transferred from the account of the buyer's bank (or the clearing bank used by the buyer's dealer) to the account of the seller's bank.

The important advantages of global electronic trading systems include the better "electronic trail" and detection of abuses. Also important are their drawbacks, such as lessened liquidity or the tendency to escape regulation through the deflection of trades to other markets.

A Matching Zoo of Risks

The risks rise too. Between the time that a transaction has been arranged and the time of its actual settlement, the counterparty to the transaction may fail to deliver on its end of the bargain—this is called a counterparty risk. Recall that in a yen-dollar transaction, the buyer of yen receives access to the yen balances during the business day in Tokyo a half-day before the dollar balances must be delivered to the seller of the yen during the New York business day. A similar time lapse problem, about a day and one-half in the case of our New York/Tokyo transfer, can arise when securities are bought in one financial center in one hemisphere but settled in another. This temporal risk, during which payment has been made in one currency but is not yet received in another currency because of time zone differences, is often termed Herstatt risk in memory of that ill-fated German bank.

Of course when you have a problem because of a lag between securities transfer and payments deliveries (counterparty risk), the way to reduce it is to shorten settlement times. At the extreme, deliveries and payments could be made at the same time, all electronically. You hand me over computer evidence of my ownership of securities in an electronic virtual vault at the same time that I hand over to you some computer money held in intangible form somewhere else. This system of instantaneous settlement goes by the name of delivery versus payment, (DVP).

However, implementation of DVP is not a popular idea. The sticking point is the requirement for book-entry holdings of the security in a depository's electronic vault. Investors don't necessarily like the idea that their valuable securities need only be held in phantom form—many still have a strong preference for physical possession of the asset, and shun the elusive ethereal.

Market Mysteries

Among the greatest mysteries in this now ethereal business are the following: How do the capital markets interlock over all the national borders? Where are the points of contact or the stress points? What are the typical amounts and risks of the overhanging unsettled funds and, specifically, what can anyone hope to do about them?

To begin to answer these questions, one needs data on settlement times and lags (exposure) and some documentation on volume and direction among the winding "nodes" and switching points.

Central bankers are almost as puzzled by this difficult system as I am and desirous of well reasoned change. Many new and more efficient netting or on-line gross real-time settlement systems are planned, in Chicago, Toronto, Tokyo, and of course Europe, and the research and cooperation coming out of Basle are impressive. Obviously, if you must pay for either foreign exchange or securities at the same time that you gain ownership, the risk that payment won't be forthcoming is eliminated. (The incentives to trade may also somewhat shrink.)

I talked with leaders in this effort, Dr.Patrick Parkinson and Dr. Patricia White, in June 1995.[9] We discussed the practical problems in navigating the "cross-border" flows (over national boundaries), which include the lack of synchronization, the timing mismatch in settlement arrangements too numerous to mention. Since the sun comes up at one time in New York, at another time in Paris, New Delhi, or Bangkok, the working days are out of sync, too. Always present is the nagging question of what interest rate changes in the various currency zones, say, a sudden hike in the central bank rate, may do to the value of your contract. Differing legal structures—frequently in different languages and with distinctive cultural twists—cause much confusion, although the multinational corporations, it seems, are used to dealing with them. Everyone settles as best they can and the receiving country usually doesn't object.

In short, the serious gray areas afflict all as they wander through multiple jurisdiction arrangements, no matter which side of the globe. Multiple clearinghouses, each with their own rules and procedures, can be a problem even within countries, and over countries the difficulties of all types are compounded. The rising flood of derivatives muddies the waters even further.

Derivatives: Their Angst and Virtues

Derivatives such as hedging against interest rate or exchange risk have been around for centuries, but recently have become a peculiarly sensitive area for regulators. The technique is largely nondeserving, most say, of the bad rap it has received, but the angst is not about to go away.

The notational amounts of outstanding over-the-counter derivatives contracts stood at $40.7 trillion on March 31, 1995, and the exchange-traded interest rates and futures contracts outstanding were another $16.6 trillion.[10] Their daily turnover, is well over a trillion dollars. The calamitous are certainly a pittance compared to the properly used, but the fallout has been great. Among the most publicized has been Procter & Gamble's suit against Bankers Trust in 1994 over losses suffered on two swap contracts. Orange County, a rich California district, ran up spectacular investment losses on leveraged interest-rate instruments before it declared bankruptcy.

A breach of fiduciary responsibility, possibly deceit, was alleged, and the effects were disastrous for some corporate buyers, pension funds, and unwitting local governments. However, a serious threat to other banks or other people never existed—a threat, in other words, that the whole system would be brought down. Why not? In derivatives, the actual cash flows tend not to be great and contracts usually are renewed. The deals are strictly bilateral, although in a string of these bilateral contracts there can be many counterparties.

A derivatives transaction has a value based on some underlying asset or reference rate. Today, the underlyings are wide ranging—interest rates, exchange rates, commodities, equities, and other indices. The contract may be either privately negotiated or actively traded on organized exchanges.

Charles Taylor of the Group of Thirty explains that every derivatives transaction can be built up from two simple building blocks: forwards and options.[11] Forward-based transactions include forwards and swap contracts, as well as exchange-traded futures. Option-based transactions include privately negotiated, OTC options (including caps, floors, collars, and options on forward and swap contracts) and exchange-traded options on futures.

In practice, we create different types of derivatives by pulling out a building block here and there, and combining them in creative and useful arrangements. Instead of barns, animals, and houses, we work the building blocks into a wide range of underlying assets, rates, or indices. In the oldest and simplest example, I buy wool from you in England, to be delivered in three months. I don't know what the value of the pound sterling will be at that time, so I hedge my position by buying pound sterling futures at the time I expect payment to be made.

For their clients, bankers usually hedge for at least some portion of interest rate and currency risk when they make loans. According to Toronto Dominion Bank's Joan Griffin, how much of a loan is required to be hedged depends on how sensitive that borrower is to a movement in interest rates. It is an age-old concept, extended when the physical trade involves many commodities in many different currency zones. Suppose that you build a bridge in Chile and the financing involves lenders in New York, Paris, Santiago, and Buenos Aires, with a term of, for example, twenty years. The hedging contract must now be more complex—a series of six-month contracts that run for twenty years in all the currencies and for different interest rates that you can live with.

That is a practical and necessary business-related derivative method for limiting risk. Someone may buy the contract and that buyer may bet that rates will go in the other direction; the markets are lubricated by the presence of such buyers and sellers. Deals are bilateral and normally not much money changes hands. Some experts will argue that people— those who make or lose the money—are affected but not the underlying markets, however complex the bets or equations on which the deals are based. The information, provided by hedging or arbitrage, speeds up market equilibrium and efficiency, according to a well-developed body of theory. The losses, while great for individuals, firms, or institutions, are small overall, and, what's most surprising, have sprung mostly from simple derivatives, not the fancy ones with the long and quite incomprehensible equations.

At the same time, others feel quite troubled by the transfer of vast sums of wealth from one group, the pension funds or central bankers, say, to another, the currency speculators. Some question whether these speculative flows are all that stabilizing. It is entirely possible that any huge outpouring of private funds against currencies can produce market expectations that are self-fulfilling and thus damaging to the hopes of those wishing to stabilize currencies.[12] With positive feedback effects, some believe that the downward slide of a nation's currency can be exacerbated by such attacks.

Universal Money and World Capital Markets

Maybe you can do something about that kind of private market distorting behavior, but traders must first be induced to believe that the central banks mean to stay the course—that their activities are fully credible. I find a touch of *déjà vu* in all this. The central bankers of a half century ago were thought able to influence market rates through altering traders' jumpy expectations about the future. Keynes talked about it in *The General Theory*. Now perhaps they can influence the expectations of the nonrational noise traders, who also may be quite susceptible to the persuasions of central banks. Only the labels change.

Some traders may *not* be fully rational agents who respond to the market fundamentals, according to the modern theory. For example, traders may be chartists, elaborate model builders, or herd-like followers of the indistinct "tea leaves" of central bankers' data. In that case, despite their thin reed of a foreign exchange base, the central banks still may manage to chill the currency attacks by convincing the markets they mean business. In March 1996, the Bank of Japan managed to persuade markets that it was going to stay the course in its efforts to prop up the dollar. However, that success is not easily come by, given present circumstances.

Electronic Currency Attacks

Currency attacks have been with us always of course, but their current ferocity is unusual. The sheer size of the transactions, and the degree to which private power plays can be leveraged through derivatives in order to unhinge a rate peg, adds a new dimension.

Professors Obstfelt and Rogoff note that "when the postwar system of fixed exchange rates collapsed in the early '70s, few imagined just how volatile currency values would be in the ensuing floating-rate era. . . . Stuffing the genie of floating exchange rates back into its bottle is, however, easier said than done. . . . For most countries, it is folly to try to recapture the lost innocence of fixed exchange rates."[13]

Things will never be the same. The largest private hedge funds single-handedly may command enough resources to wipe out the foreign exchange reserves of all but about twenty central banks. The attackers can be held at bay by only one condition—that central banks are willing to subordinate most normal goals of monetary policy. What can they do to repel the attack? Despite the odds, they have still some defenses up their sleeve. Central banks can use their own limited reserves of foreign exchange to buy back their high-powered monetary base from the speculators. They may also draw on "swap-line" arrangements with other central banks, allowing them to quickly borrow foreign currency needed for intervention. In a more drastic mode, they can repel attack by raising interest rates to a level so high that speculators will find it prohibitively expensive to go short in the domestic currency.

However, in either case both interest rate and money growth targets must be put on hold, hostage to speculative attacks. Further, a speculative attack on the central bank's foreign reserves can set off a general domestic bank run if it appears that reserves will become insufficient. Meanwhile, unfortunately, the drain from the money base may have forced interest rates up to politically unacceptable levels, weakening the economy in the process and heightening its susceptibility to future attack.

Because unanticipated hikes in interest rates are so costly, the goal of a central bank in a currency crisis is to convince speculators as quickly as possible that it is not going to fold. If investors refuse to believe that the central bank is willing to stay the course, however, even the most determined short-term defense will fail. It is always a question of how long a central bank can hold out when attacked by forces from within the country as well as outside it. The Bank of England reportedly took a more than $5 billion hit within a few hours in its vain attempt to prevent the collapse of the pound in September 1992.[14]

When the pound came under attack on September 16, British authorities were reluctant to allow a rise in interest rates. Instead, the authorities engaged in massive intervention, supposedly involving over $70 billion. However, the success of central banks depends on their ability to use the same leveraging tools as their private adversaries. Speed and volume help repel attacks. So, like the private traders, central banks use derivatives (forward market contracts in particular) to enhance the nominal amounts going into "sterilized" intervention. (Sterilized intervention means that the currency purchases are not allowed to have an impact on the monetary base.) Of course, this type of leveraged exchange-rate defense can quickly and dramatically increase the government's exposure to intervention losses, just as any derivative can. Like the private traders who make costly bets on future rate changes, the central banks also stand to lose a lot of money if they fail.

The Swedish experience shows that even the most heroically determined defenses can fail. Following up on its application for entry in the European community, Sweden began to peg its krona to European Monetary System (EMS) currencies in May 1991. In September 1992, it made a dramatic attempt to defend the krona's peg against massive speculative pressure. The Sveriges Riksbank raised its marginal overnight lending rate to 500 percent, yet this unusual interest rate surge left the economy in a much weaker position to resist the next assault. Sensing this weakness, speculators resumed their attack in mid-November. This time the Riksbank could not bring itself to raise interest rates above 20 percent, and allowed the krona to float. The swift and sharp depreciation of the krona relieved the pressure on Sweden's economy. However, the Riksbank suffered substantial capital losses on its foreign exchange positions.

The 1994 Mexican currency crisis was different. The peso exchange level was considered clearly out of line with the "fundamentals" (its real value) so the speculative attack probably merely served to speed up the ultimate downward readjustment, not cause it.

The Bank of Japan's attempts in March 1996 to support the dollar reveal another possible, and happier, result. The BOJ's success, at least short term, was in part because the BOJ *did* manage to convince speculators that it was willing to stay the course. The BOJ's pragmatic monetary policy that is not tied rigidly either to specific exchange rate or money growth levels was also thought helpful.

Recent models suggest that currency crises, like bank runs, can be self-fulfilling events in which the crisis itself creates the economic pressure, and quickly.[15] It seems clear that modern transaction capabilities contribute both to the swift onset and magnitude of crises and, probably, in equal measure to the rapid speed of correction. The bad and the good, together.

Suggested Remedies

To minimize the bad, the experts seek solutions. Carefully reasoned suggestions have come from Basle, the regulators, and private banks and firms. Payments study groups, under the auspices of the Group of Ten (central banks), pose reasoned options.

An important factor is the push toward real-time gross settlement (RTGS) throughout the day whose object is to slash away at the unsettled float (or exposure, as its usually called). Most favor central securities mechanisms to reduce settlement time lags and enhance clarity of payments routing, yet many prefer the more drastic remedy of DVP, simultaneous delivery of and payment for securities.

Others beleive we already have global money and banking in practice, in the sense that wholesale money careens over national borders anyway. The December 1995 agreement on the Euro-currency, or EURO, with its economic and monetary union (EMU) recognizes that fact. A 1999 fait accompli on some of these matters on one continent may pave the way for more permanent world currency solutions. But, once again, the road seems rocky and harmonization of domestic policies is far from assured.

Also important but not easy to unravel in the calculations for risk management are the interdependencies among capital and money flows with common participants. The same institution may have debits and credits arising each day across different systems in different markets (say, CHIPS for foreign exchange, Participants Trust Company for mortgage-backed securities, Depository Trust Company for commercial paper, and so forth). These so-called cross-system risks are likely to be matched with cross-border risks over national boundaries, as well.

Experts push the notion of foreign-exchange clearinghouse consolidations, ideally with a direct link to central bank wires. Without a common currency, however, this raises fundamental questions about the payment infrastructure in different countries that must be used to effect the actual settlement. Most everyone favors extending central bank hours in order to reduce temporal or time-delay risk and Fedwire has done so. This approach also delivers good and "final" funds with more dispatch. These are modest steps in keeping with capital's swift passage that can't be stopped with the clock.

From Basle comes a stern B.I.S. communique of March 1996 that asks for common private derivatives standards and strict internal surveillance. Some claim that banks and securities houses are usually quicker than most regulators to spot trouble. The Bank of Credit and Commerce International was treated as a pariah by most other banks long before it was closed down by regulators. And, Barings' huge positions in Japanese futures contracts was privately observed by more than a few in the weeks leading up to its extinction. Surely, much of the driving force for change comes from the private sector, such as J.P. Morgan, Britain's Association of Payment Clearing Services, the Deutsche Bank, Exchange Clearing House Ltd., or the Bank of Montreal, just to name a very few.

The banks and institutions, for their part, have sophisticated analysts to guide them, and the profit motive must always be balanced by the fear of self-destruction if the markets are gauged incorrectly. From his Frankfurt prison Nicholas Leeson put it rather well, in a taped BBC interview with David Frost. "It was advantageous to me that the people, the senior people in London that were arranging these payments, didn't understand the basic administration of futures and options, and that was probably the biggest failing: they wanted to believe. . . . As stupid as it may sound, none of this is really real money." By the time the auditors at Barings began to break through his screen of deception, he said, he was avoiding reality.[16]

No one wants to become the next Barings to slide from the face of the financial earth. Senior surveillance tightens, and new global mechanisms and capital markets arrangements are taking shape. The strange world of money laundering comes into international public eye as well, while authorities manage to serve up schemes as clever as the strategems of those who would seek to introduce their ill-begotten gains into mainstream markets.

11

The Strange World of Money Laundering

International money laundering is very big business. In its $300 billion annual world "production," class distinctions are few, and it employs both blue collar "smurfs" and white-collar types such as brokers, accountants, or lawyers. You may even have met some of them without knowing it—and some of those unwittingly engaged in the business may not know it either.

The prestigious world of "private banking" for wealthy clients was stunned in June 1994 when two private bankers working as agents for American Express Bank International were convicted on eleven counts of money laundering, four counts of deceiving Federal Reserve examiners, and two counts of bank fraud. For a customer identified as a gasoline station attendant in Mexico, the agents were said to have formed companies, opened bank accounts in Switzerland and the Cayman Islands, and sent and received "countless wire transfers of seven fig-ures." American Express International itself was not criminally charged, but entered into a settlement agreement that required the company to pay the unprecedented sum of $35.2 million. Embarrassed, American Express, its parent company, has since put the problem-ridden bank up for sale.[1]

More flashy is the work of devious no-profit hackers, the creators of bugs, worms, and viruses, or any activity that goes against the unwritten moral code of cyberspace. Cornell University undergraduate William Morris managed to bring hosts of corporate activities to a standstill through his cleverly devised worm. The tales of Phyber Optik and other swashbuckling types of the high electronic frontier have become legend, and much publicity was accorded the Robin Hood exploit of the M.I.T. student who gave away licensed software on the Internet because he thought it cost too much. The irony is that technology seems not to have helped much in detecting clandestine money; instead, the vast and until recently anonymous electronic wire transfers actually help in concealing it.

The Basics

What is money laundering? In the definition of the Office of Technology's comprehensive 1995 study, to launder money is to disguise the origin of, or conceal the ownership of, illegally gained funds to make them appear legitimate. In the United States, there may be $100 billion or more from all sources that are sanitized in some fashion or other each year. If legitimately acquired money is hidden to avoid paying taxes on it, that also qualifies as money laundering. For the criminal hard-core, the bulk of their illegal stash will consist of bank notes, or "street money." Through different channels, their job is to convert cash into bankable funds that can be reconfigured into untainted assets.[2]

As Ingo Walter, author of *The Secret Money Market,* explains, these channels are quite varied. The funds may be laundered through employ of a smurf whose job it is to run around delivering bags of cash below the $10,000 legal limit to a variety of banks and their branches. Next, the funds will be used to purchase cashiers' checks or other anonymous forms of bank assets. Thus cleansed, these funds will be exchanged or invested within the country or wired abroad at a later stage.

There may also be direct physical transport of bank notes by land or air to foreign jurisdictions for conversion into bankable funds; the funds are then sent back home, for appropriate reinvestment through interbank wire transfers. To do this, one needs the following prerequisites: the rate of exchange ought not be too unfavorable, the reporting requirements nonexistent (or, if they exist, the foreign bank overlooks them), and the political climate sufficiently friendly that the funds can be transferred without the need for colossal bribes. Another approach involves making arrangements (with white-collar financial criminals) for disguised wire transfers of funds directly from the United States to relatively secure havens abroad.

More ambitious still, but also very popular, is the creation of sham foreign corporations or other ingenious means of seamlessly blending the laundered with the legitimate. Once done, the money is invested here or abroad, again with the aid of sophisticated experts in the financial services industries.

As in any industry, the quality of the services depends on the price willing to be paid. The person wishing to conceal the source of the funds may be charged a high fee for an unnumbered account in Switzerland where privacy is absolutely guaranteed. (Note that there are also plenty of perfectly legitimate reasons for wishing privacy). The price in a newly created offshore island account may be much lower, but the product may not measure up. The "bank" of deposit may exist in brick and mortar form (in which case the cost probably is higher) or it may be on paper only without a track record for either security or secrecy.

We must include particular industry supply costs such as bribes, expertise, shoeleather, back strain from carrying around sacks of large garbage bags filled with cash, and the risk of jail sentences. It is dangerous to try smuggling duffle bags full of cash over the border by foot or four-wheeler or in the keel of a boat, and it's not much better to hire a small plane and attempt to do the laundering that way—one is liable to meet the authorities on the way down.

With the massive and commingled flows on electronic wire, the chances for a successful journey improve. If the illegal money can successfully be shifted onto that electronic flow, the good and bad money soon mingle. For this reason, Ingo Walter believes the best chance of impeding the money laundering process is at the initial currency conversion point.

The authorities try to choke off the flow by making their presence conspicuously known in key points (Miami and the Atlanta Fed branches are among them). What they can do to uncover any illicit cash resting comfortably in secure havens abroad is another matter. The Treasury has phased out the issue of bills in denominations greater than $100, yet it is no secret that a very large amount of the biggest currency notes still outstanding reflect earnings from illicit activities. Some remain "sterilized" (out of circulation) in the manner of the large gold flows into the United States in the 1930s. No one can predict quite when or where the cash may again turn up.

Clandestine Money: Variants

Under all these circumstances, what is "clandestine money"? Clandestine money is money somehow served up from illegal means; it includes not only drug money but also the ill-begotten gains from embezzlement, fraud, tax evasion, or whatever else the human mind can engineer. Unlike most of the other money forms discussed in this book, its originating manifestation is usually quite physical. Except in the case of white-collar crime, clandestine money typically starts off in the form of cash—$5, $20, and $100 bills—anonymous money that the authorities cannot easily trace. The cash is part of our money base, the reserve money of Chapter 6 on which our money system stands and through which bank deposit money is normally settled.

It is a touch of irony that drug money starts off as kingly high-powered money at the very top of the money and banking pile as genuine reserves. You might say that the banks should be delighted to accept it, and indeed for a time some were. However, there are difficulties in spending it, let alone using it as bank reserves. It may not be generally acceptable since $100 bills can be a problem in stores these days, if you offer too many of them. At least one very upscale retail store is said to notify authorities immediately when buyers peel off layers of $100 bills for expensive goods, say, diamond jewelry and furs.

Electronic wires are an easier route to safe spending; the clandestine money then becomes indistinguishable from the other deposits, legal and illegal. Or the transfer to the legal may be achieved by bribery, at a substantial discount; in the business one never knows with certainty what the precise percentage charge for converting the money may be. It may be better to transfer the clandestine money directly into investments so that the tainted and the legitimate money can be fused, and processing charges avoided. However, in direct investment, if too few questions are answered or if names need be concealed, a price must be paid. That price may be expressed in terms of higher placement costs, lower investment caliber, or decreased yield for comparable asset quality, not to mention possible incarceration.

It seems self-evident that the more conversions through the electronic and/or business chain, the greater the safety achieved—it is useful to put the dirty money through the washing machine as many times as you can. However, these costs may rise, too, since you can wash money or clothes too often. The greater the numbers of conversions, the greater the inefficiencies and the costs. The original cash value may shrivel because of unfavorable exchange rates, bribes, disadvantaged purchases (bearer bonds at exorbitant premiums), or high agent or fiduciary fees.

Why Bother?

Why go to all this bother and expense? Ingo Walter lists some reasons (not all of them criminal) for wishing to hide money:[3]

— To prevent the erosion of business and personal asset values through legal means (such as lawsuits or divorce proceedings).
— Capital flight from one country to other countries, triggered by adverse changes in economic, political, and social conditions.
— Securities law violations, especially insider trading.
— Government undercover activities such as spying and support for "freedom fighters," or the private smuggling of contraband.

Until 1986, money laundering was not illegal apart from the underlying crimes it helped conceal. Surprisingly, it was first defined as an independent crime in the Money Laundering Control Act of 1986, and the penalties include ten to twenty years in prison and substantial fines. In 1988, Congress extended the use of civil asset forfeiture to money laundering.

The Way It's Done

Law enforcement officials describe three steps in money laundering.

— Placement: introducing cash into the banking system or legitimate commerce.
— Layering: separating the money from its criminal origins by passing it through several financial transactions, for example, transferring it into and then out of several bank accounts, or exchanging it for travelers' checks or a cashier's check or anonymous digital cash.
— Integration: placing the illegal rewards into mainstream investment somewhere in the world.

Step One: Placement

The first task is to filter the money from the dirty to the clean, through appropriate placement in something that appears respectable and ordinary. Profits from organized crime (drugs, racketeering, unlicensed gambling, and prostitution) are commonly in the form of cash, mostly in small denominations. Street sales of drugs are usually conducted with $5 or $20 bills. A million dollars in $20 bills weighs 111 pounds, in $5 bills 444 pounds. The trick is to get this heavy money into the stream of legitimate commerce or into banks, or to wire transfer it to another location. It is not thought prudent to unload large trash bags stuffed with currency at a neighborhood bank these days.

Before 1970 many U. S. banks would accept cash deposits without question, not wishing to turn away either good customers or needed cash reserves. That has changed with the 1970 Bank Secrecy Act (BSA), which required financial institutions to report currency transactions of over $10,000 to federal law enforcement agencies. The government showed it meant business when, in 1984, the Bank of Boston was fined $500,000 for failing to report an international transfer of funds. Other banks were also fined or given warnings. Their public thrashing served up a moral and compliance improved dramatically.

Other subtler scouring methods then began. Money launderers responded to the new legislation and its enforcement by dividing large deposits into several smaller ones under $10,000. They might use a number of messengers to make repeated deposits in several branches of the same bank or in several banks. In legal terms, this is termed structuring a deposit; on the street it is called smurfing, a name derived from superactive little blue-green cartoon characters. The work is heavy and the smurfs' risks of incarceration quite high, but the pay is pretty good—OTA reports that smurfers usually earn 1 percent of the funds they are able to deposit in banks.

The Treasury Department issued "Know Your Customer" rules in 1995 to discourage smurfs and launderers, but some people remain skeptical about their effectiveness. As experienced launderers become more familiar with these customer identification procedures, they adopt new approaches. They may even revert to the old strategies of smuggling cash across borders (or via small rented planes above them) and into foreign banks.

What about ATMs? In theory, money can be smurfed into banks by cash deposits through ATMs, then withdrawn through an ATM in another country. However, physical limitations on ATM deposits (stacks of bills will not go through the deposit slot) and monetary limitations on withdrawals (usually $300 to $500 a day) present real practical problems. (The prospect that digital cash may be manipulated and transferred around the world through the Internet without such limitations is a frightening one for the authorities.)

Step Two: Layering

The next step is to "layer" the money through so many successive incarnations through countries with so many varying and uncertain degrees of regulation that nobody can ever hope to track it down. If the illicit stash can be moved from New York to offshore islands to Hong Kong to London to Paris to an unnumbered account in Switzerland, and then to legitimate investment on the other side of the world—all within a matter of seconds—its origins can be most difficult to track down.

In 1989, the American Bankers Association argued that halting the placement of illicitly secured cash through the bank teller's window was a top priority, but nevertheless acknowledged that wire transactions had emerged as the primary method used by high-volume launderers.

A more traditional method of getting money into the banking system is to provide a legal cover. Money launderers may use a legitimate business as a front or "shell companies" (those that exist only on paper) that are often chartered in another country. In choosing a legitimate business, they usually look for one with high cash sales and high turn-over. Some have been said to use jewelers and gold merchants, since the buying and selling of gold is usually conducted in cash to avoid frequent price fluctuations. According to Ingo Walter, currency and foreign exchange dealers have also functioned in this capacity. The size of the business is also relevant: a newsstand or laundromat gets cash but not all that much, and a newsboy depositing thousands of dollars a day will soon attract suspicion.

International money launderers also make clever use of false and inflated invoicing. Florida International University developed an analytical computer program to identify "irregularities" in government trade data. It found some, such as the extraordinary pricing of the drug Erythromycin at $1,694 a gram for imports as compared to eight cents a gram for exports.

Dissimilar techniques apply to white-collar crimes such as embezzlement, fraud, or tax evasion. Here, payment typically takes the form of checks, deposited in several bank accounts and then sent by wire transfer to an account (perhaps unnumbered) in a country with strong bank secrecy laws. Anonymous "bearer" bonds (without registration) can be handy if any still are to be found in the municipal bond business where they once were very popular for coupon-clippers. In a brazen mode of real estate fraud, developers may take out huge loans, wire the money out of the country, and then declare bankruptcy.

Whether diverted to electronic wire or a front or shell business, the layering process passes the money through a number of transactions to confuse its trail. Once the illegal proceeds have been mixed with other money flows, they are extremely difficult to trace. As an aid in anti-crime activities, law enforcement officials are instructed on the nuances of electronic wire transfers and electronic money.[4]

Step Three: Integration

Once this tricky stage is over, owners still need to figure out how best to use their illicit gains in some legitimate way, that is, to integrate them innocuously into the mainstream economy. Launderers can be just as dissatisfied with low interest rates from CDs or bank accounts as the rest of us. Here is where the highly educated experts step in to apply their creative talents. Professional white-collar criminals can often provide the link between the underworld and commercial and financial opportunities in the legitimate sector. Lawyers or accountants, even private bank officials, can supply the needed expertise. OTA was told by law enforcement personnel as well as a convicted money launderer (who himself, he said, fit this profile) that money launderers (except for smurfers and smugglers) were usually well-educated professionals.

Ingo Walters believes that an indeterminate amount of this money may find its way into hotels and beach-front development through the creative skills of experts contracted to invest the money judiciously. The money's destination may also include other varied development projects. Once commingled, and set on their way on the EFT nets, the freshly laundered money performs the same sort of useful investments as all the other capital moving around to the far corners of the earth.

"Financial institutions and their wire transfer systems provide the battlefield for the struggle to control money laundering," according to the director of the OTA study, Dr. Vary Coates. "The internationalization of financial services has created an open pipe for the movement of the profits of international crime."[5] The electronic wires suck them up, like some giant vacuum cleaner.

Detection

Law enforcement detection strategies formerly focused more on the flow of illegal funds out of the United States than on its return flow for reinvestment. As a practical matter of course, much of the money does come back—the problem is that it's more difficult to detect on the return trip. Hence, law enforcement agencies have redirected their attention to the funds that do come back. They zero in on white-collar accomplices and on those who knowingly look the other way. In early 1995, the New York Stock Exchange for the first time took action against a member for failure to monitor the receipt of suspicious cash and wire transfers.

No one is immune. The Anti-Money Laundering Act of 1992 requires securities houses to report large currency transactions. They must also report the use of foreign bank accounts by American customers. Brokerage houses may be prosecuted for participating in money laundering, even if all that is involved is "willful blindness" in accepting suspicious wire transfers of funds. Customers' funds held by the brokers as collateral (i.e., margin) may be seized in forfeiture actions with a showing of probable cause. At present, no tax withholding is necessary for foreign investors; their Social Security number need not be recorded, and the securities can be registered under the name of the investor's lawyer or a fictitious company. This bypass makes owner identification more difficult.

Bank accounts such as "threshold accounts" are particularly scrutinized. These are programmed so that when funds reach a predesignated level, they are automatically wired to a foreign account. Also in the spotlight are master correspondent accounts in a U.S. bank, established by foreign firms as "payable-through accounts." The foreign customers may be known to the U.S. bank only as a name, thus subverting the "know your customer" policy. The authorities are not certain about the number of such accounts held by foreign banks or how many of their customers have been allowed to make wire transfers through it. In March 1995, the Federal Reserve and the Office of the Comptroller of the Currency issued new guidelines to tighten their rules governing the use of these accounts and the information required to be gathered about every user.[6]

Among the most controversial regulations have been the relatively new ones monitoring the wire transfers. The idea started some years earlier when in 1988 the Treasury Department's Office of Financial

Enforcement (FinCEN) began asking banks to voluntarily report any suspicious funds transfers. Not until 1993 did the Treasury and the Federal Reserve Board jointly publish proposed regulations to provide useful information from wire transfer records, as had been mandated by the Annunzio-Wylie Act of 1992. They were issued in final form on January 3, 1995, and were a basic shift in attention from cash at the teller's window to crime hidden in the details of legitimate commerce.

Each bank involved in a wire transfer is now required to include all identifying information in the payment order as sent to the next bank. The information thus "travels" with the payment order from beginning to end. Some banks need new systems capabilities to search their data bases, and there still is much dissatisfaction about the massive quantities of data to be collected. However, officers of most large banks regard the new regulations as "livable."

These new rules apply not only to banks but to *all* domestic financial institutions, funds, and brokers and dealers generally. The effort has been to prevent a funds diversion to a much less highly regulated sector, and the shift in detection emphasis has been quite dramatic.

Loopholes

In addition, the U.S. enforcement authorities have attempted to quench the flows into international banking havens, which have led to large loopholes. With communication links shortening distances, obscure little island nations surged to prominence in international banking. Jack Blum, a former investigative counsel with the Senate Foreign Relations Committee, argues that the bank secrecy offered by these jurisdictions attracts either those seeking to avoid regulation/taxation or those whose source of funds is itself illicit, such as the narcotics trafficker. In exchange for that secrecy, Ingo Walter observes that offshore banking carries dramatic risks: political risk, risk of loss by embezzlement, or the failure of unregulated and uninsured banks. Interest rates can also be lower—an "opportunity cost" of this way of doing banking.

Besides the advantages of maintaining anonymous accounts (or accounts held in fictitious names), banking havens frequently offer the protective mask of anonymous and bearer corporations for relatively trivial amounts of money. According to Blum, a fully anonymous shell corporation may be bought in small offshore Islands for as little as $10,000, a scant sum in relation to the huge sums that may be laundered through it. (A bearer corporation is owned by whoever holds the corporation's shares, i.e., they are not listed to a particular owner.)[7]

There is, however, concern that a further escalation in government scrutiny of transactions by or for off-shore banks may increase the flow of assets into the loophole secrecy jurisdictions abroad while taking business away from legitimate capital markets. It's therefore thought that anti-crime enforcement efforts between nations ought to be collaborative, especially given the presence on the scene of electronic flows.

International Anti-crime Activities

Authorities cooperate as never before to unravel the secrets of clandestine money flows yet, at the same time, step carefully so as not to unnecessarily violate their citizens' privacy. There are many such organizations already up and running. The Financial Action Task Force (FATF) seeks to improve contact between law enforcement authorities in order to hack away at the roots of the money-laundering jungle. Included in its membership are the G-7 and the European Union, Hong Kong, New Zealand, Australia, Singapore, Switzerland, and Turkey. Among FATF's forty recommendations are those that would make drug money laundering a criminal offense and ones that encourage banks to report suspicious transactions while discouraging the use of anonymous accounts. FATF urges the formation of regional task forces patterned after itself, such as the Caribbean Task Force and the Gulf Cooperation Council. The western hemisphere followed suit with its Inter-American Commission on Drug Abuse Control.

The Commission of the European Communities has issued directives compatible with (and in some cases exceeding) the FATF recommendations. The Council of Europe also passed a multilateral money-laundering convention signed by OECD members. The Bank of International Settlement (BIS) has a task force for building international cooperation to control money laundering. Europol, the multinational European police force, is now given powers over money laundering in addition to its former jurisdiction over drug offenses.

Conflicts and Trade-offs

Nations thus recognize the destabilizing threat of money laundering, but a basic conflict still exists. That conflict is between a nation's sovereign right to shield its own domestic data and a right, perceived as being equivalent, to enforce its own laws.

In crime detection, one problem is the natural reluctance of all nations to divulge information about the personal affairs of their citizens. "Data protection initiatives" (we call them information privacy rules) govern the uses of electronically stored data and their transborder flow. The urge is natural to protect any data created within one's own borders, especially when that data cross country lines.

International bodies are quite carefully looking into matters of electronic data protection; OECD Guidelines and the Council of Europe's Convention began doing this more than a decade ago. The Council of Europe has set forth recommendations for the access and dissemination of specific types of data. Generally, the Council expects that member countries will follow its lead in data protection and prohibit exports of personal data when the receiving country does not possess adequate data protection laws.

Generally, these recommendations include what is called *protection of personal data used for payment and other related operations.* Within this rubric are consumer systems: point of sale, automated teller machines, credit card, and, prospectively, smart card and digital money. The status of the wholesale wire transfers does not seem entirely clear. Some lawyers suggest that detection of money laundering would require communicating wire transfer records to the authorities in the interest of crime prevention. Others think such criminal conduct would probably go undiscovered anyway in the flood of wire transfers passing through a receiving bank's wire room.

Foreign bank secrecy and the host of data protection initiatives throw roadblocks in the way of any monitoring system. However, U.S. efforts to forge ahead unilaterally and scrutinize wire transfer records could undermine what successes international cooperative efforts have achieved so far. Further, the U.S. Government has its own privacy versus law enforcement struggle in the international terrain. For example, the White House's controversial 1993 proposal for a "Clipper Chip" prohibited the export of advanced encryption software.[8] It also put the code-cracking encription key (digital security code) in escrow in a place where the government could get it, if law enforcement activities needed it in cases of money laundering. (Encryption keys are streams of bits, generated at random, that are used to scramble and unscramble data.)

However, encryption companies want their software to be able to compete in international markets, so they have not been happy about the Clipper Chip proposal. Privacy groups also object to the government's holding the key to private data. To mollify both groups, the administration has said it will allow the exporting of software with the more difficult-to-break 64-bit encryption schemes. And although the electronic key must be held in escrow, the government will need a search warrant to obtain it.

Others disagree. The National Research Council, in its June 1996 report, stated that it was time to revise government encryption policy to fit the new universe.[9] After careful review, the Research Council's panel urged the commercial development of powerful encryption software, even though it would make wiretapping more difficult. It also recommended that Washington ease restrictions on exports of encryption technology. Foreigners already have access to more powerful encryption systems than those American companies are allowed to sell. The best way for the government to protect itself is to stay technically ahead, and export restrictions, they argue, do nothing to keep encryption software out of the hands of criminals, but needlessly drive American exports out of foreign markets. As of 1997's start, the debate continues, unresolved.

Artificial Intelligence and Privacy

As a final irony, what the computer helps conceal, it may also help uncover. If EFT aids in hiding and merging the illegal funds, the new technology may also play a part in detecting them. Artificial intelligence (AI) is "clearly where we have to be headed," says Stanley Morris, director of the Treasury's Financial Crimes Enforcement Network (FinCEN) that oversees laundering efforts.[10] But the efforts to harness AI for the common enforcement good haven't been too promising thus far.

Moreover, the trade-offs between privacy and crime detection are publicly debated, with intensity. The government can't access the records of individuals under current law, unless it issues a subpoena or obtains a search warrant, much like when it taps telephones. And most banks won't voluntarily turn over corporate money-transfer records without a subpoena or search warrant. In both cases, a judge or magistrate must be involved.

One quite drastic option is a full AI-based system that would monitor wire-transfer traffic, comparing messages to "profiles" of illicit transfers. However, no one has been able to detect distinct money laundering patterns through AI or any other means. If enough data were to be collected, intrusion of privacy would be a serious problem. At FinCEN an additional issue would arise—the possible creation of an unlimited national data base.

On a more limited scale is a plan to provide wire transfer records electronically to FinCEN in response to specific subpoena requests. Selections would be based on FinCEN's existing AI system, plus the usual tips law enforcers are generally handed. "Link analysis" of other government and commercial data bases might also be a part of this option, which most closely approximates current law enforcement practice. An electronic subpoena direct from FinCEN to the banks would streamline the subpoena process, in the view of the Office of Technology Assessment who studied this whole question in depth.[11] Banks and/or wire transfer systems might as a first cut screen the wire-transfer traffic to eliminate the "nonsuspicious" transfers—those originated by established and well-regulated banks and by well-known customers. The remaining transfers would be copied and sent to FinCEN where they would be further filtered by an AI system to identify suspect subjects and accounts. The suspect records would then be analyzed by FinCEN's link analysis operations that are matched with data from government and commercial databases for contextual information.

Will any useable patterns emerge from this complex information? Configurations of money laundering behavior may perhaps be gleaned; criminal "profiles" may build up over time. The computer could produce tangible rewards, and the search for predictability through AI may yield law enforcement breakthroughs.

We come full circle. Ironically, the zealous law enforcer's quest mirrors the ongoing search in other global spheres for financial market predictability. Both seek useable patterns, although of different types and for dissimilar rewards. In a legend next recounted of the search for order within chaos, the ingenious race is on for some sort of money-making market predictability before the patterns all evaporate into thin air.

12

The Search for Chaotic
Market Patterns

What do financial markets, spiral galaxies, populations of fruit flies, and the red spot of Jupiter have in common? The link may be a rather new and complex theory called, in something of a misnomer, chaos theory. What you get isn't chaos in the sense of formlessness, of course. Indeed, a chaotic system has its own patterns, bounds, and sense of extraordinary and visually beautiful motion. The red spot of Jupiter swirls, forever quite self-contained, within the gaseous oceans of the giant red planet: a dramatic physical example of a bounded chaotic system. Populations of fruit flies, gypsy moths, and some viruses expand in swift and geometric progression, reach a peak, then turn around and back away, before resuming their upward plague. Galaxies and solar systems have their own self-limiting tracks, and some have said that the brain's ability to behave creatively may originate in complex chaotic patterns, also meticulously bounded within brain wave tracings.

Think of the possibilities. If you can find evidence like this of bounded structure in finance, your model will have conjured up a mathematical gem. Market meandering within fairly precise limits, for however brief a time, may serve up priceless information about future market prices and their direction. There is, however, a catch. You must be prepared to sweep in any assumed profits before the money-making relevance of the model begins to erode, as it surely will. You must get the trading message to the market fast enough to glean the profits before the predictive model shrivels and loses all its power. Before EFT, it just wasn't possible to move fast enough—neither trading nor money delivery speeds were sufficient.

Chaos and Capital Markets

Chaos in its modern guise is defined broadly as an evolving (dynamical) system that is very sensitive to initial conditions. When represented in an abstract manner—what scientists refer to as "phase space"—a chaotic system traces out a trajectory as it evolves. The lure of chaos theory is the patterns it can divine from a seemingly random stream of computer-generated data. Those patterns may even serve up predictability, although it is of a very short-term and evanescent nature.

Why should anyone in the business of looking at money and financial markets care? They care because precious information may be divulged. Financial people are interested because a rather small event, say, a central banker's innocuous remarks about inflation, can fuel some rather large market reactions and hence profit opportunities (or losses) all out of scale. In strength, the reaction is out of sync with the initial event that provoked it; mathematically speaking, the reaction is nonlinear.

The straw that breaks the camel's back is an example of a nonlinear event. The result of that event is way out of scale, grotesquely magnified. Nonlinearities abound all around, from a dripping faucet or swinging pendulum to the bends of the financial cycle. A better understanding of some very special kinds of market nonlinearities—spurts in market volatility, for example—might help in predicting market behavior under certain circumstances and with a bit of luck.

Traders always have been interested in unusual or frenetic (nonlinear) behavior at market peaks and troughs, that is, at the cycle's turning points when direction changes. Hence, chaos theory fitted in nicely with the "chartist" intuition that a sudden burst of market activity—or volatility—may foreshadow a change in market direction. The mathematical tools of chaos theory served up the means for testing the trends, and the computer was ready and able to do the tedious work. It was a tantalizing fit: computers, the fast money flows, and the new theory.

In the lore of chaos theory, it is said that a butterfly flapping its wings in Hong Kong can cause tornadoes in Kansas City. More accurately, by failing to account for the butterflies, your future predictions will fail to predict a tornado in Kansas City. Similar effects may be present in financial markets. The buzzword of the theory is initial conditions. Especially in a "dirty" or error-prone soft science such as economics, you can never get either initial conditions or butterflies' agitation exactly right, but some other interesting information may surface.

For example, the newer theories, some people think, may tell us about conditions that tend to *forewarn* market downturns or suggest an upward turnaround. With all its flaws, if time horizons are short enough, either the pure and beautiful chaos model—or some less elegant nonlinear country cousin—may work just well enough to make some money.

The big question, still largely unanswered, is the following: Is there really some predictability in financial markets or are some people just fooling themselves? You must first decide whether markets can be described by low-dimensional chaos models—i.e., those with some underlying order, even if the behavior appears on the surface to be random. It is now considered unlikely that low-dimensional chaos can be *rigorously* applied to financial markets. However, it is just possible that the mathematical *tools* of chaos can be used to assist in short-term forecasting—if, that is, we are talking about a very fleeting instant in time.

The stepping-stones for this exciting possibility were first laid down over thirty years ago. A rather obscure meteorologist blazed the scientific trail, but an innovative economist had looked at the dynamics of interacting systems much earlier.

The Foundations

For both, the scene of discovery was Cambridge, Massachusetts. Professor Edward N. Lorenz of the Massachusetts Institute of Technology was a meteorologist who wanted to understand more about the predictability of weather. He yearned to know why weather forecasters never got long-run predictions just right, and what to do about it. Lorenz began with a very simplistic model of atmospheric flows consisting of three interlinked equations. Lorenz's computer had vacuum tubes that made a lot of noise and broke down regularly, but he put the primitive thing to work to simulate the future course of the weather based on his three interdependent equations. Much to his astonishment, the results of this simulation led to the formulation of a fascinating concept of "sensitivity to initial conditions." Lorenz found that the slightest error in taking initial measurements can ruin the model's predictive capability, a critical aspect of chaos theory.

He made this discovery quite by chance. One winter day Lorenz cut corners. He did another weather run using the same information as his previous one, but instead of starting the whole run over, he began midway through. To give the machine its initial conditions, he typed the numbers straight from the earlier printout. Then he went out to get a cup of coffee. As James Gleich tells the story, when the meteorologist returned an hour later he was astonished at what he found.[1] Lorenz saw his weather diverging so rapidly from the pattern of the last run that all resemblance had disappeared. His first thought was that a vacuum tube had gone bad.

After several months of testing and additional simulations, the truth emerged. There had been no malfunction; the problem lay in the numbers he had typed. In the computer's memory, six decimal places were stored: .506127. On the printout, to save space, just three appeared: .506. Lorenz had entered the shorter, rounded-off numbers, assuming that the difference—one part in a thousand—was of no consequence. But that seemingly minuscule difference did matter. A difference between the real and measured initial conditions can cause the paths of the simulated variables to diverge wildly.

Lorenz then decided that long-range weather forecasting was doomed since it's never possible to measure initial conditions without some sort of error. If other chaotic systems are anything like Lorenz's model, these initial errors will grow enormously, destroying long-term predictability. However, we do have the very short term to think about.

To me, chaos theory has always appeared as a close kin to Nobel Laureate Paul Samuelson's dynamic accelerator/multiplier model, which appeared well over two decades before the Lorenz model. The paths of output can be damped or explosive and feedback effects are significant: the level of net investment depends on the change in expected output, while the change in income (or output) is related to the change in planned autonomous spending. As in chaos theory, the interacting oscillating fluctuations depend for their trajectory on the values of initial conditions.

I sought the current views of Professor Samuelson, also of M.I.T., and he commented: "For strict chaos you must have differential equations that are both nonlinear and involve at least three variables. The 1939 multiplier-accelerator was linear and involved two degrees-of-freedom only. Nevertheless, chaotic sensitivity of determinate systems to initial conditions will have, I predict, a place in future economic theory."[2]

We have seen that a chaotic system is a special type of nonlinear dynamic system that displays sensitivity to initial conditions. Most interesting, the paths of these variables trace out a pattern within a confined area of phase space known as the strange attractor. These patterns are very complicated; nevertheless, it is possible that we may extract some order from them.

Ideally, the patterns will be "clean" or relatively free from random noise, and there will be few variables (or dimensions) to deal with. With high-dimensional chaos, you have too many variables to handle and the system may be so complex that it can be impossible to deal with, even by computer. It may be turbulent, as, for example, a system of waves after breaking in the ocean with a burst of nonpatterned foam—or the stock market in the throes of crash in 1987 or 1929.

We hope for low-dimensional chaos, with few variables to handle that will yield patterns we can track and predict for the future, even if that future is very brief indeed. Of course, the predictive capabilities of even the purest of pure chaos models must disintegrate eventually because of inevitable initial measurement errors. We can never get it exactly right since every manmade simulation must contain within it the seeds of its own destruction. What the initial errors do to system reliability after only a few steps (iterations) in the process can be quite dramatic.

In this game, scientists have more to play with than economists or financial people. The computer can generate streams of data, with a dedication that never wanes, sleeps, or takes holiday or weekend breaks. With better initial measurements, the system may retain its predictability longer and the patterns of science show up better. One has to strain to see a fractal in money supply data, constrained as it is by infrequent data points, and many are skeptical. However, if one's imagination is pretty good, the tracings are suggestive, for M2 particularly, and Professor William Barnett's work along these lines has attracted both attention and controversy.[3]

A true chaotic system stretches and contracts like a rubber band, moving back and forth, and folding in on itself, as though repeatedly kneaded like a metaphysical loaf of bread. It is characterized by wide swings in volatility, especially at or close to the turning points. However, the true chaos trajectory must always return to some point bordering on the baseline. That point of return traces out a pattern so complex that, however much you take the whole apart, you perceive an underlying similar pattern, the so-called fractal first identified by IBM's Benoit Mandelbrot.

Complex fractals are everywhere around us in the real world, in the shape of leaves, the gentle finely patterned waves of the Pacific Ocean, the beautiful snowflakes of a winter's snowfall. Underlying structures make the physical world what it is—wondrous to behold and symmetrical in general format. The snowflake will always have the same general star pattern within all its smaller segments; the minutest portion of coastline or leaf will look the same as the larger whole. Of course the world is complex like this and nonlinear, the scientist will tell you—why should economics, or finance for that matter, be any different?

Finance and Fractals

The paradox is sublime: a theory that suggests the futility of long-range economic predictions also holds forth the promise of garnering very large short-range trading profits. Understand the workings of chaos and maybe you will have come up with an ephemeral money-making prize of major dimensions. Now, just how is that absurd result possible, and what does it have to do with computer money?

First, let's ask another question. Just how short is short? Maybe we're talking about five minutes, a minute, or a millisecond—it can't be pinned down. Even scientists working with their pure data speak of fairly rapid model disintegration, and say that it all depends. When asked, chaos experts talk in terms of numbers of iterations, or successive stages. A trader has to pick up information very fast to make his money; he needs a lot of information, whether crude data mining or more careful analysis, and must also act on it with dispatch. Indispensable are the "fast flows" of computer money to consummate the deal in timely manner.

Underlying the whole lot are some supremely complex nonlinear models and a vast quantity of raw data for computer machinations to digest and analyze. Also involved is the vital input of mathematical experts who build the models and deal with all the complex information—all this before the model's predictive power evaporates. The pay is very good for these experts, called "quants," or often rocket scientists. Many are lured from universities or from within the former Soviet bloc and their job is to divine any underlying financial patterns, or any hints about likely future cycles.

Business Cycles and Chaos

Some think that chaos theory may offer insight into the mysteries of the business cycle. After all, the patterns of economic fluctuations over time can look a great deal like the fractals of nature, in the specific sense that they restate basic structures over and over, however small the portion. With a dash of imagination, you can see that the underlying structures of the three-year inventory cycle, the eight-year business cycle, and the long fifty-year Kondratieff cycle are somewhat alike. We note an overlay of patterns traced by the economic data. Neighboring business cycles often have common structures, although generally uncommon causes. And business fluctuations never return to the same equilibrium point twice: "shifting equilibrium," it used to be called.

Dr. Benoit Mandelbrot was once invited to give a lecture at Harvard University about his new work at IBM on fractals. He noticed that a graph of fractal patterns was already displayed. "What do you mean," he reportedly commented to his host Hendrik Houthakker, "by putting up my graph before I even so much as got here?" But it was not Mandelbrot's graph that was posted—it was a graph of cotton prices over the past century.[4]

It is tantalizing to imagine that there really was a connection between Mandelbrot's theory and price or market movements. Suppose the business cycle, if one could get the data just right, actually does trace out a fractal over time. Imagine that you could discover in advance, by using an appropriate model, the peaks and valleys, the turning points of business upturns and downturns. Is that so very far-fetched?

This notion—the economics "pot of gold at the end of the rainbow"—is steeped in classical tradition. Jean Pierre Grandmont, the French chaos economist, credited Haberler and Hayek and the whole Austrian school, along with Keynes and Samuelson, as stressing cyclical bursts of investment activity and sudden market turnarounds. All shone the spotlight on the markets' cumulative bursts of activity, which can cause the process to feed on itself. Expectations shifts and nonlinear spurts of behavior, volatility by another name, often can drive markets.[5]

Dr. Milton Friedman's famous "inside" and "outside" lags in monetary policy also put expectations and time lag effects specifically in focus.[6] In monetary policy context, his insights drew grudging recognition even from within the Federal Reserve Board's staff, which he criticized. Milton Friedman is right of course, we said in 1957 and 1959, when the Federal Reserve Banks raised their discount rate at the very moment when (in retrospect) the economy was just turning down. The Fed's action took place at the wrong time. The effects of credit tightening take time to filter down—another example of nonlinearity.

How can we prevent overreaction of just this sort, which exaggerates the peaks and valleys of business cycles and can make matters worse instead of better? Many people wish to curb the power of the central bank, and most want to require those at the helm of monetary policy to supply more information to market participants. All of us recognize the difficulties with frequent, perhaps unsettling, policy shifts, and monetarists, rational expectations economists, and chaos theoreticians agree on the need for timely, unexpurgated data.

The Evidence

Dr. Chera Sayers is a highly respected economist at the top of the nonlinear dynamic field who has developed important statistical tests for detecting chaotic economic systems and applied them to exchange rates, options, and futures as well as money and other economic data series. Is there evidence of any repetitive nonlinear structures in money and finance? Chera answered that we can't say for sure—maybe we'll never know. Maybe everything around us is nonlinear, maybe very little. In economics, maybe we have some chaos but can't detect it, because the data are too dirty or there is "nonstationarity" in the systems (i.e., things such as policy are always changing). You can't pin down the data as you can in the harder sciences. Chera does say, however, that we do begin to discern some evidence of nonlinear structures in disaggregated data especially. Compared with ten years ago, the techniques have improved dramatically.[7]

In contrast, the mathematical quants do not reveal whether they find anything useful in their quest for predictable patterns. They don't publish articles or give lectures about their work. If they are successful, they won't tell you and are probably as loathe to admit failure. Lined up in their offices are numbers of different nonlinear models all working for them at the same time, to hedge their bets. They are said to be embarrassed at their sudden wealth, which can be considerable compared with the unprepossessing wages of academia.

The popular press, and some firms, extol the benefits of computer-aided trading and data show that it is rising sharply. Still, some economic experts at the cutting edge of the field, remain skeptical. "I haven't seen any gaudy forecasting successes in the market," says Dr. Ted Jaditz, economist at the Bureau of Labor Statistics, "not yet. I'm going to have to be convinced." [8]

Model usefulness gets down to the numbers of "degrees of freedom," or, to say essentially the same thing, the numbers of dimensions, the numbers of events people are likely to react to. What helps is that traders are in some sense predictable in their reactions. The market devoutly listens to the central bank chairman and looks at certain key items in central bank balance sheets, what I call tea leaves. If they are indicative of Fed tightening, for example, the market will sell off bonds in anticipation of higher interest rates and capital losses. Many have commented on the herd instincts of traders, their raw exuberance and the way they abruptly change course. The way to beat the market, Keynes in effect said in his *General Theory*, was not to choose the most logical investment strategy but the one based on what you thought everyone else in the market was going to do. People are nonlinear; they follow the crowd.

The Computer's Tricks

What, specifically, are the tricks of the trade if you wish to use the quants' talents properly? Even if you can't construct the proper model, the computer still may help merely by virtue of the mass of data it can dredge up. Data mining, the scooping up of all manner of data, is a pejorative term that is sometimes handy. You may follow the fortunes and relevant data of many companies and select a few that look interesting or undervalued for some reason. In other cases, the idea is to discern, by sheer eyeballing, patterns of more a general nature.

Rigorous statistical theory scoffs at this helter-skelter approach. If you search for (or mine) the data for economic growth versus the movements of the stars, you will eventually find some correlation. Whether it is meaningful is another matter. The English economist Jevons found some correlation between the eight-year business cycle and the sunspot cycle, also eight years, and it is of course possible that sunspots affected crops. But whether that caused measurable fluctuations in business activity is highly speculative and has certainly never been shown.

A more scientific, and also more time-consuming, form of search for nonlinear structure is also possible with current computer power. The patterns of pure deterministic chaos may elude us, but we may still find some evidence of interesting nonlinear structure relevant to the habits of financial markets.

Many such searches begin with an application of the Grassberger-Procaccia dimension estimation algorithm. Dimension estimation tells us whether we may have low-dimensional chaos, which is manageable, or high-dimensional chaos with an impossibly high number of messy variables to deal with. Another popular test for estimating dimension has the difficult name of Lyapunov exponents. Studies include a test statistic for independence, the BDS test.[9]

When we come down to it, most of the broad economic series such as GDP, employment, or money supply suffer from a major limitation of economic data: the data are sparse, short, and usually noisy (error-ridden). Noted economists in the field have taken unusual care in avoiding sweeping claims of any sort, and the thoroughness of the work by such economic experts as Jaditz and Sayers has kept down the number of false positive tests of chaos.

In financial markets, however, the trade-off is different—investment managers are much more enthusiastic than economists. The finely grained financial series provide longer and cleaner series than the broad macro data, and the capital markets can generate data in continuous streams. Just as in the physical sciences, the computer can spew out all manner of statistics on foreign exchange trading or stock market or publicly traded derivatives prices. Reactions of traders are faster than those of consumers or long-term investors who drive the macro markets. The stakes are also higher. For traders, with millions of dollars at their disposal, the monetary rewards from success can be significant and worth the considerable expense. Almost without exception, leading brokerage houses and big bank research departments use the talents of the quants and aren't afraid to relinquish the considerable sums of money needed to keep them going. What are the kinds of models most used? Everything is the answer—chaos, neural net, nonlinear time series, a variety, often running simultaneously.

Where may the capital markets rewards lie? One is the ability to recognize the so-called volatility persistence that you would expect from chaos theory or its less pure cousins. This is the telltale and coveted fingerprint that may foreshadow sudden market changes, and equally sudden ways to make money from market turnarounds.

Volatility Persistence

One of the largest deviations from pure randomness in financial series is volatility persistence, as it is known in the trade. Nobody pretends to be able to predict rate of return very well; however, some think they may have found predictability in the *magnitudes* of rate of return movements or, to put it in another way, their volatility. Your chances for a ten strike appear to be the greatest in foreign exchange markets where high trading levels, and volatility, make up for the costs of trading in those markets.

Professor Blake LeBaron issues an important caveat, however. Before you try to make a mint of money, beware for the following reasons: (1) the actual implementation of a forecasting rule for trading may involve unforeseen costs; (2) taking on these dynamic strategies may involve exposure to extensive risks. The large expected returns might evaporate since there are no guarantees. It is a risk/reward strategy blown up to the hilt.[10]

The tools of this trade are not easy. One of the most important is GARCH theory, Generalized Auto-Regressive Conditional Hetero-skedacity, an important new technique for analyzing volatility clustering. It infers that prices tend to be volatile when they have just been volatile and not when they have not. Suppose we divide the market into periods of high and low volatility. A pattern may then emerge. When volatility is low, the market tends to follow trends: it persists in rising for longer than random or falling for longer than random. However, when volatility is high, trends persist for shorter than expected periods. High volatility means change is in the wind, low volatility means the market will probably just chug along on its present path. In both cases, the market is partly predictable.

It is not return but volatility that runs in trends. Find the onset of volatility, and then you will know where the action is going to be—market orders will be clustered. You will have a clue, perhaps, about when to get out of the market and when to get back in.

Professor William Brock, who has been adopted by the chaos physicists as one of their own, suggests the unthinkable. In the words of *The Economist*, "Might chartists, that disreputable band of mystics, hoodwinking innocent fund managers with their entrail-gazing techniques and their obfuscatory waffle about double-tops and channel break-outs, be right more often than by chance?"[11] Taking advantage of new computer power and a greater density of data, LeBaron and Brock tested some of the most popular chartist techniques on ninety years of data from the Dow Jones index. Although many other studies have termed technical analysis as useless, Brock suggests that this conclusion may have been premature; or, to put it differently, trading profits are not consistent with a "random walk."

Returns during buy periods are less volatile than returns during sell periods. People are more eager to make money when markets are moving up than they are to admit danger and get out when the market plunges. That is nonlinearity if ever there was such a thing. But is this science or the herd instinct or something best described as a fundamental psychological aspect of human nature?

The chartists, who also go by the name of technical analysts, justify their techniques with arguments about the behavior of investors. People who trade in the market are subject to a "burst of animal spirits," with sudden volatility their hallmark. When an index breaks through a previous resistance area and heads for new heights, investors think of profit taking. The more that people share a belief, the more the belief is likely to be true and a self-fulfilling prophecy is set in motion.

Chaos: Its Neural Kissing Cousins

As computer power grows, much interest tends to shift to "neural nets," also nonlinear and complex, patterned after the human brain. Neural nets, although useful for many simple aspects of pattern recognition, are not very bright on their own. Despite their present intellectual limitation, neural nets have avid fans replete with on-line electronic journals and live conferences. Perhaps as computer power grows, their predictive skills will also increase. However, Ted Jaditz cautions about taking any of the potential rewards from the models too seriously at this time.[12]

Like chaos theory, neural networking recognizes patterns. A neural network is a form of artificial intelligence (AI) like that described in the last chapter, designed to take a pattern of data and generalize from it. To "educate" the AI program, the computer painstakingly varies the strengths of connections between individual processors until the input yields the right output, or just the right answer. But the results can sometimes look silly or embarrassing—you have to keep teaching the computer things we take for granted, for example, that a credit applicant with no mortgage and not many credit cards may not be a thoroughly bad lot but merely one old enough and sufficiently gender-sensitive to have paid off the mortgage and put the credit cards in his wife's name.

A little genetic engineering can do wonders to brighten up the critical powers of a brain-deficient net. With the aid of a genetic algorithm you can design your own neural network and "breed" your own system, reproducing the species with the fittest of the fit. Those systems that do the best in predictive capability are bred to propagate their own kind; those that fare badly are selected out for extinction. Genetic algorithms employ trial and error, this time in a direct analogy with how evolution works by mutation and natural selection.[13]

Computer power and the analysis of brilliant minds can take us along the complex adaptive systems route as well. From Dr. Murray Gell-Mann's simple quark to intricate jaguar, this theory holds that organisms adapt to the environment in ways of increasing complexity.[14] Populations of fruit flies and gypsy moths rise and fall in adaptive feedback loops; large-scale interconnected systems, and their ups and downs, may also be metaphors for economic behavior.

The complex systems approach looks at what some call "the edge of chaos," that thin line of greatest creativity just before the onset of true chaos in the physical sense. With dynamic simulations, the Santa Fe Institute assembles ideas and sponsors research into imaginative ways in which species and systems adapt. According to Dr. Gell-Mann, complex adaptive systems may permit diversity in species and successful evolution of all that we see growing around us, whether flora or fauna. Atoms get more complex as one moves away from the Big Bang, and so do the ways they are put together to produce great diversity and species, including humans.

Economic systems also may change as the woven threads in cyberspace proliferate and grow, and when communications rise in complexity, whether they are signals or money. As we add more links and interconnect more people and machines around the world, one wonders what may happen. The problem is one for electrical engineers, but the fallout will affect money delivery. Most experts say that increased Internet capacity and data compression will eradicate any temporary difficulties; others, such as M.I.T.'s *Technology Review*, remain concerned. The underlying threat is that as more people plug into electronic commerce, the chance for systems gridlock or outright instability may tend to rise. This basic engineering problem is foremost and it is an axiom that those who can build the most carefully engineered and safe system will fare

The Search for Chaotic Market Patterns

best. Another proven way of dealing with the problem is to build redundancies into the system. If one route fails, another will always be available to deliver your most precious ideas or your money.[15]

Chaos researchers are now looking at these new questions, too, and scrutinizing the abrupt shifts in phase, a hallmark chaos characteristic. They are examining the dynamics of a neural network as the overall connectivity is changed, that is, as the numbers of people in central system locations (nodes) are increased along with the numbers of those from outlying nodes that feed into the network. Brock finds a link between nodewise connection strengths and the onset of overall chaotic dynamics in the economic system.[16] Although no one explicitly interjects this thought, the implications for an increasingly wired world can be interesting.

If we surrender control to computers in market decision making, perhaps no one human will be able to unravel the complex process completely as the distinguished mathematician Professor Roger Penrose suggests.[17] Perhaps we will face a threat of rapid shift from stable to unstable systems, as the economy is held hostage to the computers' delivery forms with their web-like intricate flows of information. From central nodes, the bank wires and, more important for the future, the Internet thread anything and all, from foreign exchange markets to central banks' trading desks to your own PC. It is an awesome journey.

Wisdom from Patterns

Perhaps the soothsayers can divine wisdom from tea leaves or patterns, after all. Certain physical motions such as planetary rotations or fluids flows, if modeled accurately, can yield deterministic predictions for the future. Maybe market players can achieve the same miracle and knowledge. The new models getting a play on Wall Street can stagger the imagination. Time lags (except in the matter of actual money settlement) and market reaction times shrink to nothingness. Money flows and market transactions spurt, although most certainly not in an explicitly predictable way as one would hope. True chaos of the deterministic type seems unattainable in finance and economics. But in the place of the very pure is something else, other nonlinear models crafted from the mathematical tools of chaos theory. They, too, are useful, and in financial markets they mostly serve still as a "screening" adjunct to the human decision-making process.

Universal Money and World Capital Markets

The complex nonlinear techniques borrowed from the hard physical sciences present great opportunities for those with computer power, brains, and deep pockets. If we cannot hope to attain deterministic chaos, perhaps we can strive for fleeting glimpses of nonlinear structure. But these mirrors to another world evaporate fast, if not at the speed of light, then close to it. Similarly destined to ephemeral life is virtual money, which feeds the traders' dreams and generates "real" forces that are quite powerful indeed.

Virtual Money
as a Market Force

Virtual reality and virtual banks are very much in the public eye, even though they seem the stuff of science fiction. However, the notion of virtual elementary particles underlies the concept of modern physics, and that rich scientific heritage provides some interesting insights. In this chapter we think of e-money forms in the lingo of cyberspace and in analogy to the even stranger physical world of the very small.

Virtual Money: The Concept

What exactly is virtual money? One must shift gears quite abruptly to think in such odd terms. Is virtual money only issued by virtual banks or virtual branches of brick and mortar banks? I think not. Computer money with no immediate interface with conventional money I define as virtual money. Virtual money is money that isn't there in any real monetary sense. It is not—and cannot be—measured as part of the permanent money stock.

Our ordinary bank deposits are simply accounting money, and surely not very physical either; however, they are measured and sit squarely on bank balance sheets. What about EFT, the electronic money flows? You might say that they don't qualify as virtual money either since the flows just provide the means of quick passage to conventional money. On the other hand, we do see multiple money overhang prior to reentry into the standard balance sheet M's. Does that fuzzy multiple qualify as virtual money?

There can be no doubt about the official money aggregates. They are real money, even though no gold hovers close by. Conventional balance sheet money is firmly rooted in our banking system and is backed by the money of central banks. It maintains a recorded public presence. In contrast, virtual money is not measured money. It may in part be electronic float, exposure in the bankers' terms. Or it may be generated for a brief time by the fast-as-light speeds of EFT before its inevitable denouement at collection time. Virtual money is money that slips around the globe without a permanent real money interface. Virtual money can do many things and it is not to be ignored. It also has a sterling scientific backing.

The concept goes back to modern physics and in particular the work of Richard Feynman and, later, Roger Penrose, Stephen Hawking, and Murray Gell-Mann, among many others. Sci-fi borrowed from the scientists, and scientists were first to conceive the idea, bizarre as it may seem.

Stephen Hawking defines a virtual particle in modern quantum mechanics (the world of the very small) as "a particle that can never be directly detected, but whose existence does have measurable effects."[1] From such a definition I derive the virtual money concept. Often our phantom money can't be directly detected either, but its effects are real enough—volatility of foreign exchange or capital markets prices. The tangible effects can thwart the stabilizing activities of central banks as they defend their own currencies and markets. A real effect from the global stir of all the virtual brief-lived money particles doubtless does exist. It includes unusual heavy spurts of traders' flows and the engineered derivative models that capture the possibilities of rapid money turnaround.

Virtual particles in physics may seem at first to be little more than a mathematical curiosity. However, virtual particles have a profound effect on basic physics and, in fact, are considered responsible for all the fundamental forces of nature. By analogy, it is plausible that virtual money, although not "real," may have a significant impact on the real monetary system of most nations today.

Phantom Money's Creation

How does the system conjure up some "virtual" money? It's very simple.

The electronic money transfer message moves very fast. The legal and institutional mechanisms don't always work that fast, especially when many currencies, languages, and laws enter in. The result is fast-as-light money flow but not quite so fast balance sheet transfers through a string of banks and wires.

Consider the huge flows on CHIPS and Fedwire and their foreign counterparts. They overhang at many multiples of the underlying money base. As the speed ratchets up, and money turns over faster and faster, we have a form of money mass that isn't quite there, money that never becomes a permanent balance sheet entry, never really gets to be counted, money that self destructs. In short, injected into the staid money business we have virtual money, unaccounted for and unmeasured except sporadically as gross transactions values.

The e-flows on the Internet may add to the stock of this ephemeral money, which escapes the measured M's, a retail variant. Up to now the Fed has paid little heed to retail flows since they are relatively small, only about one-twentieth of wholesale flows. Most are fully backed, and paid for, by the credit or debit card holder's underlying bank deposits. There hasn't seemed to be much chance of systemic risk, which is a payment guardian's proper concern. However, electronic commerce on the Net can be fueled by cybermoney; this is incapable of being directly measured. The retail money can thus blow up to some multiple of its formal money backing and the shopping galleries in the cyber-world could serve up their own special potions of virtual money too. All told, the uncounted money may zoom around the world several times a day prior to extinction, buying and selling financial assets at myriad links along the way. This idea, first expressed by the New York Fed's Paul Henderson fifteen years ago, is a powerful one.[2]

There can be no question that the buyer's money flow always has a buying counterpart. Its creation arises from the existence of matching transactions that demand payment. The monetary MV (money x velocity) side of the equation of exchange must exactly match the real PT side (transactions for which they represent payment x their average price). Financial assets are included along with everything else. It is continuous money, but is it really money? Does the "money" exist if it is doomed to collapse from all its multiple worlds at the end of the day, or whenever final settlement may take place?

Perfectly reasonable economists differ among themselves about this. I now believe that the continuous money flow or electronic credit is money—virtual money if you wish to use the language of cyberspace—on the condition that it is acceptable for goods and services throughout the day. When the Bank of America gets some federal funds through Fedwire from First National Bank B, it doesn't know or care that they are fueled by an evanescent overdraft. It just goes ahead and uses the money now expressed as credits on Fedwire. First National Bank B (or a customer) may also spend the same "money" until the Fedwire overdraft expires.

Central bankers tend to believe none of this is money until it has been collected in good and final funds and one knows that one's check (or its electronic equivalent) isn't going to bounce. Central bankers may also believe that money isn't money unless it's able to be measured. Paper float may be spent and the paper check kited but should one count money twice if it is twice spent? Is the involuntary "loan" of float matched by an equally temporary bank liability that can be spent as a form of value until the float's collapse catches up with you? In the paper-based era, most of us did not give this matter much thought. Within or outside a central bank, we relied on official discrete or end-of-day Fed accounts. Now that the electronic overhang is huge, does it make a difference? One would certainly think so. On a day-in day-out basis, the trillions of dollars plus are hard to ignore.

I pose the following important questions. Given the thin and shrinking interface with official "real" money, what is the nature of money flows in a computer-generated money mode? Should the e-flows not be considered spendable value until someone spends them on something and pays from genuine netted-out balance sheet accounts of banks? Or, are they the phantom-world but practical mirror image of that already sent on its way to purchase assets? Money takes many forms, and its nature can be quite equivocal during the course of its travels.

Virtual Particles: An Analogy

This ambiguous money state reminds me of the famous physics theory of quantum electrodynamics created by Richard Feynman for which he won the Nobel Prize.[3] I am told that Feynman first developed the concept of virtual particles and said that electrons have a cloud of virtual particles surrounding them. An electron is always sending out these virtual photons, but they don't really exist unless they are grabbed by another electron. When this occurs, the virtual photon becomes a real photon and that kicks the two electrons apart. In the meantime, before the photon self-destructs, the little particle can do such impressive things as tunneling over edges of glasses or out of black holes or the nuclei of atoms.

Virtual money, like the virtual photon's time horizon within the "real" world, is strictly limited. The virtual photon achieves its life through a form of borrowing—the physical world's equivalent of an overdraft. In fact, physicists often use this banking analogy to describe the loan of energy. The virtual particle can "borrow" energy from the Heisenberg uncertainty principle that relates energy and mass, they say—but it's only for a certain constrained time. How long the photon can hold onto the loan and extend its shadowy lifespan will depend on the loan of energy's size: the greater the "energy" overdraft from the physical world, the shorter the loan's duration. In the meantime, before the world can know, the little particle may tunnel its way up and out.

If you are a bank sending money on wire and are over your credit cap, you may borrow on overdraft (in the United States). But you must pay back the sum you borrowed. Any netting system such as CHIPS gives you similar free rein—but only within the day. The funds thus spent in capital or currency markets, say, are living on borrowed time, but they can do their buying (and matching selling) "thing" before their inevitable end-of-day demise.

Like Cinderella at the ball, the virtual money has but a certain length of time in which to play. It buys and sells assets, whether currencies or thirty-year Treasury bonds. It stirs things up in markets and responds to expectations shifts. In a brief time span, it captures not a prince but a profits prize. In similar fashion, computer cybermoney may enjoy a life "borrowed" for a time from the underlying money before it, too, vanishes in a cloud of settlement smoke.

A Life of Its Own?

The evidence that virtual money may tunnel into markets is as shadowy as its substance. But there can be little doubt that wholesale money multiples have tangible market effects, especially when foreign exchange speculators or hedge fund traders are at work. The virtual money multiples help to fuel market volatility. They contribute to the "churning" of currency markets and span the globe in reactions that are nonlocal. Bit by bit some data emerge from Basle and the Federal Reserve that indicate the remarkable extent of this virtual money play.[4] Computerized foreign exchange transactions—without benefit of human hand—move toward the trillion-dollar mark daily, and derivatives transactions are not far behind.

The dual intertwined themes of benefits and risks recur. At the Federal Reserve Board's March 1994 International Payments Symposium, former Fed Governor Angell stated that the capital markets link "with a new perfection." But "volatilization of financial asset prices is not likely to disappear and will continue to result in rapid turnover in financial markets." In echo of the common theme, J. P. Morgan's Dennis Weatherstone observes "that we are in an age of borderless finance and an acceleration of cross-border flows. With it comes a growing dominance of capital markets and a new prominence for risk management."[5]

To reduce risk is to reduce the money overhang, the unsettled money that looms at many untold multiples of official measured money. Bankers call it exposure, which they want to control and lower. Indisputably, this is virtual money of a sort, money that no one will or can measure with any certainty. Will any brief or within day financial churning of this money overhang do anything "real" for a while in the world below? Recent unsettling foreign exchange volatility suggests that the effects in, for example, currency markets are all too real.[6] The situation concerning derivatives is more puzzling: the derivatives contracts may be bought and sold many times during the day in gross, but little money (net) actually moves between the two parties. Very little in the way of real assets or commodities underlying the contracts move either. When asked, experts say they think all that activity wouldn't have much effect on the underlying markets, but no one can be quite sure. Right now, it is not possible to know in any empirical sense.

The complex web that money has become creates many mysteries along with opportunities and the wrenching quest for understanding.

In sum, the virtual money mysteries are the following:

— What are the underlying money links in global dimensions, to the extent that anyone can even set them forth?
— How do the complexities of these links in cyberspace produce the overhanging or virtual money that we see all around (and above) us?
— How may travel speeds alter the risk as well as size of the over-

hanging unseen mass, and what can anyone hope to do about it?

— Does this phantom money have any life of its own in the money or capital markets before it self-destructs, as eventually it must?

— Before its inevitable demise, is there evidence at all that virtual money tunnels into real-world markets and impacts in some tangible way on the planet and its people below?

— Finally, how may we usefully reorient our world view in light of the dramatic evidence that things are no longer, and can no longer be, what they once were?

The Real World Below

Even to ask these questions will require a little more detail about the rapidly changing money world. I return to the links of the money and banking person to help tell the story.

"Snapshot" Money

Let's portray money at rest as a child's compressed "Slinky". It expresses in more casual form the layers of Figure 6.1's pyramid. When compressed as tightly as possible, we see quietly resting balance sheet (or "snapshot") money of some sort. For their balance sheet snapshot, bankers choose the end of day, month, year. We start with reserves at the base, the official money M's, then the bank-linked plastic. With time we will perhaps gravitate to the superimposed new layers, cybermoney and free money or e-barter, about which we know very little.

We have to get from one level to another, and for this task money must be set in motion. We also may call the now stretched-out value continuous money, which represents money times its use throughout the day. To get an idea of what's involved, pull the Slinky out as far as you can. The mechanisms, physical or wire, sandwiched in between the balance sheet money show us how we can go from one "money at rest" layer to another. To move from one balance sheet layer, we must send a signal through an intervening "money in motion" or money flows layer. What follows are wholesale wires, such as central bank wires and CHIPS, and the retail check, GIRO, credit, and debit card systems. Next in potential succession are the bank-linked Internet modes such as smart cards and the hypothetical free flows that do their own thing without the need of banks. When you stretch the vision into the future, newer technologies will certainly add levels and links, as money transfer instructions seek their most efficient paths.

Money in Motion

The way that the balance sheet, or snapshot, money makes the journey from one money form to another (vertically, in money layers) is mainly through communications signals. Money's journey across the face of the globe (horizontally from place to place) also takes the signals route.[7]

The messages to transfer money from Jon's account in New York to Sandra's account in Australia travel as an electromagnetic wave. In the case of satellite transmission, the messages have been prepared expressly for the journey on a transmitter at the ground station that services the electronic wire of Jon's New York bank. When they meet their final destination at the other side of the globe, the electromagnetic waves carrying the message hit the station in Australia. There, the oscillating electromagnetic field created by the EM wave jiggles the electrons in the receiver. (Recall the analogy in Chapter 6 of the buoys bobbing up and down in response to the water wave.) The stream of electronic 1s and 0s then enters into the books of banks or whomever it is that is keeping track of Sandra's "money." They register the newly arrived snapshot money and credit her account. Meanwhile, another message tells Jon's bank in New York to debit his account by an equivalent amount.

Consider all the ways each of the different money forms, ranging from traditional paper to the most ghostly cybercash, may either convert into another form or travel to another place. The systems range from simple to complex. The bank's internal system will transfer money from one form to another, from deposits to cash. However, the minute another bank is involved, say, to produce cash at a "foreign" ATM (one not owned by your own bank), the signals route comes into play.

Complexity is certainly the byword when money moves through layers of banks, settlement banks, and central bank wires, up and down again over continents. (In the case of fiber optics lines, recall that the message moves *below* oceans but the complexities don't change.) Indeed, the mechanisms can become most complex even if all that's wanted is to get some "real" money back in return for computer money assets.[8]

Bridges from Virtual to Real Money

The cloud-like free flows without official bank backing may hop around on the Internet or via other technologies the open Net may eventually come to compete with, Direct Broadcast Satellite (DBS), cable modem, cellular phone, personal communicator, or whatever else may materialize to do the job in this age of creative imagination.

In this manner, the "free money" starts out as unregulated private money on the Internet. But holders may want something more firmly rooted and they can choose to convert the cybermoney into smart cards, electronic checks, or other e-cash arrangements that hook up with banks.

The flows may migrate around here for a while before moving down another level toward the conventional. Cybermoney returns to the familiar world through "closed" financial systems containing plastic, GIRO, home banking, debit card, and ATM. In the plastic bank-linked world may also come to rest the e-wallet or electronic check, depending on how firmly the bank ties are welded. To make the descent back down to conventional money at retail level, we need only use the well-established transfer routes of credit card company, GIRO, EDI, ACH, or paper check transfer.

The wholesale money that moves the big markets has another transfer tier to go, say, CHIPS or SWIFT. Then it hits a central bank wire as the final means of net settlement into the reserves of many countries. Reserves grounding at the foundation of any money system is thus attained.

In short, the *method* of money transfer isn't going to be all that different in the latest round of e-money creations. What can vary is the added numbers of layers they must travel. Also different is the expanded numbers of systems interface (nodes) through which the computer-generated money must travel before settlement inexorably collapses the flows.

What is this rising complexity going to do to money mechanisms as we know them, including risk?

The Stacked Sandwich

To get a feel for the possible hazards facing holders of private or free money, think of the layers as a many-stacked sandwich. Unfortunately, we don't always quite know precisely what we get when we bite into it. The e-money systems will promise to convert their money IOUs into "real" bank deposit money, whenever it's requested. Some may hold the user's deposits in escrow, for ready redemption on request. Several questions must be asked, however. What is the percentage available for conversion at any one time (i.e., how great are the underlying "escrow" deposits owned by the e-money creator)? How many steps in the process must we take before we finally get back to "real" money? Finally, what happens if promises are not fully backed up by fact? What is the legal recourse to any holders who may be parted from their money?

In money forms, the range is from reserves (high-powered money), to conventional money, credit and debit cards, and bank-linked e-money. But what of the money freely roaming the Internet? Consider first the *form* of backing: is the e-money to be backed by central bank reserves, conventional money of banks, or liabilities of some other issuer, say, a computer company? Consider next its *use*: is the backing held sterilized in escrow, or invested (temporarily) in assets that may range from Treasury bills to loans or venture capital, if no one is looking? Consider also the issuer's *percentage range* of backing, and, finally, the number of layers the "money" may have to travel before it finds the ultimate backing—reserves.

The point of this discussion is that e-money's grip on conventional money can get quite diluted. To put it more bluntly, the private money creation may produce deep trouble, if something goes wrong somewhere in what may be a lengthy chain—and nobody is paying attention.

There are several reasons why trouble may sometimes occur. The greater the numbers of layers, the greater the risks, including not only security but exposure (i.e., overhanging float or unsettled balances). Also, the greater the numbers of layers, the larger the numbers of individuals or systems that must reliably do their jobs and, more important, not fail or suffer gridlock. The more layers, the more points of contact, with their potential impact on other markets or systems. Finally, the more layers, the greater the complexities and "feedback effects" that are neither foreseen nor capable of rollback.

In short, the more the system is layered with virtual money, money that isn't measured or tracked, the greater are the things we do not know or cannot understand. Now add the following caveat: the more complex is the system, and the greater the numbers and varieties of computer links, the greater the trust that we have transferred from humans to computers in the expansive world of cyberspace.

Science: The Parallel Mysteries

We're drawn back to the virtual money mysteries. The question of when money is money and not just a directed electromagnetic wave or computer entry has always bothered me. It is similar to the philosophical query asking whether thunder is thunder if there is no one around to hear it. What happens when a money transfer signal hits the receiver at the earth station?

The first answer is that, for money, you don't really need to know what happens in that nanosecond when contact is made and the transfer reconfigures the balance sheet assets of the parties. Money transfer is a macro-scale event. The balance sheets are adjusted and we can consider any money photon/waves that go astray in their journey as totally trivial. We are talking about the equivalent of losing five drops from the whole Pacific Ocean.

Dr. Murray Gell-Mann expands the general thesis with a different example. Take the case of predicting racetrack outcomes. We don't need to concern ourselves with the practically infinite alternate histories of all the underlying elementary particles (photons, electrons, quarks, and so on) that make up horses, riders, and everything else involved in racetrack outcomes. For such large-scale macroevents, coarse-grained histories are good enough.[9] Sparkplug wins the race, and the electromagnetic waves get the money message to the proper place. By analogy, money moves around, quite properly. Signals directed into space will work as well as checks. It's all the same—probabilities get you to where you ought to be.

The portfolio theory of economist James Tobin says something similar. Professor Tobin also looks at the probabilities, this time at brokers' offices, not racetracks; risks are reduced (for a given yield or return) when you hold a diversified or balanced portfolio because, mathematically, the pluses and minuses in the fortunes of individual assets tend to cancel out.[10]

For me, the still nagging questions of money's content remain, even if we average away the probabilities. What happens when the receiver makes a measurement at the earth station? Physicists can't say why, when we make a measurement of a photon quantum, whether through instrument or ear or eye, we change what is known as its state. For any one photon the wave function is said to collapse. When it hits the cones and rods of the retina, or the eardrum, or the receiver, something fundamental happens. How does the state of the photon change, and why does it change when we measure it? We have evidence that it happens, but no one can answer that question either. We have stumbled onto a fundamental mystery that has bothered scientists for years.[11]

Quite surprisingly, the matter of creation and destruction of the virtual particles is developed theory. Even though we don't understand the details, the theory works. This physical process was established by Richard Feynman in the 1950s.

Creation and Destruction

Professor Feynman illustrated the manner of constant creation and destruction of the virtual photons that surround the electrons like a cloud. They are all around us but we can't see or even detect their presence without very special and carefully prepared experiments.

Also quite unseen is the constant explosion and deletion of money around us. The presence of much electronic float means the same money bit can coexist in many places and in different points in time. Virtual money is akin to virtual elementary particles that emerge from nowhere and just as quickly vanish into nothingness—but not perhaps until assets have been frequently bought and sold, in some cases by following computer-fixed order with nary a human hand intervening.

According to particle behavior, the vacuum of space is a seething mass of virtual particles in its own right even when there are no real particles. They create and self-destruct, jostle one another, hop around in time and space, and do things very briefly to the real world that one cannot always understand. Can it be that our virtual money, before the time of its eventual demise, may also have a life of its own for those who look for, and are able to take advantage of, short-term opportunities? If so, the quants may make or lose a lot of money for the firm and the hedge funds may do well. But what of the world at large?

All we can know is that something specific happens at each and every interface. The uncertainty ends when the message hits the earth's receiving stations or computer, except, of course, the uncertainty about how and when—and where in the globe—the money will be spent.

The World View: A Reorientation

When zooming over political borders in cyberspace, we may have global money in reality, whether we care to admit it or not. Politicians may not be aware of it, but the central bankers are. Their collaboration in seeking mutual solutions is enormous.

But what comes first, global money or global opportunities? The answer is another fundamental mystery. Is the effective money flow created because of the broad investment opportunities existing around the world and the ease and speeds with which they can be seized? Or is the reverse true, a form of tunneling to the real world below? Could the enormous breadth of assets around the planet exist precisely because of the vast opportunities to create virtual money of almost infinite variety and size, given computer speeds? Or do both happen, more or less spontaneously?

History tells us that money permutations range from the slowest to the fastest, from tangible to intangible, of life ranging from the very short to the rather long. Over the ages both have evolved from the simple to the complex, much as the intricate jaguar develops from the elementary quark and primitive life forms in Murray Gell-Mann's fascinating *The Jaguar and the Quark*. Creation is at its most profuse, in the new science of complexity, when the world (or society) is just at the border of chaos and order. In the money world, we are at a similar time of exploding possibilities, filled both with ferment and also great creative imagination. The new money creatures of technology take on a life of their own. At the same time, the matter of controlling—even of understanding—the unknown physical forces of money creation elude us.[12]

In the physics of the very small—i.e., quantum mechanics—the act of observing a system forces it to select one of its options which then becomes real. The probability of one event crystallizing from all others can be computed by a simple recipe, conjured up by what some call quantum cooks. The recipes work just fine both for communications signals and electronic money deliveries. The virtual money disappears from its multiple worlds when it's settled out of existence. When measured, the ghosts disappear and the money flow crystallizes into real or balance sheet money.

Feynman explains the basic recipe (of the quantum mathematical equations) simply. In quantum mechanics, an event is a set of simple initial and final conditions, no more and no less.[13] We can know the initial and final conditions, but we don't really know what is going on in between. Schrödinger's double-slit interference experiment is a classic example. Particles are fired through slits and they appear at a screen on the other side. However, there is no way you can know which slit one particular particle—now wave—has gone through. Existing in its travels as a smeared-out probability wave, perhaps the particle has traveled through both. Since any measurement will ruin the experiment, there is no way to find out. In fact, it is pointless to even ask the question.

The packet-switching techniques of new telecommunications and the Internet advance the analogy. These virtual routes carry most large noncheck money delivery instructions. They are cheaper and more efficient. They let the computer decide the paths, and it makes decisions on the spur of the moment, at each information-switching station (or I-way intersection) the message hits in its travels. Packet networks are entirely self-routing. No one knows in advance how each of the many little packets will travel.

The packet switching system is also layered. Each layer (which constitutes a separate point of interface or switching) can both carry and signal the data's future travel routes independently. Each lower layer nests into the layer directly above it, and within each layer the controlling software is only cognizant of the layer below and the one above it. Not only is the route not known in advance, but the order of arrival of the instruction packets is not known either. Individual packets that compose a message may travel over different routes, all chosen on an ad hoc basis. They may arrive at the proper destination out of order but for computer, not human, reassembly at the final end point.[14]

A New York broker's money transfer message will be carved up into little packets, each on its own special virtual route before it ever zings its way around to recombine, miraculously, in Tokyo. But every last bit of the message must get there; surely nothing indeterminate exists about the process.

In an interview with former New York Fed Operations Director Paul Henderson, I mentioned that physicists believe that you need not worry about any of the most minuscule indeterminacy of money flows. It goes without saying that if there ever was any doubt, we wouldn't have workable EFT. I was somewhat surprised that the question was not entirely academic. We do have determinant results, but operations people have had to think about the matter—they have resolved the uncertainty. Are there ever any qualms about what shows up at the receiver's end point? Yes, he replied, but that's taken care of, because whatever number the receiving bank gets at the point of contact the sending bank will normally agree to accept. Might the receiving bank ever fudge in its own favor or be careless about this? No, the banks deal with each other all the time; they trust each other. If necessary, the Fed would enforce the understanding to remove any doubts.[15]

The handshaking protocol between computers of sender and receiver settles, if necessary, any minor differences that may arise because of noise, electromagnetic radiation, software, or human error that the circuitous routes may generate. In the end, the photon flows give you the same message certainty and clarity as the paper flows. But not in between.

When the transfer message moves as an EM wave in cyberspace, the signals are neither independent nor time extended. They just merge along with much else that is up there. In that act of fusion, however, the money flows are in some sense also tied together by a web of electromagnetic signals. They are connected along virtual paths carved out by computer selection to deliver money—along with a great assortment of other digital messages—in the best manner. In an almost holistic way within the web, our money is unified around the world in fact, if not by law.

From the bumpy and winding voyage of money transfer's ephemeral journey over currency zones and continents come other unknowns, also of major proportions. Not the least of our concerns is privacy and security, which initiates the discussion of electronic money's uncommon consequences (Part V).

Part V

The Consequences
of Electronic Money

14

Privacy and Security

One of the most closely shielded bank secrets is its electronic money transfers. And no private bank is more ringed with elaborate security than the giant Citicorp, which boasts more extensive international connections than just about any U.S. bank. But nothing is sacrosanct any more. According to complaints unsealed in September 1995 in federal court, Citicorp's cash-management system fell prey to the wiles of a young Russian computer operator. The master hacker's name was Vladimir Leven and he lived in St. Petersburg. The charge was illegal entry into the bank accounts of Citicorp customers, in all about $12 million, of which $400,000 was actually withdrawn.

Mr. Leven added some nice touches of realism, to mimic the usual pattern of fund transfers: for example, when he posed electronically as Banco del Sud SA in Buenos Aires, transferring $304,000 through Citicorp to another account in San Francisco, he did so at his St. Petersburg computer at 1:10 A.M., Russian time. But the ingenious attempt to simulate time delays didn't help much in the end. FBI agents and the Russian police tracked the trail as it led from Argentina, Jakarta, New York, to San Francisco. Arrests were also multinational, sweeping up suspects in the Netherlands, Tel Aviv, San Francisco, New York, and Britain.[1]

The Information Skein

This particular conspiratorial ring was fortunately able to be apprehended; however, it may be more difficult to trace any tapping into our own personal cocoons of information. Before we had computers, people used to collect some information about others in the course of doing business, but it usually took too long or was too costly to compile or evaluate much within the paper stacks. Now, all that's needed to pull up the database of any of us is a few clicks of the mouse. The computer has mass-produced transactional information and also made its rapid and cheap access by outsiders very easy.

Martin and Weingarten (1991) compared records that documented American life 100 years ago with the present, and note that the changes in recordkeeping are especially dramatic.[2] What did the world at large know about individual people a century ago? Not too much. The few records that existed kept track of births, deaths, marriages, land boundaries, and ownership. Few school records were maintained, and 75 percent of the population was self-employed. There was no insurance, few government benefits, no driver's licenses, and no medical records. Today, less than 5 percent of the population is self-employed, 66 percent have life insurance, 90 percent have health insurance, 95 percent have Social Security accounts, and 60 million students are enrolled in schools and colleges. Records are kept by government agencies such as the Internal Revenue Service, Social Security, Selective Service, welfare, motor vehicle agencies, as well as universities. Private companies maintain millions of medical, insurance, and credit records.

Such personal and financial information funnels incessantly into a maze of databases, and documents the daily lives of almost everyone in the United States. This web of information is formed during one's lifetime by means of increments to all the interconnected databases and much of the private data contained on one net within the web (say, bank balances, subscription lists, registrations, or mail-order purchases) can pass to owners of other nets, through sale or tacit permission, or often in ways quite unknown to its rightful owners. The object of the information knows little or anything about who holds all this data concerning his lifestyle and tastes.

Privacy expert Dianne Martin provides a chilling metaphor for all this record-keeping in *Cancer Ward* (1968) when Solzhenitsyn states:

... as every man goes through life he fills in a number of forms for the record, each containing a number of questions. . . . There are thus hundreds of little threads radiating from every man, millions in all. If these threads were suddenly to become visible, the whole sky would look like a spider's web. . . . They are not visible . . . but every man . . . permanently aware of his own invisible threads, naturally develops a respect for the people who manipulate the threads.[3]

A National Database

Professor Alan Westin dazzled listeners at a conference sponsored by the Columbia University's Center for Law and Economic Studies in 1977. He talked of the implications of an electronic funds transfer system, with remarks that made him both pioneer and prophet.

> Often, public debate . . . has seen the fanciful speculations of "total system" EFT enthusiasts met by equally fanciful (though horrified) reactions from civil libertarians. . . . The trouble with the debate of the 1960s and early 1970s is that it was over a straw man. . . . No "total system" EFT plan had any possibility of being installed then.

He also added the admonition that our social policies concerning individual rights in personal data must be made unmistakably clear and brought up to date *before* major new data systems are allowed to be installed.[4]

The prophecy that EFT, when finally realized, would bear little relationship to the all-accounts-automated "cashless" model that characterized much of the writings in the 1960s was right on target; however, his caveat about being legally ready for the privacy problem has yet to be implemented.

The concept of privacy as a legal interest deserving of independent remedy was first enunciated by Brandeis and Warren in 1890 as "the right to be let alone." Although a right to privacy is not set forth in the Bill of Rights, the U.S. Supreme Court has found sources for a right to privacy in the First, Third, Fourth, Fifth, Ninth, and Fourteenth Amendments. Congress has tried to prevent the unauthorized or incorrect use of government records; however it has failed to take action on a number of bills seeking to protect knowledge of our personal spending habits from private vendors who would use or sell the information for profit.

In fact, privacy concerns led to Congress' refusal to create a national database in the 1960s and its later passage of the Privacy Act of 1974. This act was originally written to cover information-handling practices by private industry as well as government, but was pared down to include only the federal government.

Somewhat paradoxically, in the end we have a de facto national database anyhow, mostly outside the rule of law. Big Brother isn't the government—it's the assembly of private data collectors and traders that use linked computerized databases, electronic record searches and matching, and computer networking. Our Social Security number generally provides the electronic national identifier. Credit bureaus, mailing lists, law enforcement officials, medical insurance, and governments help feed the threads of data encircling. As our shopping cart moves from crowded aisle to aisle, electronic scanners can pick up information about our personal spending habits and tastes. Vendors can trade information about our tastes and lifestyles. Insurance companies and banks can clue each other to facts that may make us good or bad credit—or insurance—risks. Depending on how well the security works, the electronic purse or check can carry the potential for information tracking. Indeed, one of the advantages of Electronic Benefits Transfer to its issuing states is their ability to monitor the spending of the money stored in the card to be sure the electronic food stamps aren't bartered for cigarettes, or worse.

Boundaries between types of information and places are blurring. As the numbers of interconnected computers and users expand, telephone conversations, video segments, and computer data are merging to become simply digital information. Lower costs have moved computing from the hands of experts to everyone who owns a home PC. Lower cost computing also empowers those who wish to invade our personal financial lives.[5]

Privacy Preservation

There are, however, some limited ways to cope with the hovering privacy menace. A first step is to be aware of what our personal dossier says about us by examining records of credit bureaus and government agencies. To get off a mailing list is a daunting experience, but it can be done to a limited degree if impending legislation is beefed up. To be removed from a carefully culled list for telephone solicitors can be a problem, but the Telemarketing Association gives us options by offering a card to be filled out. Legislators can help protect us and they have passed a number of privacy laws; still others remain in Congress, awaiting enactment. The 104th Congress introduced legislation to restrict the use or sale of lists collected by communications carriers (H.R.411) and the U.S.Postal Service (H.R.434). Another bill would detail acceptable usage of credit report information (H.R.561). In addition, in 1995 the Office of Management and Budget published notice of draft privacy principles and draft security tenets for the national information infrastructure (NII).

Under Joan Winston's leadership, the Office of Technology Assessment's privacy and security study finds that increased linkage of government information is arguably not addressed by the Privacy Act. The study recommends restructuring the law so that it addresses the sharing and matching of data, as well as permits tracking the flow of information.[6] Most privacy experts conclude that we ought to be able to know what is said about us, buried deep within the database, as well as have a means for correcting what is false or inaccurate. Of course, that's easier said than done. The computer interface produces much personal information that other computers, without our knowledge, can lawfully tap. The first National Bank of Podunck could only extract the information from a check that we specifically wrote on it. Our blended database, in one nanosecond, serves up much more information than we can possibly imagine. If we don't want the receiver to know, we must make sure the software doesn't send it—it is a matter of controlling the technology.

The reader may be astonished to learn what manner of information is known by credit bureaus about income, debts, payments, bank balances, and daily financial habits. One cannot believe that this broad-sweeping data source could be quite as accurate about the most personal of financial material and at the same time be subject to serious and often dangerous errors. But that is the nature of the computer, an idiot savant in some respects.

Digital Glitches and Software Calamities

Going beyond privacy, digital glitches can present a hassle of massive proportions. Private firms have worked very hard—and quite effectively—to establish security on the early EFT systems such as credit cards and CHIPS. On the Internet, the young cyber-sleuths, exchanging intercepted information on-line, ferret out other security weaknesses and promise to hold a club over all to help ensure privacy.

Some unauthorized access to networks or change or duplication of electronic data by outsiders is inevitable. Users must be able to verify the accuracy and origin of any data they may receive, be allowed to call back up the transactions they already have made, and protect their anonymity so the world at large will not know their affairs. Possible misuse or bungling by insiders, competitors, and of course hackers and incompetent programmers is an ever-present concern.

In November 1985, my students were analyzing the combined Fed system balance sheet when someone noticed that discounts of the New York Federal Reserve Bank for the week had jumped by well over $20 billion. This was extremely unusual since Fed bank discounts normally range from $100 million to at most $2 billion. At the time, in order to calm the curious, the Fed was quoted as saying the rise in discounts was merely a "technical" matter. Fuller details emerged later. A computer failure at the Bank of New York, it seems, snarled thousands of government security transactions. The problem was with the software, which was new and not adequately tested, and the bank hit a volume threshold that caused the system to crash. Securities kept backing into the Bank of New York, decreasing cash, but it could not back them out again for credit. It also could not process and reroute the securities for payment so it kept being debited for the securities it received with no offsetting credits. It plunged deeper and deeper into overdraft.

As a temporary band-aid, the Federal Reserve extended massive overnight credits. If the central bank had not done so, other networks such as CHIPS would also be in peril, since the Bank of New York would not have been able to pay other system members for what was owed them. Systemic "contagion" could have been the end-result of something that started out as inadequately tested software and its impact could have ricocheted to many banks.

Although neither Fedwire nor CHIPS have been plagued with such software misfortunes that we know about, other private institutions have been less lucky. Recently, a software glitch delayed the opening of the Big Board on December 18, 1995. "The snafu halted the opening of trading for 60 minutes, paralyzed action at several other markets and contributed to no small amount of hair-pulling on Wall Street," according to the *Wall Street Journal*. The software mishap stemmed from a communications problem between the securities industry's central processing unit and the Exchange's electronic display books at specialists' posts. As the Big Board feverishly worked to bring its systems on line, the financial markets reacted. By the time the New York exchange came on board at 10:30 A.M. EST, the Nasdaq Composite Index was down more than 27 points and the bond market a full point.[7]

Operations Gridlock

Computer systems can also crash because of electrical failures, hardware failure, deliberate abuse, and storms. For money delivery, delays of this type (or operations gridlock) can present a far more serious problem. Overload the system, or engineer it improperly, and its stability may be threatened. The original designers of Arpanet twenty-five years ago were aware of the problem and built in safeguards; so did the Federal Reserve, with its robust security and backup capability in case of failure at any single point. Under the technical title of "operational risk," great care has been exercised to provide plenty of systems redundancy.[8] A good system must be a little like the human brain in this respect. If one path is overloaded or out of commission, another will put it through. This concept lies behind the virtual or carved-to-order worldwide paths of most modern telecommunications routes, including the Internet.

Dr. Paul Henderson, also an M.I.T. engineer, reveals a nice story along these lines from the early days of automation as it was then called at the New York Fed. In about 1978, Paul wanted to buy a couple of expensive computers, at a cost of several million dollars each. The other Fed Banks objected because they thought the new machines were too expensive. One day the older system that held the Federal Open Market Committee data went down and Paul demanded to know what you do if you cannot process FOMC operations, which is the New York Fed's job.[9]

The other Fed Banks didn't need much convincing and the Operations Division quickly procured their two expensive computers. One provided a backup and systems cross-check in a kind of bridge to detect any fraudulent or illegal entry; the other computer did the actual work. Then President of the New York Fed Paul Volcker was extremely supportive of getting the highly automated equipment up and running, and Governor George Mitchell pushed for the necessary approval at the Board level. By way of footnote, there has been no serious problem of this type since; however, other significant vulnerabilities remain, especially for the less strictly controlled systems.

Through network viruses, worms, or sniffers, and the like, the latest in technology can create vulnerabilities that defy the imagination. Human errors and design faults, intentional and malicious acts, insider and natural disasters are only part of the picture.

A Common Tongue: Interoperability

Once past these hurdles, there still remains the matter of getting the motley systems to talk to one another. Hearings before the House Committee on financial Services stress the difficulties that common standards and protocols seek to address.[10]

One company's technology is usually layered atop other technologies and services provided by still other companies. Take an everyday example, the telephone. We expect a common dial tone when we pick up the phone. Even a simple telephone network combines privately owned local networks, public switched phone lines operated by one local company, and interstate services offered by possibly yet another. When we talk from state to state, the equipment tied on the ends of these lines may be made by different companies. Each is designed to do different tasks, but any diverse technologies must be made compatible: they must speak the same language.

Standards and Protocols

Standards are technical specifications for electrical engineers, written or understood by formal or informal agreements. Standards allow different products to work together, making products and services easier to use and less expensive. Standards are particularly important in networks since the many people sending out financial data must store and communicate information using compatible formats—called *protocols*. Even the otherwise anarchistic Net has a careful protocol worked out by an erudite board of the highest calibre that uses formats built on the Transmission Control Protocol/Internet Protocol (TCP/IP).[11]

The standards-setting process can be a tricky business, and much of the necessary information may be proprietary. Designers must make compromises so that the different protocols can work together, without costing too much or surrendering trade secrets. They must be user-friendly, flexible, work at adequate speed and capacity, and protect the most markets and the most people possible. Market-driven de facto standards, DOS or UNIX, can be better than well-protected standards whose users cannot communicate with very many other users.

A wide variety of good but incompatible standards will only frustrate people. In general, vendors in countries with markets and bodies that develop standards quickly can gain an advantage over those in other countries lacking quality standards. So it's very important that they get together to do the job in a way that does not fall afoul of the Antitrust Division. A recent example is the pairing of rival Sony and Toshiba factions in the CD optical technology. They compete, but they also wish to avoid the market confusion and withdrawal that plagued the VHS and Beta VCR technologies for a time.

The numbers of standards setters are quite daunting. We have bodies such as the Internet Engineering Task Force and the Internet Architecture Board, the International Organization for Standardization (ISO), and the American National Standards Institute (ANSI). Also included will be the European Computer Manufacturers Association (ECMA), the European Telecommunications Standards Institute (ETSI), the Institute of Electrical and Electronics Engineers (IEEE), and the American Bankers Association (ABA).[12]

Encryption

Encryption also draws together money-securing bedfellows of extraordinary variety. I used to think encryption was the sole province of the military and the national security experts, but in today's money world it perhaps is not surprising that this mathematically arcane science joins the other forces of technology to help deliver our money intact, in one intangible but secure phantom whole.

The recorded history of cryptography is more than 4,000 years old. Manual encryption methods using codebooks, letter and number substitutions, and transpositions have been around for hundreds of years. The Library of Congress has letters from Thomas Jefferson to James Madison containing encrypted passages. Modern, computer-based cryptanalysis began in the World War II era, with the successful Allied computational efforts to break the ciphers generated by the German Enigma machines.

In the post-World War II era, the U.S. locus of cryptographic research has been the Defense Department's National Security Agency (NSA). In its modern setting, cryptography is a field of applied mathematics/computer science. Encryption transforms a message or data files (plaintext) into a form (ciphertext) that is unintelligible without special knowledge of some secret key (the decryption key). Two common forms of encryption include: (1) secret-key, or symmetric, encryption and (2) public-key, or asymmetric, encryption. Note that key management—the generation of encryption and decryption keys, as well as their storage, distribution, cataloging, and eventual destruction—is crucial for the overall security of any encryption system.

Encryption can be used as a tool to protect the confidentiality of information in messages or files. For this task, both the early DES and the new Escrowed Encryption Standard (EES) use a secret key (a mathematical code or algorithm). Encryption can also guard the integrity of information and prove that unauthorized people have not made changes, or deleted or added items. It can authenticate the information's origin—that is, determine that it comes from the stated source or origin and is not a forgery. Digital signatures, most commonly using the RSA or Digital Signature Standard (DSS) algorithms, can accomplish integrity and authenticity functions.[13]

From Carol to Ted, Safely

The federal Data Encryption Standards (DES) was first approved in 1976 and reaffirmed in 1993. With DES, users can generate their own encryption keys. The secret encryption key for DES is fifty-six bits long, and the DES does not require the keys to be escrowed or deposited with any third party. OTA describes the simple secret key (symmetric) encryption system as follows. Carol encrypts her messages to Ted with their shared secret key; Ted decrypts messages from Carol with the same secret key, and sends messages back to Carol in the identical way. Some secure form of key distribution is needed so that Carol and Ted can share their key.

In electronic commerce, the more complicated—and theoretically harder to break—public-key system is commonly in use. Its level of security is supposedly higher. In the public-key (or asymmetric) system, everyone uses two keys: one private and one public. Everyone has access to a user's public key, which can be found in a sort of electronic phone book. However, your corresponding private key is maintained under the greatest security and kept secret from others. For example, if an associate sends Carol a message encrypted with Carol's public key (which he and other people can find in the equivalent of a phonebook), in principle only Carol can decrypt it because she is the only one with the correct private key.

A Digital Signature

But how can you prove that the message, say, an e-check for $100, is really yours? You must authenticate the money transfer just as in any check-writing system, and the digital signatures must provide a high degree of authentication. They also allow the resolution of disputes about whether you really did send the money and whether it was perhaps spent twice or forged. Public-key cryptography allows secure, efficient digital signature techniques to be used on e-checks and electronic documents. How does it work?

To "sign" a message, a user may transform it with his private key, that is, provide a digital signature, and send it on to the intended receiver. The receiver validates the message by acting on the transformed message with the sender's public key (obtained from the electronic phone book) and matching that result with the original message. Because the signing operation depends on the sender's private key (known only to the sender), it is impossible for anyone else to sign messages in the sender's name—provided the private key is kept private![14]

There is also the matter of how best to exchange the private key. The most widely used commercial digital signature system (based on the Rivest-Shamir-Adelman, or RSA, algorithm) can also encrypt. Therefore, the RSA techniques can be used for secure key exchange as well as for signatures and many companies have licensed the RSA technology. On the World Wide Web, Netscape (in collaboration with RSA Data Security Inc.) handles encryption of "secure" pages where, in theory, you may entrust your credit card information, and flags them with unbroken key symbols against a blue background. The visual display of key captions conveys a reassuring aura when buying something that you may fancy, but is the comfort-level warranted? Only if its implementation is done correctly.

Security Shortcomings

Is security on the Web good enough for us to trust credit card or digital money transfer? I consulted a master hacker for his insights. My informant, who prefers to remain anonymous, tells me e-money in home memory is spectacularly vulnerable because, in his words, "Any computer geek can figure out how to get in there. And they will do it too. Especially if it downloads to your own PC. Now I would not feel comfortable going to an ATM machine with a screwdriver and fiddling with the software there but at my own house I would feel comfortable, absolutely. When you talk about home-brew money, the security had better be bloody good, whether it's Bill Gates's or someone else's."

These words would prophesy what was yet to come. A couple of first-year graduate students, Ian Goldberg, 22, and David Wagner, 21, of the University of California at Berkeley, identified a serious flaw whose nature shortly resonated through the Internet. It threatens, according to the *New York Times,* "to cast a chill over the emerging market for electronic commerce."[15]

Goldberg and Wagner said they had decided to put the Netscape software to a test in an effort to raise public concern about placing too much trust in unproved electronic security systems. Netscape's security is based on public key cryptography, in which as we saw earlier a new key is created for each information exchange, based on a mathematical formula that is combined with numbers supposedly known only to the sender or recipient.

But how was it possible to crack the code so fast? The students first figured out how Netscape's formula generated the number used as a starting point for creating a key. That accomplished, they were then able to greatly reduce the potential combinations that would unlock the code. It turned out that the starting-point number was based on the time and date of the transaction, combined with several other unique bits of information from the user's own computer system.

Once you knew how the starting-point number was created, the job was simplified and from that point, the code-breaking task takes anywhere from a matter of seconds to about four hours, depending on whether you believe the code-breakers or an embarrassed firm whose previous assurances had been shown to be overoptimistic, to say the least. A standard computer work station was the code-cracking medium.

Just one month earlier in August, another student at the École Polytechnique in Paris had to use a network of 120 computers to generate a Netscape secret key. Damien Doligez employed a "brute force" attack. His job was much harder since he couldn't narrow down the search field as fast. To break the code took him eight days.

In neither case was any actual customer information stolen. All that

was known were details of how to break through the protective envelope that surrounds transmissions. A reward was offered to anyone else
who could find and fix security breaches and software designed to fix
the problem would be in the electronic delivery pipeline within the
week.

Some think the transgression was not so serious. The chances that
your number might be pulled were slim, perhaps lower than those
incurred by dispensing credit card numbers over the phone to someone
you would never meet. The cash reward provides the kind of public
scrutiny that such a security system needs, and may be a brilliant ploy.
Others have been less sure. Recurrent security glitches continue to
receive press publicity. People have not been flocking to the Internet
Shopping Network in droves just yet; the 1996 Christmas shopping season on the Web was a disappointing one.

The technology continues to move on. Newest on the money horizon
is quantum cryptography, which can potentially break just about any
existing code and erect some much stronger ones.[16] It's uncharted territory for money—and so is much else about the business, when you put it
all together.

15

The Reconstructed Whole

Popular imagination and the press often focus on what they perceive to be a dying money form: cash. Whether the 180-degree swing in money perceptions, from physical to out-of-sight ethereal, will stand up over time is a matter of conjecture. Within the digital money assortment to be plucked by consumers—tired of the dirty paper bills and endless paper fumbling—are Cybercash, Proton, Digicash, and innumerable others. VisaCash smart card lies waiting in the wings, with an e-money graft on its own familiar credit card, while MasterCard aligns with Mondex.[1]

Less in the public eye, but of a greater potential significance, is what the present speed of money's transfer may do to our financial economy. The advent of high-speed communications implies a major overhaul in the way that economists acquire financial data and analyze money's impact on economic relationships. Money turns over incredibly fast, and does its global "buying thing" equally fast. The notion that $2.2 trillion dollars changes hands daily, mostly on electronic wire, takes a little getting used to. The *New York Times* says more boldly that "because each transaction involves two or more payments, bankers estimate that each day $3.2 trillion cascades through the world's foreign exchange settlement systems."[2] Just to put it all in focus, consider that the U.S. debt limit in early 1996 was raised from $4.9 to $5.5 trillion so that our government could continue to pay its bills from March 1996 to September 1997.

Fragmented Perceptions

Despite a few scares, all that enhanced transaction speed hasn't led to the feared financial meltdown. Quietly behind the scenes, experts are working on the problem. From Basle, Switzerland, the BIS has issued pointed guidelines, in order to develop consistent ways of coping with risk and reflecting on it.[3] We are forced to start thinking about the nature of the large new virtual flows engine—and what it is and may do to markets and to each of us caught up in it.

In *Hyperspace*, Professor Michio Kaku describes how established perceptions of reality can become twisted when you move into a new world format such as this.[4] Of course, cyberspace, which encompasses the entire spatial range within which any information, including money instructions, can travel, is not to be construed in the same manner as hyperspace, the term popularly used when referring to the geometry of higher dimensions. Still, one can't help feeling that comprehension in both cases can become distorted and in major need of clarification.

Economists now look at monetary images and effects in an incomplete way. In large part, this problem reflects our inability to get the kind of data we would wish in the more complex and dynamic environment. Another obstacle to overcome is our continued reliance on concepts that no longer reflect the way economic relationships really work.

The current tools for measuring monetary transactions are seriously inadequate. Most economists are examining end-of-day money data instead of continuous money flows (effective money). In the process, they miss much of the important dynamics. This situation is strikingly similar to the fictional two-dimensional Flatlander faced for the first time with a three-dimensional world. His difficulties were recounted in 1884 by Edwin Abbot, headmaster of the City of London School, in his popular novel *Flatland: A Romance of Many Dimensions by a Square*. Because of the intense public fascination with higher dimensions, the book was a instant success, with numerous editions.[5]

The novel's hero is Mr. Square, a conservative gentleman who lives in a socially stratified, two-dimensional land where everyone is a geometric object, but in only one or two dimensions at most. Discussion of a possible third dimension is strictly forbidden. One day, Mr. Square's life is permanently turned upside down when he is visited by a mysterious Lord Sphere, a three-dimensional character. Lord Sphere patiently tries to explain that he comes from another world called Spaceland, where all objects have three dimensions. However, Mr. Square remains skeptical and stubbornly resists the idea that a third dimension can exist. Frustrated, Lord Sphere proceeds to peel Mr. Square off the two-dimensional Flatland and hurls him into Spaceland.

As the flat Mr. Square floats in the third dimension like a sheet of paper drifting in the wind, he can visualize only two-dimensional slices of Spaceland. Seeing just these cross sections of three-dimensional objects, Mr. Square views a fantastic world where objects change shape and appear and disappear into thin air. An apple materializes as a red circle, gradually expands, then contracts, turns into a small brown circle (the stem), and finally disappears.

Just as the Flatlander can't truly understand a sphere by looking at two-dimensional slices, we find it difficult to comprehend what is happening within the macroeconomy just by looking at the end-of-day (discrete) money. The unusual through-day (continuous) dynamics of the high-speed money flows—along with their staggering size and buying power—have vastly altered the workings of the monetary world. The effects of continuous money flows are neither fully recognized nor quantified. With the fragmented snapshot data at hand, we simply are not, and currently cannot, grasp the whole picture.

By analogy to our financial world, the official money and velocity numbers can be visualized as brief tracings—or small cross sections—of a large cyberspace cloud that generates real purchasing power in markets. Fragments of events are frozen within one instantaneous slice of time, determined by whenever the balance sheet is drawn up and the official reporting is done. The dynamics that effectuate quite dramatic changes in markets aren't captured and everyone seems puzzled; the phrase "no one knows" recurs. The private firms who run the actual operations aren't fully in the know either—they too can see merely fragmentary slices of a much bigger and unreconstructed whole.

The Reconstruction

The money whole is getting bigger. Links in the money chain are becoming more numerous and more complex and the spendable value leverage over reserve and money base is growing, as Part II described.

The primary way to rationalize the new money whole is to introduce new concepts such as continuous money flows (or effective money), which we met in preliminary form in Chapters 6 and 7. A second priority is to analyze much more explicitly the implications of communications and computerization on the proper *measurement* and characterization of money (Chapter 3).

A third task, also not easy, is to develop economic models that indirectly account for virtual money and its very real effects. An analysis of the electronic transactions data—with their vast multiples over underlying money—is one plausible way to proceed.

Virtual money's role in this reconstruction may not at first appear significant, since this type of money is ephemeral. It's not on the usual end-of-day balance sheets and sooner or later will be settled out of existence. However, like the virtual particles in physics whose introduction explained the fundamental forces of nature (Chapter 13), virtual money may hold the key to understanding some fundamental processes in the world economy.

The macromodels I am aware of don't presently allow for the economic effects—and massive buying power—of the daily trillions of light-speed ephemeral transactions. Logically, they ought to do so since a stretching of the money categories running through the macroeconomy could enhance our somewhat myopic vision.

Elastic Money

This volume has considered broadened categories of value that can serve as a medium of exchange, money if you will. First, is *conventional money*: cash, deposits and other components of the published money aggregates, or the official money supply. Also important is *electronic money*, which remains outside the basic money stock as commonly understood and published. Electronic money includes all credits on the wholesale electronic nets without conventional money counterpart, and as yet uncollected—often called exposure. It also includes all retail e-monies where value rests outside conventional banks, on plastic (smart card) or computer chip (cybermoney), as well as anything that turns over within the system without an apparent base. It includes multiple money counting of all types, thus embraceing the virtual money we have been focusing on.

To summarize, virtual money, with its real market impacts, currently consists of four general types.

1. The daylight overdrafts (daylight money) supplied by the Federal Reserve and guaranteed on Fedwire. Temporary credits under the ceiling of other central banks would be included here as well.

2. The settlement e-float that exists when virtual money is sent out on private electronic wire in the morning as payment for real expenditures, but not collected until the end of day or later (see Chapter 3).

3. The multiple private e-float in secondary use down the flows stream by private banks and their customers. When enhanced by rapid turnover, the money flows are swelled to the trillions of dollars of transactions that we daily see. Eventually included here would also be any unspent balances on smart card or computer cybermoney before they return to the banking system to be deducted from the books of their issuers (see Chapters 4 and 5).

4. The unknown but growing, barter electronic transactions that net out the credits and debits, as a paper clearinghouse might do. They help reduce settlement burdens, yet, at the same time, mask some very important real wholesale transactions from the statistical base (see Chapter 6). The task of information gathering by governments, individually and collectively, is well underway (see Chapter 10).

Information Gleaning

The matter of adding retail e-money information to total wholesale flows presents some special problems. The Bank for International Settlements provides extensive data on the plastic world-wide credit card dissemination. Quite possibly, it's too early to do much about the e-cash and cybermoney issues except to analyze the mechanisms critically and ask the necessary questions so that rules or regulations if needed can be applied more successfully.

E-cash or the plastic electronic wallet may become a quasi-money form. Does that mean someone should collect data on the flows as well as amounts outstanding? The privacy issues involved are hotly debated. The new electronically stored value may be considered in the same category as physical cash that now enjoys, and always has enjoyed, anonymity once it moves outside the banking system. Given this view, we should treat the e-cash like ordinary cash, anonymous and free—but that assumes it won't rise to significant proportions.

There is also the seignorage, or investible float awaiting the money's actual use and transfer, that we must consider. In the case of physical cash, the government prints the money and enjoys the seignorage from the use of the money holder's idle funds, say, the $100 notes buried in the backyard. The Treasury will invest the holder's original deposits yielded up in return for the paper, safely, probably in U. S. Treasury obligations. However, when the profits and investment opportunities from the float are enjoyed by the e-vendor, and possibly known only to the vendor, more questions arise. Consumers have a right to know how and where their original funds—the backup for their e-cash or computer money—are invested.

When and if the regulators finally step in depends of course in large part on how big the e-cash and cybermoney eventually comes to be. Long before this money ever gets to be a significant portion of our effective money supply, regulators will want to know more about the new products, what backs them, and what recourse users will have if promises are not kept. Central bank members of the European Community are openly on record for continued monitoring, and much sentiment suggests that only the regulated banks should be permitted to issue e-cash.

In this volume I propose that a reevaluation—and expansion—of concepts as we know them may clarify the practical issues and help us ask the proper questions.

Markets in Flux

Clearly, people are not sitting on their hands as markets seethe in flux. Congress is holding ongoing hearings on the future of electronic money, and bringing together knowledgeable people in the field. "Don't forget, we're dealing with some very creative but also some very young people. The atmosphere is highly competitive; we have to get used to the idea that the creators may not all be around a few years from now," as House Subcommittee on Monetary Policy's Chairman Michael Castle has observed.[6]

Banking regulators are studying the emergent e-money questions with great care, but are naturally quite reluctant to talk prematurely about their views. Public officials may be hesitant to reveal their tentative ideas in the absence of current data of the type financial economists, and the courts, normally require before they forge binding standards of conduct. On the other hand, in a classic chicken and egg situation, they want to know what's going on before the need for such binding rules becomes obvious.

The Consequences of Electronic Money

Of course, by itself, the government is not in any position to make definitive judgments since markets change so rapidly. The antitrust authorities are also altering their sights, in nimble action, while the market players move just as fast (see Chapters 8 and 9). While the Department of Justice studied the alleged monopolistic practices of the MicrosoftNet, Microsoft and the other on-line companies shifted their base of operations to the Internet.

What's the latest in market possibilities? Regulators are working with the private vendors. They chose that course with the successful credit card technology. With a nascent market, it's often best just to observe carefully and allow the market to work out the best course. That's been the position of both our Treasury and Fed, concerning e-money's first glimmerings. Given a need for action, say, big losses or a lack of confidence in the money system, one can rest assured that the Fed as well as the regulators will jump in to assert themselves. Perhaps those assurances should come sooner.

Those who would constitute the markets of the future say they need to be convinced—they are not sure they have all that much to gain and some see much to lose. "If the new e-vendors get their way, there'll be a run on shovels," a student says. "Why shovels?" I respond, "To dig a hole in the backyard for the physical money we can trust."

At present, the private sector understandably takes the lead. "We develop the encryption and security necessary to prevent the loss of confidence," stresses Citibank's Sholom Rosen, at the Cato Institute's May 1996 Conference on the Future of Money. "It is absolutely central to our thinking. We have to get people to trust our system and the public sector wouldn't know how to do it."[7]

The Unchanging Core

What doesn't change is a necessary core of trust, the notion that you can transfer cybermoney for real official money on demand. Many technical experts expect that e-cash, once generated, will flow around quite freely, *outside* banks. Some believe that private actuarial trust will keep e-money consumers quite content outside the comfortable banking haven as we've always known it. You trust that the insurance company will have the funds on hand to pay your claim, based on the actuarial probabilities that not everybody will die at the same time, or that hurricanes aren't likely to decimate all parts of the United States simultaneously. In similar fashion, e-cash issuers can figure out the proper probabilities, perhaps.

The difficulty with this reasoning is that it negates the possibility of sudden quite irrational bank runs.[8] This particular behavioral x-factor has been known to take over in no time at all. History is replete with bank runs, during wars and periods of overissue, in the Wildcat banking era of the mid-1800's, and of course in the early 1930s when the newly elected President Franklin D. Roosevelt was forced to declare a Bank Holiday and reform the banking structure and its regulation in 1933–34. A regulatory forum could provide the same scrutiny for e-monies that their banking brethren are subjected to.

Fortuitously, thus far, most e-vendors either *are* the regulated banks or have voluntarily aligned themselves with banks, (e.g., Digicash and the Mark Twain Bank or Mondex and its North American as well as British partners).[9] But they will all get to do business on the Internet and we continue to ask how it will be possible to regulate anything flowing on the Internet. Assets can flee, anonymous, across borders to the least suffocating environment. If excessive regulation persists, any overregulated users may skip to more pristine areas—the Offshore Islands will do well.

That particular argument seems a kind of Gresham's law: that bad money drives out the good. However, financial environments that achieve reputations for relative safety, and a high market regard, may still retain their edge. Is this concept going to change in the brave new world of the Internet? I think not. A joint regulatory scheme by all the players, private, public, and global, may evolve to further protect us. It's the Internet way. And, the process has already begun, as described in Part IV.[10]

Some other things may never change either, like the urge for a demonstrably proven track record. To gain the trust of markets, the private cybermonies of the future will have to provide the proper comfort level. With their closed and private systems—not to mention guarantees in case of loss or theft—credit card companies have managed to convey a quiet aura of security. At present, we can only trust that the digital e-money issuer, who must assume the responsibility that this money is sound for all purposes, will also offer the proper guarantees. The encryption locks and keys had better be demonstrably secure, the backup money solidly in place in all its shadowy virtual vaults. Money possibilities are daily becoming more fanciful and they forshadow an age of true money wizardry yet to come.

The Consequences of Electronic Money

Epilogue

This book is being written in the midst of a technological maelstrom whose parameters—to say nothing of its outcome—cannot be predicted. I pause to catch my breath. The future possibilities seem quite remarkable, while the present reality appears often crafted from the virtual and the unreal.

The Pivotal Role of the Internet

Surely one of the most fantastic situations in this whole picture is the rise of the Internet as a potential central player. Nobody could have imagined that this all-embracing system would have been organized by the military, with the aid of academia and some dedicated people from a high-energy accelerator center in Switzerland, who simply wanted to make it easier to access important scientific information.[1]

Yet in any future money-molding mode, the bottom line stays comfortably intact: consumer markets and competition for the consumer's dollar. The credit card or plastic era started out in an elitist vein, with the up-scale eagerly wooed, and then worked its way down to the rest of us. E-money also debuts in an elitist mode, but look who the elite are now. First to be courted were the technologically adept, the zealot who navigates the Web with zest and dedication.

The knowledge of how to browse and shop the Net has filtered down to the less technologically skilled members of the public. We grew dependent on the plastic, most of us; we may get to like the idea of an electronic purse that eliminates the aggravating pennies and the need for change. Some of the more adventuresome among us may wish to manipulate some digital money from a desktop computer, or distant server, for purchases on the Net. The Web can get to be quite addictive. A quarter century from now, our present money usage may look quite quaint, our fears about the new groundless—but not necessarily.

Some nagging questions are willed to the new generation, including some of the same old doubts revisited. Way back in 1978, the National Commission for Electronic Funds Transfer looked at matters of privacy, sharing, and security. Many of its worries, like the matter of credit card competition, have been laid to rest; others continue to fester, including risk. The harsh market judgments of some vendors from that early age will doubtless also mirror, a quarter-century hence, the high but collapsed hopes of some unlucky contemporary vendors.

Nagging Questions

The fate of those pioneers now eagerly stepping forward may rest also on the working through of major unknowns. First, what is the role of government in the current high-tech wave? Will the technical and organizational innovators be trampled by the heavy stomp of bureaucrats? The Antitrust Division seems to be stepping up its interest, while the Fed treads lightly; most central banks' policy tools already have adapted to technology, rather than the other way around. For some observers, the issue may center on whether any control ought to be exercised by any government authority.

Second, how can standards best be developed to permit both safety and ease of use? It seems perfectly clear that private banks and innovative firms will bear the primary responsibility. Government doesn't have the necessary data, and the technology moves too fast—standards appropriate for one time and place may be out of date in six months or a year. Under such circumstances, the government's optimal role is one of review and possibly collaboration with the private sector, unless egregious market restraints develop.

Third, what revamping of the law or regulation is necessary to redefine the term "bank" to make it all-inclusive? I would argue that the responsibilities of the various financial players be applied evenly across the board, at least as a sought-for goal. Professor Edward Kane suggested well over a decade ago that deposit insurance should be based evenly on risk, not granted as a right. His idea sought to impose more market discipline; foolish or reckless bankers might not have the government to bail them out.[2] Those responsible will want to revamp the manner in which assets can be used and how the new accounts will be held. The security issue looms very big here. What may happen if holders of the new e-money aren't guaranteed prompt redemption, or can't safely transfer their intangible value to others?

Fourth, who will issue the e-cash, assuming there is any great demand for it—the Treasury, the banks, or anyone who can convince people that their IOUs are worth having as a store of value? Regarding the e-money specifics, to either endorse or decry any one vendor could do precisely what the Treasury and Fed does not want to do—shape the emerging markets and take the early decision-making away from users. One can be sure, however, that any sudden surge in e-cash proportions, or any sudden losses or redemption failures, will stoke a rapid reaction. Both retail and wholesale money intergovernmental study commissions are in place as of January 1997; one would hope the necessary questions are being asked.

Finally, will the banks hold their own against their nonbank e-money-issuing counterparts in a virtual money world? Those who suggest the banks must act quickly to grab for themselves the e-money prize or be left by the wayside do both banks and the public a disservice.[3] The regulated banks aren't going to rush ahead heedlessly, and the public won't permit them, which is probably a good thing. The questions and trade-offs are many, and they will take time to figure out.

Conflicts and Trade-offs

If only banks are permitted to offer the smart card or computer cyber-money, the advantages of nonbank innovations will be tempered and multi-industry consolidations encouraged. If only Treasuries or central banks can do the e-cash creating, the threats of loss of anonymity (which surrounds cash) may surface. Privacy is yielded, in a quite scary way, if a data-disseminating currency issuer or big brother arises in our midst. On the other hand, there is considerable merit in knowing who gets your e-cash in case of fraud or loss, and unbridled anonymity can create true new nightmares for those who try to enforce the law.

If banking regulations such as reserve requirements and examinations are retained but not extended to those performing analogous tasks, banks may then find their place eroded. Their costs of doing business may become higher than the costs of those piped into everyone's home through telephone, cable TV, or desktop computer company. The banks' market may also prove more spatially limited, in the customary brick and mortar context. To extend the regulations may extend the reach of government and may shackle the innovative impulses of the market, as well as its ability to serve up the optimal money menu.

If the antitrust authorities are too vigilant in preventing market mergers, they may thwart the best synergistic fit between segments of the technology that can enhance operations through working together. If they demonstrate complete disinterest, then anything and everything may go, and the result may be the rise of monopoly power. The potential fear is that that threat can prevent the efficiencies of technology from filtering down, properly, to the consumer user.

However, in such dynamic markets as these, the new entrants can be many, and their sources as varied as the many industries that join forces under the combined telecommunications/computer/banking umbrella. Those that don't provide the proper financial backing and security, whether banks or nonbanks, may be blown away by the winds of change. In this seething creative environment, other technologies should be handily available to take their place.

The Unpredictable and the Unexpected: A Reprise

The old refrain recurs: one cannot predict. The Internet may prove to be just as powerful a decade hence in shaping society as the technologies that preceded it, the telephone, radio, TV. Or it may be even more powerful. The e-cash, computer cybermoney, and electronic commerce possibilities are particularly riveting. Which of these will win consumer favor in the manner of the credit card is far from certain.

We cannot know what will happen in the end when payments instructions travel outward on jagged computer-generated paths or money dwells unseen and often distant in computer memory. The e-money infusion has demonstrated a mind of its own, and its precise workings can sometimes seem a bit bewildering.

The dynamic money flows on their unmarked virtual paths around the globe often seem to border on the chaotic. Interconnections on the journey are growing and sometimes are overworked or stressed. The conservative banks and high-tech people, not cut from the same cloth, seem almost inevitably to have melded their fortunes, but not without some pain.

Yet the story has unfolded in a quite orderly fashion and has shown ample evidence of a kind of patterned direction to the whole seemingly messy money transformation. This volume has tried to lead the reader through the story from its beginnings of well over a generation ago. It reveals a money technology sometimes unsettling, often baffling, but in the end quite harmonious in its own singular yet stunningly complex fashion.

Unity out of complexity—it is possible to construct an ordered whole. We can identify some major bits of information that we need to obtain and, with a little effort, our perceptions can adapt and stretch. The textbook T-accounts still work, although upgraded. The diagrams of money's flows can be redrawn, to illustrate the money backup however distant either in geography or the money chain. The high-tech players of the future can be fitted into the drawings and the structure and some hypothetical alternatives can be sketched out. The markets have their play to search out the best adapted of the new money species. The regulators think through the questions, in advance. The markets self-select in a manner akin to the biological. Users in the culling process know more than they often give themselves credit for knowing.

Innovative money isn't that arcane, after all. We use the plastic credit/debit card—considered quite radical in its time—every day now, and vendors have worked out the bugs mostly to our general satisfaction. The road from the predicted cashless/checkless society has had its own extravagant reaches and claims, pulled back along the way. Like the "butterfly effect" of meteorologist Ed Lorenz, the tracings of the high-tech money flows yield up their own harmonious central designs, some quite intricate, but nonetheless working like the mechanisms of a clock or automobile—or of old-fashioned money, enhanced and more efficient.

Society is fascinated by what technology has created, and is mostly served by it, but money contours are inflated over time and presently in quite a dynamic fashion. Around the planet, money users have their work cut out for them, and an important role to play in shaping how far the creatures of technology may be left alone to do their own thing.

Notes

Chapter 1: An Introduction to the World of Electronic Money

1. Dale Reistad, Interactive Television Association and electronic media consultant, interview with the author, Washington, D.C., 30 May 1995.

2. As described by the author in the entry "Electronic Funds Transfer," in *The New Palgrave Dictionary of Money and Finance*, ed. P. Newman, M. Milgate, and J. Eatwell (London: Macmillan, 1992), 745–47.

3. George White, President, George White Papers, Inc., interview with the author, Montclair, N.J., 23 April 1995 and telephone interview, 3 January 1997. George White thinks it worth noting that since the time the concept of the checkless/cashless society was launched, we have doubled our volume of checks. The check system works well; electronic bill presentment, where customers pay recurrent bills such as utilities or mortgages electronically, remains insignificant.

4. Gould, *Ever Since Darwin*, 11–45, quote from 21; Gould, "Dinomania."

5. Gould, *Ever Since Darwin*, 12–13.

Chapter 2: A Tale of Money and Banks

1. With N goods, the standard formula for the number of prices is the following: $N (N\text{-}1)/2$. For 10 goods, we must compute 45 prices, and for 100 goods the number of price computations jumps to 4,950. For an amusing account, see the Federal Reserve Bank of New York, *The Story of Money* (New York: Federal Reserve Bank, 1995), 2–7.

2. See the Federal Reserve Bank of New York, *From Rocks to Riches: An Illustrated History of Coins and Currency*, and *The Key to the Gold Vault*; Mulcahy, *Coins of the Ancient World*; Federal Reserve Bank of Boston, *History of Colonial Money* (Boston: Federal Reserve Bank of Boston, 1992).

3. Ross Robertson, *The Comptroller and Bank Supervision* (Washington, D.C.: Office of the Comptroller of the Currency, 1968).

Chapter 3: Money on the Move

1. Juncker, Summers, and Young, "A Primer on the Settlement of Payments," 857; Richards, "Daylight Overdraft Fees and the Federal Reserve's Payments System Risk Policy," 1065–77. *Risk Reduction and Enhanced Efficiency in Large-Value Payment Systems: A Private-Sector Response* (New York: The New York Clearing House Association, January 1995).

2. Humphrey, *Payments Systems: Principles, Practice, and Improvements,* Chap. 2; Henderson, "Modern Money."

3. Federal Reserve Bank of New York, *Fedwire: The Federal Reserve Wire Transfer Service,* 3–7 and *A Day at the Fed,* 24–27; Elinor Solomon, "Electronic Funds Transfer: Challenges for the Computer Age," *The Bankers Magazine,* January/February 1993: 69–77. Passell, "Fast Money," 42ff.

4. Drake *The New Information Infrastructure: Strategies for U.S. Policy;* U.S. Department of Commerce, *NTIA Telecom 2000: Charting the Course for a New Century.*

5. U.S. Congress, Office of Technology Assessment, *U.S. Banks and International Telecommunications,* Chap. 2.

6. Knudsen, Walton, and Young, "Business-to-Business Payments and the Role of Financial Electronic Data Interchange," 269–78.

7. Michael Nelson, Special Assistant for Information Technology, the White House Office of Science and Technology Policy, interview with the author, Washington, D.C., 12 June 1995. For discussion of the plans for Internet II, see "Snap, Crunch or GigaPOP," *Scientific American* 275 (December 1996): 38–40.

Chapter 4: Plastic Everywhere

1. For an early perspective, see my "EFT: a Consumer's View," Chap. 9.

2. Baker and Brandel, *The Law of Electronic Fund Transfer,* Chap. 23.

3. For the mechanics of ATM systems, see my "Future Money and Banks: 1990–2010," 820–22.

4. Lawrence J. White, *The S&L Debacle: Public Policy Lessons for Bank and Thrift Regulation* (New York: Oxford University Press, 1991).

5. Steven D. Felgran, "From ATM to POS Networks: Branching, Access, and Pricing," *New England Economic Review* (May/June 1985) and Felgran and R. Edward Ferguson, "The Evolution of Retail EFT Networks," *New England Economic Review* (July/August 1986).

6. Bank for International Settlements, *Payment Systems in the Group of Ten Countries* (Basle: Central Banks of the Group of Ten Countries, December 1993) and its *Statistics on Payment Systems in the Group of Ten Countries*

Notes

(December 1995); Electronic Funds Transfer Association, "Leaving Behind the Past to Enter a New Millennium."

7. Spencer Nilson, telephone interview with author, 7 January 1997, projections and actual 1995 data from *The Nilson Report* (Oxnard, Calif., mid-1996) based on twenty-seven years of actual tracking of the credit card business from its inception. Spencer Nilson believes that smart cards have a definite future in a closed loop situation, but as any replacement for general purpose credit cards, that future may be ten to fifteen years away.

8. Remarks by Eugene A. Ludwig, Comptroller of the Currency, before the OCC Antitrust Conference, Washington, D.C., 16 November 1995; and Stephen A. Rhoades, "Competition and Bank Mergers: Directions for Analysis from Available Evidence," for that same conference. Both speakers note the past decade's considerable rise in nationwide concentration, while the number of banking organizations declined from nearly 11,000 to around 7,900 from 1985 to early 1995. However, the U.S. banking system still remains by far the least concentrated in the world.

Berger, Kashyap, and Scalise, "The Transformation of the U.S. Banking Industry: What a Long, Strange Trip It's Been."

9. Saul Hansell, "A Shaky House of Plastic with No Quick Fix in Sight," *New York Times*, 28 December 1995, D1 and D5.

Chapter 5: Smart Cards and Cybermoney

1. *Digital Cash and Electronic Money*, the Columbia Institute for Tele-Information, Columbia University, New York, 21 April 1995. David Chaum, Digi-Cash Corporation, Keynote Address; Lee Stein, First Virtual Holdings, "How Will Electronic Money Change Competition in Markets for Banking and Payments Services?," Respondent.

See Payments System Task Force, *The Role of Banks in the Payments System of the Future* (Washington, D.C.: American Bankers Association, September 1996); Congressional Budget Office, *Emerging Electronic Methods for Making Retail Payments* (Washington, D.C.: The Congress of the United States, June 1996).

For the views of private vendors, see the Department of the Treasury, *Federal Electronic Cash Forum*, Financial Management Service, October 1995 and the testimony prepared for the Committee on Banking and Financial Services, U.S. House of Representatives, *The Future of Money*, 25 July 1995, by David Van Lear (Electronic Payment Services), William Melton (Cybercash Inc.), Rosalind Fisher (Visa USA), Heidi Goff (Mastercard International), and Scott Cook (Intuit Inc.)

2. "Electronic Money: So Much for the Cashless Society," *The Economist* 26 November–2 December 1994, 23–27, quote at 27.

3. Peter Ledingham, "Pre-paid cards," 57, 4 *New Zealand Reserve Bank Bulletin*(1994): 346–49; Tom Kokkola and Ralf Pauli, 12 *Bulletin of the Bank*

of Finland (1994): 9–14; Meeting with Stephen Rhoades, Fred Schroeder, and Banking Markets staff, Federal Reserve Board, October 1994; Moore, "Money in the Third Millennium."

4. See David Laster and John Wenninger, "Policy Issues Raised by Electronic Money," *Digital Cash and Electronic Money*; Wenninger and Laster, "The Electronic Purse," 1–5; D. Chaum, "CAFE, the Electronic Wallet for the Information Age," *Federal Electronic Cash Forum*; Jeffrey Marquardt and Heidi Richards, interview with the author at the Federal Reserve Board of Governors, Washington, D.C., 31 October 1995.

5. Conversation with Y. Oritani, Bank of Japan, Washington, D.C., August 1989; "The Future of Money," *Business Week*, 12 June 1995, 66–78.

6. Kawika Daguio, "Digital Cash and Other Potential Electronic Payments Mechanisms"; interview with the author, American Bankers Association, Washington, D.C., 19 October 1995, and telephone conversation 3 January 1997.

7. Working Group on EU Payment Systems, "Report to the Council of the European Monetary Institute on Prepaid Cards" (Frankfurt am Main: European Monetary Institute, 1994): 1–12, quote at 3; Alan S. Blinder, Statement before the Committee on Banking and Financial Services, U.S. House of Representatives, 11 October 1995, quote at 13. In the same vein is the testimony of Eugene A. Ludwig, Comptroller of the Currency, before the Committee that same day; Marquardt and Richards, interview with the author, October 1995.

8. The EBT material is voluminous, but for an overview see the Federal EBT Task Force, *EBT Report to Congress*, 1 June 1994; *From Paper to Electronics: Creating a Benefit Delivery System That Works Better & Costs Less*, May 1994. Food and Nutrition Service, *Evaluation of the Off-Line Electronic Benefits Transfer Demonstration* (Rockville, Md.: U.S. Department of Agriculture, May 1994); *The Evaluation of the Expanded EBT Demonstration in Maryland*, May 1994.

Chapter 6: Money's Synthesis

1. Among many others, Burt Edelson (Director, Institute for Applied Space Research), Henry Geller (Visiting Professor, Duke University and communications fellow, Markle Foundation), H. R. Davis, Albert Ehrenfried, hydraulics engineer, Carl Howe (Product Manager, Bolt Planet), Kenneth Buckley, Division of Reserve Bank Operations, and Thomas H. Solomon (Assistant Professor of Physics, Bucknell University).

2. For specific examples, T. H. Solomon, interviews with the author, Washington, D.C., 1 July 1995, and 2 January 1997. Pierce and Noll, *Signals: the Science of Telecommunications*. For a technical description of optical storage, see Alfred Poor, "21st Century Storage: DVD and CD-ROMS," *PC Magazine*, January 21, 1997, 164–70. Also excellent is Carol H. Fancher, "Smart Cards," *Scientific American* 275 (August 1996): 40–45.

3. Some of these ideas were expressed earlier in my "Today's Money: Image

and Reality"; and "Electronic Funds Transfer," in *The New Palgrave Dictionary of Money and Finance*, ed. Peter Newman, Murray Milgate, and John Eatwell (London: Macmillan, 1992), 745–47.

4. Edward Ettin, Deputy Director of Research, conversations with the author, Federal Reserve Board, Washington, D.C., 1990, and 3 January 1997.

5. Haberler, *Prosperity and Depression;* Paul Henderson, meeting with the author, the Department of Justice, Antitrust Division, Washington, D.C., Winter 1981; E. H. Solomon, talk and group discussion at the Electronic Banking Economists Society, New York City, 7 February 1985.

6. Moore, "Payments and the Economic Transactions Chain."

Chapter 7: Money Control Layers

1. Harvard University Department of Economics, "Inflation, Unemployment, and Monetary Policy," *Alvin Hansen Symposium on Public Policy*, 24 April 1995; John B. Taylor, "Monetary Policy Guidelines for Inflation and Employment Stability"; Robert M. Solow, "How Cautious Must the Fed Be?" from that Symposium. See also Taylor, "The Monetary Transmission Mechanism: An Empirical Framework," 11–26.

2. Henry C. Wallich, "Recent Techniques of Monetary Policy," *Economic Review*, Federal Reserve Bank of Kansas City (May 1984): 21–30.

3. For example, see Andrew Crockett, "Monetary Policy Implications of Increased Capital Flows," and Commentary by Alberto Giovanni, in *Changing Capital Markets: Implications for Monetary Policy* (Kansas City: Federal Reserve Bank, 1993): 331–77.

4. James Tobin, "Monetary Rules and Control in Brave New World," *Electronic Funds Transfers and Payments*, 155–56.

5. Goodhart and Vinals, "Strategy and Tactics of Monetary Policy: Examples from Europe and the Antipodes"; Crockett, *Changing Capital Markets*, 351

6. In summary of different views: "Symposia: The Monetary Transmission Mechanism," *The Journal of Economic Perspectives* 9 (Fall 1995): 3–96; Federal Reserve Bank of Boston, "Goals, Guidelines, and Constraints Facing Monetary Policymakers," Conference Proceedings (Boston: Federal Reserve Bank, June 1994). M. Friedman, "A Theoretical Framework for Monetary Analysis"; B. M. Friedman and F. M. Hahn, *A Handbook of Monetary Economics*.

7. For example, John M. Berry, "Greenspan Calls Economy 'Soft', Hints at Rate Cut" and Jay Mathews, "Investors Put Negative Spin on Remarks," *Washington Post*, 21 February 1996, C1; John H. Wilke, "Economy Is on Track," *Wall Street Journal,* 21 February 1996, A2; Statement by Alan Greenspan, Chairman, Board of Governors of the Federal Reserve System, before the Subcommittee on Domestic and International Monetary Policy, 20 February 1996.

8. Bank for International Settlements, *Central Bank Survey of Derivatives Market Activity* (Basle: Bank for International Settlements, 18 December 1995),

2. After adjustment for double-counting during the month of April 1995, $839 billion of over-the-counter foreign exchange, interest rate, equity, and commodity derivatives contracts were traded per day. During April 1995, reported daily *turnover* of exchange-traded interest rates and futures contracts amounted to $1.1 trillion.

9. My son and I put together a model to simulate the possibilities for similar transitions in a nonlinear illustration of monetary control—see T. H. Solomon and E. H. Solomon, "Money Stability and Control."

10. Linda Moore, interview with the author, Washington, D.C., 22 May 1995.

11. Marquardt and Richards, interview with the author, 31 October 1995. Blinder, Statement before the Committee on Banking, 11 October 1995. Alan Greenspan, *Remarks at the U.S. Treasury Conference on Electronic Money and Banking: The Role of Government*, Washington, D.C., 19 September 1996. *Implications for Central Banks of the Development of Electronic Money* (Basle: Banks for International Settlements, October 1996).

12. T. H. Solomon and E. H. Solomon, "Money Stability and Control," 102–6.

Table 7-1. Money and Money Flows Concepts:
Discrete (Snapshot) and Continuous

M = Money stock: the official M's (point in time) = M3 plus L	$\Sigma M = M + M_E$: the official M's plus all e-money (net of double-counting)
V = Rate of money stock use (velocity) for GDP/ time period	V: = continuous money velocity = rate use of all ΣM
MV = Payments: M stock x GDP-based V	MV flows = phiΦ : effective money = flows of all money through time (continuous)

Note: ΣM = all money in broadest form, both official (M) and e-money or e-float (M_E). M_E is electronic money value not entered in any way into the official M's.

V = continuous rate of use (velocity) of all this "money" in all markets (including capital markets), not just final GDP markets.

Φ = effective money = ΣMV, or all the money flows, for purchase of all goods and financial and other services continuously throughout the day.

Chapter 8: Markets and the Law

1. Important Supreme Court decisions interpreting Section 7 of the Clayton Act involving bank mergers include *United States v. Philadelphia National Bank*, 374 U.S. 321 (1963); *United States v. Marine Bancorporation*, 418 U.S. 602 (1974); and *United States v. Connecticut National Bank*, 418 U.S. 656 (1974). For present merger policy see U.S. Department of Justice and the Fed-

eral Trade Commission, *Horizontal Merger Guidelines*, 2 April 1992.

For the earliest Sherman Act case in banking, involving the alleged fixing of prices of services, see *United States v. Northwestern National Bank of Minneapolis, et al.*, Cr.4–63 Cr.6, Civ. 4–63 Civ. 52, filed Feb.8, 1963, and terminated before trial, following *nolo* pleas in the criminal and consent decrees in the civil cases. The seminal economic analysis of banking collusion was by Almarin Phillips, "Competition, Confusion, and Commercial Banking," *Journal of Finance* 19 (1964): 32–45.

2. Anne K. Bingaman, Assistant Attorney General, Antitrust Division, U.S. Department of Justice, *Antitrust and Banking*, address before the Office of the Comptroller of the Currency's (OCC) Conference on Antitrust and Banking, 16 November 1995. For further background, see Bernard Shull, *The Origins of Antitrust in Banking: An Historical Perspective*, OCC Antitrust Conference, and E. H. Solomon, "The Dynamics of Banking Antitrust: The New Technology, The Product Realignment," *The Antitrust Bulletin* 30 (Fall 1985): 537–81.

3. Informal comment by Vice Chairman of the Federal Reserve Board Alan Blinder, OCC Antitrust Conference, 16 November 1995.

4. Remarks by Eugene A. Ludwig before the OCC Antitrust Conference and paper by Gary Whalen, *Non-Local Concentration, Multimarket Linkages and Interstate Banking*, 16 November 1995.

5. Donald I. Baker, Esq., partner, Baker and Miller, interview with the author, Washington, D.C., 7 February 1995.

6. See Baker, "Compulsory Access to Network Joint Ventures Under the Sherman Act: Rules or Roulette?" especially 1002–10. Baker, "Compelling Access to Network Joint Ventures," *Regulation* 2 (1994): 53–60. For the card systems development, see Baker and Brandel, *The Law of Electronic Fund Transfer Systems* Chap. 23; duality and ATM discussion, paras. 23.02 and 23.03 especially.

7. Wayne Boucher, President, Electronic Funds Transfer Association, interview with the author, Washington, D.C., 15 May 1995.

8. Stephen A. Rhoades, Assistant Director, Research Division, interview with the author, Federal Reserve Board, Washington, D.C., 27 June 1995. Rhoades, *Competition and Bank Mergers: Directions for Analysis from Available Evidence*, OCC Antitrust Conference, (*Antitrust Bulletin*, Summer 1996).

9. Press release, Department of Justice, *Justice Department Files Antitrust Suit to Challenge Miscosoft's Purchase of Intuit*, 27 April 1995. Cook and Microsoft executive quotes, from p. 3 of that press release.

Chapter 9: Partners and Rivals

1.Baker, interview with the author, 7 February 1995; Baker, *Shared ATM Networks — The Antitrust Dimension*, OCC Antitrust Conference; Baker and Brandel, *The Law of Electronic Fund Transfer Systems*, Chaps. 13 and 21.

2. James McAndrews, "Antitrust Issues in Payment Systems: Bottlenecks,

Access, & Essential Facilities," *Business Review of the Federal Reserve Bank of Philadelphia* (September/October 1995): 3–12; "Antitrust Issues and Payment Systems Networks," *Review* (St. Louis: Federal Reserve Bank of St. Louis, November/December 1995); Solomon, *Electronic Money Flows*, Chap. 8; Stephen Felgran, "From ATM to POS Networks: Branching, Access, and Pricing," *New England Economic Review* (May/June 1985); and Felgran and Ferguson, "The Evolution of Retail EFT Networks" (July/August 1986).

3. *National Bancard Corp. (NaBANCO) v. Visa USA, Inc.*, 596 F.Supp. 1231 (S.D.Fla. 1984), aff'd 779 F 2d 592 (11th Cir.), *cert. denied*, 479 U.S. 923 (1986). See Baker and Brandel (1988): 21.03 [1][a] and NaBANCO, p.1259. In NaBANCO, the court found broadly that the product market was payments systems, i.e., "all payment services used in retail sales guarantee cards." In the PULSE arbitration, Professor Kauper concluded that "ATMs are themselves a relevant, if fragile, market for antitrust purposes." 55 Trade Reg. Rep. (BNA) No. 1380 (Aug. 25, 1988): 356.

4. A similar access question was at issue in *Household Bank F.S.B. v. Cirrus Sys. Inc.*, No 87C2353 (ND Ill., filed March 1987). The question was whether the shared system was an "essential facility" so critical to those in the business that all competitors should be given equitable access to it. See Baker and Brandel (1988) 25.01 [1].

5. Arbitrator's Opinion, PULSE, 80–82. The procedure for implementing the decision is noted on p. 84.

6. *Valley Bank of Nevada v. PLUS and Visa* (U.S. District Court for Southern Nevada), March 1989. Defendants were charged with conspiring to fix prices in violation of antitrust laws. In September 1990 the Ninth Circuit Appellate Court found in favor of appellee Valley Bank for, among other reasons, "legitimate state interests" including tourism and gambling within the state of Nevada (filed 11 September 1990, p. 10970).

7. "Cost of using bank teller machines may rise," CNN, U.S. News Briefs, 6 December 1995; Kawika Daguio, American Bankers Association, telephone conversation with author, 21 December 1995.

8. Department of Justice, *Justice Department Files Antitrust Suit Against the Largest Regional ATM Network in the U.S.*, Press Release, Thursday, 21 April 1994. *United States v. Electronic Payment Services, Inc.*, Civ. No. 94–208, Competitive Impact Statement, 21 April 1994.

9. Final Judgment, in the U.S.D.C. for the District of Delaware, Civ. No. 94–208, 14 October 1994.

10. Anne K. Bingaman, *International Cooperations and the Future of U.S. Antitrust Enforcement*, Address before the American Law Institute, Washington, D.C., 16 May 1996.

11. *Wall Street Journal*, 27 July 1989, B7. Bankers had urged MasterCard and Visa to accept an offer from the attorneys general to settle the federal antitrust suit filed against them. *American Banker*, 2 October 1989.

12. John Markoff, "Microsoft Joins Visa to Propose a Standard for On-Line

Notes

254

Paying," *New York Times*, 28 September 1995, D1. Jared Sandberg, "Infighting Unravels Alliance Seeking Standard to Protect Internet Purchases," *Wall Street Journal*, and "MasterCard, Backed by IBM, Enters Fight for Internet-Payment Rules," 4 October 1995, B12; "Visa's Dominance May be Liability," *Wall Street Journal*, 6 June 1996, B1.

13. "Visa's European Members Drop Plan to Block Cards," *Wall Street Journal*, 30 May 1996, A3.

14. But see, "Researchers Find Big Security Flaw in Java Language," *Wall Street Journal*, 26 March 1996, B4. Unscrupulous people who discovered the flaw could booby-trap a Web page on the Internet, essentially seizing control of the browser software of any PC that tapped into that page. Once pointed out by the Princeton team, the flaw was promptly fixed. But a third flaw was found by an independent software consultant working with the Princeton group in May 1996.

Chapter 10: Money of the Global Village

1. Federal Reserve Bank of New York, *April 1995 Central Bank Survey of Foreign Exchange Market Activity*, 19 September 1995. Between 1992 and 1995 the use of automated brokerage has grown rapidly, from virtually nothing, to almost half the volume of brokered spot transactions in April 1995.

2. Oishi and Komai, *Networks and Society*. The theory of networking is analyzed by Drs. Oishi and Komai in the Introduction (ix–xiii) and Professor C. Christian von Weizacker in Part I, "Networks," 3–6.

3. George, "International Banking, Payment Systems, and Financial Crises," 73–79; Mussa, "The Integration of World Capital Markets," 245–330; Robert Solomon, *The Transformation of the World Economy, 1980–93* (New York: St. Martin's Press, 1994); R. Solomon, interview with the author, Washington, D.C., 26 October 1994.

4. See *London Financial Times* in daily running account, 27 February–3 March 1995; "The Bank That Disappeared," *The Economist*, 4 March 1995, 11–12. Greenspan quote from John Berry and Clay Chandler, "Bank Failure," *Washington Post*, 1 March 1995, C3.

5. "Who Lost Barings?," *The Economist*, 22 July 1995, 16.

6. Allen B. Frankel and Jeffrey C. Marquardt, "International Payments and EFT Links"; Marquardt and Richards, interview with the author, 31 October 1995; Jeff Stehm, interview with the author, Federal Reserve Board of Governors, Washington, D.C., 16 May 1995; Bank for International Settlements, *Cross-Border Securities Settlements* (Basle: Group of Ten, March 1995).

7. Yoshiharu Oritani, "Financial Networks and the Financial System: Japan's Experiences" and "Globalization of Payment Network and Risks." Oritani, conversations with the author, Washington, D.C., August 1988 and at the Bank of Japan, Tokyo, 2 March 1990. See Oritani, "A Japanese Central Banker's View of the EMS," in *Financial Regulation and Monetary Arrange-*

ments After 1992, ed. C. Wihlborg, M. Fratianni, and T. D. Willet (Amsterdam: Elsevier Science Publishers B.V., 1991), 335–37.

8. Simpson, "Trends in Global Securities Markets"; Bank for International Settlements, *Delivery versus Payment in Securities Settlement Systems* (Basle: Group of Ten, September 1992). In another example of globalization, ADRs (automated depository receipts)—where some banks serve as trustee and custodians for shares listed on foreign exchanges—are growing in popularity and link the exchanges as well as borrowers and investors of many countries. See also David Folkerts-Landau, Peter Garber, and Dirk Schoenmaker, *The Reform of Wholesale Payment Systems and Its Impact on Financial Markets* (Washington, D.C.: Group of Thirty, 1996) and Basle Committee on Banking Supervision, *Supervision of Cross Border Banking* (Basle: Bank for International Settlements, October 1996.)

9. Patrick M. Parkinson, Associate Director of Research and Statistics, and Patricia White, Assistant Director, interview with the author, Federal Reserve Board, 27 June 1995. Parkinson and Stehm, *Clearance and Settlement in U.S. Securities Markets.*

10. BIS, *Central Bank Survey of Derivatives Markets Activity*, December 1995, 1 and 2.

11. Charles Taylor, *The Globalization of Derivative Securities*, Remarks to the National Economists Club and conversation with the author, Washington, D.C., 11 April 1995; Global Derivatives Study Group, *Derivatives: Practices and Principles* (Washington, D.C.: Group of Thirty, July 1993).

Cathy E. Minehan and Katerina Simons, "Managing Risk in the '90s: What Should You Be Asking about Derivatives?" *New England Economic Review* (Boston: Federal Reserve Bank of Boston, September/October 1995). Eli Remolona et al., "Risk Management by Structured Derivative Product Companies," *Economic Policy Review* (New York: Federal Reserve Bank of New York, April 1996): 17–37. *Framework for Supervisory Information about the Derivatives Activities of Banks and Securities Firms*, Joint report by the Basle Committee on Banking Supervision and IOSCO, May 1995; Edwards, G. and G. Eller, "Derivatives Disclosures by Major U. S. Banks, 1995,"*Federal Reserve Bulletin* 82 (Washington, D.C.: Board of Governors of the Federal Reserve, September 1996): 791–801.

Joan Solomon Griffin, Director, Toronto Dominion Bank of Canada, interview with the author, 11 August 1995, New York City, and 9 January 1997, Washington, D.C. Ms. Griffin notes that, although risk hedging goes way back in time, its popularity and need rose greatly in the 1980s "when banks' funding costs started to fluctuate wildly and banks moved from fixed to floating loan rates. . . . Then the derivatives layered on top of bank lender floating rates eliminated the interest rate variability risk to their borrowers."

12. Shleifer and Summers, "The Noise Trader Approach to Finance," 19–33; C. L. Osler and John A. Carlson, *Rational Speculators and Exchange Rate Volatility* (New York: Federal Reserve Bank, May 1996).

Notes

John Ammer, Federal Reserve Board, interview with the author, George Washington University, Washington, D.C., 18 December 1995; Alan Maltz, Federal Reserve Bank of New York, telephone interview with the author, 29 March 1996; Charles A. E. Goodhart, "The International Transmission of Asset Price Volatility," in *Financial Markets Volatility* (Kansas City: Federal Reserve Bank of Kansas City, 1988): 79–132; and Alexandre Lamfalussy, "Globalization of Financial Markets," in *Financial Markets Volatility*: 133–140.

13. Obstfeld and Rogoff, "The Mirage of Fixed Exchange Rates," 73–96, specific quote from 73–74.

14. Obstfeld and Rogoff, 73, 77 and 80. See the Bank for International Settlements, *Settlement Risk in Foreign Exchange Transactions*, Report prepared by the Committee on Payment and Settlement Systems of the Group of Ten (Basle, March 1996).

15. Lewis, "Occasional Interventions to Target Rates,"; Juann H. Hung, *Intervention Strategies and Exchange Rate Volatility: A Noise Trading Perspective*, Federal Reserve Bank of New York, Research Paper #9515, June 1995; Catherine Bonser-Neal, "Does Central Bank Intervention Stabilize Foreign Exchange Rates," *Economic Review, Federal Reserve Bank of Kansas City* 81 (First Quarter 1996): 43–47.

16. Nicholas W. Leeson, interview with David Frost for British Broadcasting Company, shown on CBS's *Sixty Minutes*, 10 September 1995; "Barings Trader Questions Monitoring by His Superiors, *New York Times*, 11 September 1995.

Chapter 11: The Strange World of Money Laundering

1. U.S. Congress, Office of Technology Assessment, *Information Technologies for Control of Money Laundering* (Washington, D.C.: U.S. Government Printing Office, September 1995), 16, note 48. See also Peter J. Quirk, *Macroeconomic Implications of Money Laundering*, prepared for the Financial Action Task Force for Money Laundering (Washington, D.C. International Monetary Fund, June 1996). In a broader, but not unrelated focus, Porter, R. and R. Judson, "The Location of U.S. Currency: How Much Is Abroad?" *Federal Reserve Bulletin* 82 (October 1996): 883–903.

2. Walter, *The Secret Money Market* and OTA, *Money Laundering*. These books provide two primary, and also fascinating, sources of information about techniques.

3. Walter, *The Secret Money Market*, Chap. 1.

4. Joe Cleaver, Executive Secretary, Federal Financial Institutions Examination Council, conversation with the author, Washington, D.C., 16 November 1995. See OTA, *Money Laundering*, 19, and Chap. 1 for techniques and experience of law enforcement officials.

5. Vary Coates, interview with the author, Washington, D.C., 29 May 1995. OTA, *Money Laundering*, 12–17, presents the profiles and strategies of the professional money launderers; for the role of the federal agencies, along

with relevant laws and regulations, see Chap. 3, "Money Laundering and Law Enforcement."

6. See "Reading the Legal Roadsigns on the Information Superhighway," *Federal Bar News and Journal* 41 (August 1994): 481–519 for an overview. OTA, *Money Laundering*, 15; Federal Reserve Board, *Proposed Rulemaking to Revise Its Regulations on Reporting of Suspicious Activities*, Press Release, 28 June 1995; Edward W. Kelley, Jr., Member of the Board of Governors of the Federal Reserve System, Statement before the Committee on Banking and Financial Services, U.S. House of Representatives, 28 February 1996 from *Federal Reserve Bulletin* 82 (April 1996): 322–25.

7. OTA, *Money Laundering*, 106 and notes 23 and 24. For international anti-crime activities and data protection, see Chap. 6.

8. Lance Hoffman, *Encryption Policy for the Global Information Infrastructure*, Institute for Computer and Telecommunications Systems Policy, George Washington University, January 1995.

9. Commissioned by Congress, the report prepared for the National Research Council opposes existing administration proposals. The report, "Cryptography's Role in Securing the Information Society," recommends that Washington ease restrictions on exports of encryption technology and calls for the widespread commercial adoption of technologies used to prevent illegal wiretapping of computer data, telephone, cellular, and other wireless communications. Editorial, *New York Times*, 10 June 1996, A16, which notes "the danger . . . that Washington might move to outlaw encryption technology it has not approved, a step that would grossly violate American civil liberties."

10. Statement of Stanley E. Morris, Director, Financial Crimes Enforcement Network, before the Subcommittee on Domestic and International Monetary Policy of the Committee on Banking and Financial Services, U.S. House of Representatives, 11 October 1995.

11. Five technological options are presented by the Office of Technology Assessment, *Money Laundering*, Chap. 7, 136–44, including the comments of FinCEN's Director Morris, 143.

Chapter 12: The Search for Chaotic Market Patterns

1. Gleich, *Chaos: Making a New Science,* 15–18; Baumol and Behhabib, "Chaos: Significance, Mechanism, and Economic Applications," 77–105; Brock, "Introduction to Chaos and Other Aspects of Nonlinearity."

2. Paul Samuelson, conversation with the author, Cambridge, Massachusetts, 24 April 1995, and correspondence, June 1996. "Interactions Between the Multiplier Analysis and the Principle of Acceleration," *Review of Economic Statistics* 21 (1939): 75–78.

3. Barnett and Chen, "The Aggregation-Theoretic Monetary Aggregates Are Chaotic and Have Strange Attractors"; Ted Jaditz and Chera L. Sayers, *Fore-*

casting Monetary Aggregates, University of Houston and Bureau of Labor Statistics, March 1995.

4. Benoit Mandelbrot, *The Fractal Geometry of Nature* (New York: Freeman, 1977); Houthakker story from Gleich, *Chaos*, 83–86.

5. John Maynard Keynes, *The General Theory of Employment, Interest, and Money* (London: Macmillan, 1936). Haberler, *Prosperity and Depression*; Jean M. Grandmont, "On Endogenous Competitive Business Cycles," *Econometrica* 53 (1985): 995–1045; M. Woodford, "Three Questions About Sunspot Equilibria as an Explanation of Economic Fluctuations," *American Economic Review* 77 (May 1987): 93–98; Brock and Sayers, "Is the Business Cycle Characterized by Deterministic Chaos?," 71–89.

6. Milton Friedman, "The Quantity Theory of Money, A Restatement"; *A Program for Monetary Stability* (New York: Fordham University Press, 1960).

7. Chera Sayers, interview with the author, Washington, D.C., 15 March 1995.

8. Ted Jaditz, interview with the author, Bureau of Labor Statistics, Washington, D.C., 25 May 1995.

9. For both theoretical review and empirical tests of this nature, see Brock, *Pathways to Randomness in the Economy: Emergent Nonlinearity and Chaos in Economics and Finance*, Social Systems Research Institute, 410 (1993). Sayers, "Testing for Chaos and Nonlinearities in Macroeconomic Time Series," in *Business Cycles: Theory and Empirical Methods*, ed. Willi Semmler (Norwell, Mass.: Kluwer Academic Publishers, 1993); Ridley, "A Survey of the Frontiers of Finance: On the Edge"

10. Blake LeBaron, *Chaos and Nonlinear Forecastability in Economics and Finance*, SSRI 9446, University of Wisconsin-Madison, October 1994, and "Technical Trading Rule Profitability and Foreign Exchange Intervention, SSRI 9445, October 1994.

11. Brock, Lakonishok, and LeBaron, *Simple Technical Trading Rules and the Stochastic Properties of Stock Returns*, *The Journal of Finance* 47 (December 1992): 1731–64. Also discussed in "Frontiers of Finance," *The Economist*, 9 October 1993, quote from 9.

12. Ted Jaditz, interview with the author, 25 May 1995. "More in a Cockroach's Brain than Your Computers Dream of," *The Economist*, 15 April 1995, 75–77. Laurence Davis *Handbook of Genetic Algorithms* (New York: Van Nostrand Reinhold, 1991); Blake LeBaron and Andreas S. Weigand, *Evaluating Neural Network Predictors by Bootstrapping*, Social Systems Research Institute, Working Paper 9447 (Madison: University of Wisconsin, 1994).

13. Some investment managers are enthusiastic about the prospects for neural nets, despite their real limitations. John C. Barber, Vice President of Falcon Asset Management, talk before Computer Group of the Cosmos Club, 21 September 1995. Barber, "Genetic Algorithms as Tools for Optimization," *Risks and Rewards*, The Investment Section of the Society of Actuaries (June

1995). Inexpensive software packages bear names like Neuroshell 2, Brain-Maker, and Genehunter. "Efficient Markets and the Quants' Descent into Chaos," *Euromoney,* July 1993, 60–66; "The Quants May Have Your Numbers," *Business Week,* 25 September 1995, 146–47, which lists funds that take their cues from computers; Ridley, *Frontiers of Finance*; Peter Truell, "From I.B.M., Help in Intricate Trading," *New York Times,* 25 September 1995, D5.

14. Murray Gell-Mann, *The Quark and the Jaguar: Adventures in the Simple and the Complex*: 307–10. The work of the Santa Fe Institute is discussed by Mitchell M. Wadrop, *Complexity: The Emerging Science at the Edge of Order and Chaos* (New York: Simon & Schuster, 1992).

15. Randolphe M. Nesse, "Internet@Crossroads.$$$," *Technology Review,* May/June 1995: 24–31. Interviews with the author Carl Howe (Bolt Planet), Cambridge, Mass., 24 April 1995; Paul Henderson (New York Federal Reserve Bank), Washington, D.C., 16 June 1995.

16. See Brock, "Understanding Macroeconomic Time Series Using Complex Systems Theory," 119–141. These are sometimes called "sandpile" models.

17. See Penrose, *Shadows of the Mind: A Search for the Missing Science of Consciousness,* 393–411, for a fascinating discussion.

Chapter 13: Virtual Money as a Market Force

1. Stephen W. Hawking, *A Brief History of Time: From the Big Bang to Black Holes* (Toronto and New York: Bantam Books, 1988), 187.

2. Henderson, meeting with the author, Washington, D.C., Winter 1983, and "Modern Money," *Electronic Funds Transfers and Payments.*

3. Richard Feynman, *The Character of Physical Law* (Cambridge: MIT Press, second edition, 1982); John Gribbin, *In Search of Schrödinger's Cat: Quantum Physics and Reality* (Toronto and New York: Bantam Books, 1984), 183–90, 255–60.

4. Federal Reserve Bank of New York, *Central Bank Survey* (19 September 1995) and BIS, *Derivatives Market Activity* (18 December 1995); "Soros: Anatomy of a Comeback," *Business Week,* 25 September 1995; Gregory J. Millman, *The Vandals' Crown: How Rebel Currency Traders Overthrew the World's Central Banks* (New York: The Free Press, 1995); Mark Greenblatt, "Momentum Investment Strategies, Portfolio Performance, and Herding: A Study of Mutual Fund Behavior," *American Economic Review* 85 (December 1995): 1088–1105. On check-float, New York Federal Reserve Bank, "Float," *Fedpoints,* March 1992.

5. Wayne D. Angell, "Payment and Settlement Systems Policies and Incentives," *International Symposium on Banking and Payment Services* (Washington, D.C.: Federal Reserve Board of Governors, 1994), 119, and Dennis Weatherstone, "Major Themes in Changing Banking and Financial Markets, 8.

6. "Cheers and Fears," *The Economist,* 16 March 1996, 73, which reported that "In the past six weeks, central banks (mainly the Bank of Japan) bought no

less that $43 billion-worth of Treasury securities." Michael R. Sesit, "Strong Dollar Scenario Fails to Develop," *Wall Street Journal*, 26 February 1996.

In 1995, the hedge funds profited by borrowing low-yielding yen, converting the proceeds into dollars and investing the dollars in higher-yielding Treasury bonds. But in 1996 that strategy turned sour along with sharply falling U.S. bond prices, and the funds reversed those trades, selling dollars and buying yen. It has produced, according to *The Economist*, a "Nightmare on Bond Street" (74).

7. Chapter 6; Pierce and Noll, *Signals*.

8. "Banks, Consumers, and the Law," *Electronic Money Flows*, 162–63, for an example of getting cash from the electronic ATM.

9. Gell-Mann, *Quark and Jaguar*, 136–65, describes the modern alternative histories approach. See also Penrose, *Shadows of the Mind*, 256–94.

10. James Tobin, "Money, Capital, and Other Stores of Value," *American Economic Review* 51 (May 1961): 34–35.

11. T. H. Solomon, Physics Department, Bucknell University, conversations with author, 1995–96.

12. Hawking, *A Brief History of Time*, 55–61; Penrose, *Shadows of the Mind*, 331–47.

13. From Gribbin, *In Search of Schrödinger's Cat*, 173.

14. The packet "train" only knows that it is to deliver the baggage data somewhere, but cares little about how the data are packed or arranged. At each node (or switching point), instructions are given about where and how the packet is to be delivered. Because of its efficiency, Dr. Richard Jay Solomon thinks it likely that all networks will converge on the layered and packetized techniques. See R. J. Solomon, "Telecommunications Technology for the Twenty-first Century," in *The New Information Infrastructure*, ed. W. J. Drake, 93–111.

Pierce and Noll, *Signals* (206), note that a packet is a short block of data, usually of a fixed length of about 1,000 bits. Individual packets may travel over different routes and arrive at the destination out of order, which the computer at destination must assemble in the correct order.

15. Paul B. Henderson, interview with author, Washington, D.C., 16 June 1995.

Chapter 14: Privacy and Security

1. "Cyber Caper," *Wall Street Journal*, 12 September 1995, 1. An important discussion of security specifics is to be found in the Report by the Committee on Payment and Settlement Systems and the Group of Computer Experts, *Security of Electronic Money* (Basle: Bank for International Settlements, August 1996).

2. Martin and Weingarten, "The Less-Cash/Less-Check Society: Banking in the Information Age," 187–215.

3. Solzhenitsyn quote from Martin and Weingarten, 203.

4. Westin, "Privacy Aspects in EFT Systems," quote on 301.

5. U.S. Congress, Office of Technology Assessment, *Information Security*

and *Privacy in Network Environments*, OTA-TCT-606 (Washington, D.C.: U.S. Government Printing Office, September 1994) and the companion *Issue Update* (June 1995), 23–25; Andrew Grosso, "The National Information Infrastructure," *Federal Bar News and Journal* 41 (August 1994): 481–87. Martin and Weingarten, "Less-Cash/Less-Check Society," 191, 202–07.

6. OTA, *Information Security and Privacy Update*, 88–89; U.S. Office of Consumer Affairs and Issue Dynamics, Inc., *The Information Superhighway and Emerging Consumer Issues*, Symposium, Washington, D.C., 26 October 1995. Aware of consumer problems along these lines, the Telemarketing Association presented cards to remove one's name from the lists they prepare, should that be the preferred option.

7. Dave Kansas, "Software Glitch Delays Opening of Big Board," *The Wall Street Journal*, 19 December 1995, C1. Also Elizabeth Corcoran, "NYSE Computer Glitch," *Washington Post* 19 December 1995, C1.

8. The Federal Reserve Board Chairman told Congress, "Like it or not, computers and their software systems—with the possibility of mechanical or human failure—are an integral part of the payments mechanism. The scale and speed of transactions permit no other approach," from *Washington Post*, 13 December 1985, D7–8.

9. Henderson, Interview with the author, 16 June 1995.

10. William P. Crowell, National Security Agency, *Statement* to the House Committee on Banking and Financial Services, *On the Future of Electronic Forms of Money*, 11 October 1995; statements of Sally Katzen, Office of Management and Budget, and Robert H. Rasor, Department of the Treasury. National Information Infrastructure, Security Issues Forum (Washington, D.C.: Executive Office of the President, 14 June 1995). These issues were discussed earlier by Martin and Weingarten, "Less-Cash/ Less-Check Society," 198–200.

11. OTA, *Information Security and Privacy*, 160–71; *Update*, 1–42; David Banisar, "Roadblocks on the Information Superhighway," *Federal Bar News and Journal* 41 (August 1994): 495–504.

12. OTA, *Information Security and Privacy*, 87–95.

13. See "Safeguarding Networked Information," *Information Security and Privacy*, 25–68 and its *Update*, 43–65 for history, analysis, mechanisms, and suggested encryption policy options, in depth.

Lance J. Hoffman and others, "Cryptography Policy," *Communications of the ACM* 33 (September 1994): 109–13. Thomas Beth, "Confidential Communication on the Internet," *Scientific American* 273 (December 1995), 87–91.

14. OTA, *Information Security and Privacy*, 36–40 and 53–56 for specific types of private and public key encryption techniques, including digital signatures; David Chaum, "Achieving Electronic Privacy," 270 *Scientific American* (August 1992): 96–101. In something of a shocker, however, twenty-two–year old Paul C. Kocher has demonstrated the manner in which the public-key encryption code can be broken—see John Markoff, "Secure Digital Transactions Just Got a Little Less Secure," *New York Times*, 11 December 1995, A-1.

Notes

15. John Markoff, "The New Watchdogs of Digital Commerce," *New York Times*, 17 October 1995 and 19 September 1995, first Business page; "Discovery of Internet Flaws Is Setback for On-Line Trade," *New York Times*, 11 October 1995, 1.

16. As discussed by Seth Lloyd, "Quantum Mechanical Computers," *Scientific American* 273, 140–45 and Penrose, *Shadows of the Mind*, 355–56 and 394. Because most public key encryption systems—such as those protecting electronic bank accounts—rely on the fact that classical computers cannot find factors having more than, say, 100 digits, quantum-computer hackers would give many people reason to worry.

Of course, whether or not quantum computers (and quantum hackers) will ever come about is a hotly debated question because of massive design and insulation difficulties. Any disturbance will damage the delicate "multiparticle quantum states," causing quantum "decoherence" and computer failure (145). However, Dr. David Deutsch of the Mathematical Institute at Oxford University (with other scientists in the United States and Israel) begin to try to model them. Seth Lloyd believes that exploring their properties is a goal that lies within our current grasp.

Chapter 15: The Reconstructed Whole

1. James Gleick, "Dead as a Dollar," *New York Times Magazine,* June 16, 1996, 26 ff.

2. Michael R. Sesit, "Central Banks Issue Warning on Trading," *New York Times*, 28 March 1996, C1.

3. Bank for International Settlements, *Settlement Risk in Foreign Exchange Transactions* (Basle: Central Banks of the Group of Ten Countries, March 1996). This pathbreaking volume sets out alternative recommendations and explicit guidelines on defining and measuring foreign exchange settlement exposure. It provides model options on how the private and public sector, combined, may begin to define concepts in a uniform and measurable fashion so that participants can view the new risks and problems more clearly, and in the same way.

4. Michio Kaku, *Hyperspace: A Scientific Odyssey through Parallel Universes, Time Warps, and the 10th Dimension* (New York and Oxford: Oxford University Press, 1994), Chap. 2 and 3 especially.

5. From Kaku, *Hyperspace*, 55–59.

6. Michael N. Castle, *The Future of Money in the Information Age*, Cato Institute's 14th Annual Money Conference, Washington, D.C., 23 May 1996.

7. Sholem Rosen (Citibank), "Creating an Electronic Monetary System," at the Cato Institute's *The Future of Money*.

8. These interesting issues, a Domain of Actuarial Trust vs. a Domain of Guaranteed Trust, are discussed by William Melton (CyberCash, Inc.) at the Cato Institute's *The Future of Money*.

9. For the many arrangements, see Payments System Task Force, *The Role of Banks in the Payments System of the Future* (Washington, D.C.: American Bankers Association, September 1996). "An Introduction to Electronic Money Issues," prepared for the United States Department of the Treasury Conference, Washington, D.C., 19–20 September 1996.

10. Treasury Secretary Robert Rubin looks at the appropriate role of government that will address concerns and, at the same time, help us to realize the great potential of the exciting new technologies. Robert Rubin, Keynote Address, *Toward Electronic Money and Banking: The Role of Government*, 20 September 1996. According to the Honorable Michael N. Castle before that conference, "I believe that the market will produce bargains, however Faustian, that a significant segment of consumers will choose to accept. . . . The fact that governments are becoming restive and are reaching to regulate cyberspace argues urgently for a good faith effort by international private sector interests to come together and draw their own outline for progress."

Epilogue

1. The remarkable, but understated, achievements of Tim Berners-Lee are told by Steve Lohr, "His Goal: Keeping the Web Worldwide," *New York Times*, 18 December 1995, D1.

2. Edward J. Kane, *The Gathering Crisis in Federal Deposit Insurance* (Cambridge: MIT Press, 1985).

3. For example, Eli M. Noam (Director, Columbia Institute for Tele-Information), "Electronics and the Dim Future of Banks," presented at conference on Electronic Banking of the Fujitsu Research Institute, January 1996.

References

Baker, D. I. "Compulsory Access to Network Joint Ventures Under the Sherman Act: Rules or Roulette?" *Utah Law Review* 4 (1993): 1006–1133.

Baker, D. I., and R. Brandel. *The Law of Electronic Fund Transfer Systems*. Boston: Warren, Gorham & Lamont, 1988.

Bank for International Settlements. *Central Bank Survey of Derivatives Markets Activity*. Basle: Group of Ten, December 1995.

———. *Cross-Border Securities Settlements*. Basle: Group of Ten, March 1995.

———. *Delivery versus Payment in Securities Settlement Systems*. Basle: Group of Ten, September 1992.

———. *Payment Systems in the Group of Ten Countries*. Basle: Group of Ten, December 1993.

———. *Settlement Risk in Foreign Exchange Transactions*. Basle: Committee on Payment and Settlement Systems of the Central Banks of the Group of Ten, March 1996.

———. *Statistics on Payment Systems in the Group of Ten Countries*, Basle: Group of Ten, December 1995.

Barber, J. C. "Genetic Algorithms as Tools for Optimization." In *Risks and Rewards*. The Newsletter of The Investment Section of the Society of Actuaries. Annapolis, Md., June 1995.

Barnett, W. A., and P. Chen, "The Aggregation-Theoretic Monetary Aggregates Are Chaotic and Have Strange Attractors." In *Dynamic Econometric Modeling*, ed. W. A. Barnett, E. Berndt, and H. White. Cambridge, England: Cambridge University Press, 1988.

Baumol, W. J., and J. Behhabib. "Chaos: Significance, Mechanism, and Economic Applications." *Journal of Economic Perspectives* 3 (Winter 1989): 77–105.

Berger, A. N., Anil K. Kashyap, and Joseph M. Scalise. "The Transformation of the U.S. Banking Industry." *Brookings Papers on Economic Activity* 2 (1995): 55–218.

Beth, T. "Confidential Communication on the Internet." *Scientific American* 273 (December 1995): 87–91.

Brock, W. A. "Introduction to Chaos and Other Aspects of Nonlinearity." In *Differential Equations, Stability, and Chaos in Dynamic Economics*, ed. W. A. Brock and A. B. Malliaris. New York: North Holland, 1988.

———. "Understanding Macroeconomic Time Series Using Complex Systems Theory." *Structural Change and Economic Dynamics* 2 (1991): 119–41.

Brock, W., and C. Sayers. "Is the Business Cycle Characterized by Deterministic Chaos?" *Journal of Monetary Economics* 22 (1988): 71–89.

Business Week. "The Future of Money," June 12, 1995, 66–78.

Cato Institute. *The Future of Money in the Information Age.* 14th Annual Monetary Conference, Washington, D.C., May 23, 1996.

Chaum, D. "Achieving Electronic Privacy." *Scientific American* 270 (August 1992): 96–101.

Columbia Institute for Tele-Information. *Digital Cash and Electronic Money,* Columbia University, New York, April 21, 1995.

Crichton, M. *Jurassic Park.* New York: Ballantine Books and Random House, Inc., 1990.

Crockett, A. "Monetary Policy Implications of Increased Capital Flows." Symposium, Kansas City Federal Reserve Bank, 1993, 331–77.

Daguio, K. "Digital Cash and Other Potential Electronic Payments Mechanisms," *Digital Cash Conference*, Columbia Institute for Tele-Information, Columbia University, New York, April 21, 1995.

Drake, W. J., ed. *The New Information Infrastructure: Strategies for U.S. Policy.* New York: The Twentieth Century Fund Press, 1995.

The Economist. "The Birth of a New Species," The Software Industry Survey, May 25, 1996.

———. "More in a Cockroach's Brain than Your Computers Dream of," April 15, 1995, 75–77.

Electronic Funds Transfer Association. "Leaving Behind the Past to Enter a New Millennium." EFT Report 13 (1990): 1.

EU Payment Systems, Working Group. "Report to the Council of the European Monetary Institute on Prepaid Cards." Frankfurt am Main: European Monetary Institute, 1994.

Federal Reserve Bank of New York. *April 1995 Central Bank Survey of Foreign Exchange Market Activity*, September 19, 1995.

———. *A Day at the Fed.* New York: Federal Reserve Bank, 1991.

———. *Fedwire: The Federal Reserve Wire Transfer Service.* New York: Federal Reserve Bank, March 1995.

———. *From Rocks to Riches: An Illustrated History of Coins and Currency.* New York: Federal Reserve Bank, 1992.

———. *The Key to the Gold Vault.* New York: Federal Reserve Bank, 1991.

References

Frankel, A. B., and J. C. Marquardt, "International Payments and EFT Links," in E. H. Solomon, ed., *Electronic Funds Transfers and Payments*. Norwell, Mass.: Kluwer-Nijhoff, 1987.

Friedman, B. M., and F. M. Hahn, eds. *A Handbook of Monetary Economics*. Amsterdam and New York: North-Holland, 1990.

Friedman, M. "The Quantity Theory of Money, A Restatement." In *Studies in the Quantity Theory of Money*, ed. M. Friedman. Chicago: University of Chicago Press, 1956.

———. "A Theoretical Framework for Monetary Analysis." *Journal of Political Economy* 78 (1970): 193–238.

Gell-Mann, M. *The Quark and the Jaguar: Adventures in the Simple and the Complex*. New York: W. H. Freeman and Company, 1994.

George, E. "International Banking, Payment Systems, and Financial Crises." *International Symposium on Banking and Payment Services*. Washington, D.C.: Board of Governors of the Federal Reserve System, March 10–11, 1994, 73–79.

Gleich, J. "Cash Is Dying," *New York Times Magazine,* June 16, 1996, 26ff.

———. *Chaos: Making a New Science* . New York: Viking Penguin Inc., 1987.

———. *Genius*. New York: Vintage Books, 1993.

Goodhart, C. A. E. "The International Transmission of Asset Price Volatility." *Financial Markets Volatility*. Symposium of the Federal Reserve Bank of Kansas City, Jackson Hole, 1988, 79–132.

Goodhart, C. A. E. and J. Vinals. "Strategy and Tactics of Monetary Policy." *Goals, Guidelines, and Constraints Facing Policymakers*. Conference Series No. 38. Boston: Federal Reserve Bank of Boston, June 1994, 139–187.

Gould, S. J. "Dinomania." *The New York Review of Books,* August 12, 1993, 51–55.

———. *Ever Since Darwin: Reflections in Natural History*. New York: W.W. Norton, 1977.

Grandmont, J. M. "On Endogenous Competitive Business Cycles." *Econometrica* 53 (1985): 995-1045.

Grant, J. "Florins and Photons." *Grant's Interest Rate Observer* 10 (March 27, 1992): 7–14.

Greenblatt, M. "Momentum Investment Strategies, Portfolio Performance, and Herding: A Study of Mutual Fund Behavior." *American Economic Review* 85 (December 1995): 1088–1105.

Gribbin, J. *In Search of Schrödinger's Cat: Quantum Physics and Reality*. Toronto and New York: Bantam Books, 1984.

Group of Thirty, Global Derivatives Study Group. *Derivatives: Practices and Principles*. Washington, D.C, July 1993.

Haberler, G. *Prosperity and Depression*. Geneva: League of Nations, 1937.

Henderson, P. B. "Modern Money." Chap. 1 in *Electronic Funds Transfers and Payments*, ed. E. H. Solomon. Boston and Dordrecht: Kluwer Nijhoff Publishing, 1987.

References

Humphrey, D. B. *Payments Systems: Principles, Practice, and Improvements.* Washington, D.C.: The World Bank, 1995.

Juncker, G., B. Summers, and F. Young. "A Primer on the Settlement of Payments in the United States." *Federal Reserve Bulletin* 77 (1991): 47–58.

Kaku, M. *Hyperspace: A Scientific Odyssey through Parallel Universes, Time Warps, and the 10th Dimension.* New York and Oxford: Oxford University Press, 1994.

Knudsen S., J. Walton, and F. Young. "Business-to-Business Payments and the Role of Financial Electronic Data Interchange." *Federal Reserve Bulletin* 80 (1994): 269–78.

LeBaron, B. *Chaos and Nonlinear Forecastability in Economics and Finance* and *Technical Trading Rule Profitability and Foreign Exchange.* University of Wisconsin—Madison, October 1994.

Lewis, K. K. "Occasional Interventions to Target Rates." *The American Economic Review.* 85: 691–715, September 1995.

Martin, C.D., and F. Weingarten. "The Less-Cash/Less-Check Society: Banking in the Information Age." In *Electronic Money Flows*, ed. E. H. Solomon. Boston: Kluwer Academic Publishers, 1991.

Moore, L. K. S. "Money in the Third Millennium." Chap. 2 in *Electronic Money Flows*, ed. E. H. Solomon. Boston: Kluwer Academic Publishers, 1991.

———. "Payments and the Economic Transactions Chain." Chap. 2 in *Electronic Funds Transfers and Payments*, ed. E. H. Solomon. Boston and Dordrecht: Kluwer Nijhoff Publishing, 1987.

Mulcahy, J. *Coins of the Ancient World.* Philadelphia: Federal Reserve Bank, 1987.

Mussa, M. "The Integration of World Capital Markets." In *Changing Capital Markets: Implications for Monetary Policy.* Kansas City: Federal Reserve Bank of Kansas City, 1993.

The New York Clearing House Association. *Risk Reduction and Enhanced Efficiency in Large-Value Payment Systems: A Private-Sector Response.* New York: The New York Clearing House Association, 1995.

Nilson, S. *The Nilson Report*, bi-monthly issues, 1995 and 1996.

Obstfeld, M., and K. Rogoff. "The Mirage of Fixed Exchange Rates." *The Journal of Economic Perspectives* 9 (Fall 1995): 73–96.

Oishi, Y., and M. Komai, eds. *Networks and Society.* Tokyo: University of Tokyo Press, 1991.

Oritani, Y. "Financial Networks and the Financial System: Japan's Experiences." *Networks and Society.* Tokyo: University of Tokyo Press, 1991.

———. "Globalization of Payment Network and Risks." Chap. 5 in *Electronic Money Flows*, ed. E. H. Solomon. Boston: Kluwer Academic Publishers, 1991.

Parkinson, P., and J. Stehm. *Clearance and Settlement in U.S. Securities Markets.* Board of Governors of the Federal Reserve System. Staff Study 163, March 1992.

References

Passell, P. "Fast Money." *The New York Times Magazine*, October 18, 1992, 42.

Penrose, R. *Shadows of the Mind: A Search for the Missing Science of Consciousness.* Oxford: Oxford University Press, 1994.

Pierce, J. R. and A. M. Noll. *Signals: the Science of Telecommunications.* New York: Scientific American Library, 1990.

Rhoades, S. A. "Competition and Bank Mergers: Directions for Analysis from Available Evidence." *Antitrust Bulletin* (Summer 1996).

Richards, H. W. "Daylight Overdraft Fees and the Federal Reserve's Payments System Risk Policy." *Federal Reserve Bulletin* 81 (1995): 1065–77.

Ridley, M. "Electronic Money: So Much for the Cashless Society." *The Economist.* November 26–December 2, 1994, 23–27.

————. "A Survey of the Frontiers of Finance: On the Edge." *The Economist.* October 9, 1993.

Sayers, C. "Testing for Chaos and Nonlinearities in Macroeconomic Time Series." In *Business Cycles: Theory and Empirical Methods*, ed. Willi Semmler. Norwell, Mass.: Kluwer Academic Publishers, 1993.

Shleifer, A., and L. H. Summers. "The Noise Trader Approach to Finance." *The Journal of Economic Perspectives* 4 (Spring 1990):19–33.

Simpson, T. D. "Trends in Global Securities Markets." Chap. 6 in *Electronic Money Flows*, ed. E. H. Solomon. Boston: Kluwer Academic Publishers, 1991.

Solomon, E. H. "EFT: A Consumer's View." Chap. 9 in *Electronic Funds Transfers and Payments.* Boston and Dordrecht: Kluwer Nijhoff Publishing, 1987.

————. "Future Money and Banks: 1990–2010." *The Antitrust Bulletin* XXXVII (1994): 820–22.

————. "Today's Money: Image and Reality." Chap. 1 in *Electronic Money Flows.* Boston: Kluwer Academic Publishers, 1991.

Solomon, T. H., and E. H. Solomon, "Money Stability and Control." Chap. 4 in *Electronic Money Flows.* Boston: Kluwer Academic Publishers, 1991.

Taylor, J. B. "The Monetary Transmission Mechanism: An Empirical Framework." *The Journal of Economic Perspectives* 9 (Fall 1995): 11–26.

U.S. Congress. *The Future of Money.* Testimony before the House Committee on Banking and Financial Services, Washington, D.C., July 25, 1995.

————. *On the Future of Electronic Forms of Money.* Testimony before the House Subcommittee on Domestic and International Monetary Policy, the House Committee on Banking and Financial Services, Washington, D.C.: October 1995.

U.S. Congress, Office of Technology Assessment. *Information Security and Privacy in Network Environments.* OTA-TCT-606. Washington, D.C.: U.S. Government Printing Office, September 1994, and the *Issue Update*, June 1995.

————. *Information Technologies for Control of Money Laundering.* Washington, D.C.: U.S. Government Printing Office, September 1995.

———. *U.S. Banks and International Telecommunications*. Washington, D.C.: U. S. Government Printing Office, September 1992.

U.S. Department of Commerce. *NTIA Telecom 2000: Charting the Course for a New Century*. Washington, D.C.: U.S. Government Printing Office, October 1988.

U.S. Department of the Treasury. *Federal Electronic Cash Forum*. Financial Management Service, October 19, 1995.

Walter, I. *The Secret Money Market*. New York: Harper & Row, 1990.

Wenninger, J. and D. Laster. "The Electronic Purse," *Current Issues in Economics and Finance*. Federal Reserve Bank of New York 1 (April 1995): 1–4.

Westin, A. F. "Privacy Aspects in EFT Systems." In *Regulation of American Business and Industry*, ed. F. R. Edwards. New York: McGraw-Hill Book Company, 1979, 300–307.

References

Index

NOTE: Italicized page numbers refer to figures.

Index

Business cycles, 191–93

California Bank Card Association, 53
Capital markets: and central banks, 162; and chaos, 186–87, 194; and clearing, 159; equilibrium of, 164; and federal funds, 161; and globalization, 159–61, 162, 164, 168; problems with, 159–60; and settlement, 159, 160–61, 162. *See also* Securities markets
Caribbean Task Force, 181
Carte Blanche, 10, 51, 60
Cash: conventional, 66–67, 71, 86, 174, 175–76; cyber, 233. *See also* Electronic cash
Cashless/checkless society, 3, 4, 221, 245
Castle, Michael, 238
Cato Institute, 239
CD optical technology, 227
Central banks, 112, 213, 238, 242; as backers of money, 202, 209; and capital markets, 162; and clearing, 168; as controllers, 104–5, 108, 110, 111, 112, 114; and creation of money, 105, 204; and currency speculation, 151, 165–66; and currency unification, 158; and globalization, 151, 155, 156, 157, 158, 162, 165–66, 167, 168; and government, 104; and money flows, 110, 111; and partnerships, 134; and velocity of money, 108; and virtual money, 202, 204, 209
Central processing unit (CPU), 136, 136
Certificates of deposit (CDs), 26
Chaos: and business cycles, 191–93; and capital markets, 186–87, 194; characteristics of, 185–86; and computers, 192–94, 195–96, 197, 198; and economic systems, 197, 198; and financial markets, 194; and forecasting, 187–99; foundations of, 187–90; and fractals, 190, 191; and monetary theory, 191–92; and money

multipliers, 188; patterns in, 3–4, 198–99; and predictability, 186, 187–88, 189, 190, 195; and quants, 190, 192, 193, 194, 212; and risk, 195; and securities markets, 3–4, 192–93, 195–96, 198; and virtual money, 213; and volatility persistence, 194
Chase Bank, 44, 46, 157
Chaum, David, 63, 79
Checks, paper, 11, 35, 39–40, 39, 86, 87–88, 108, 177; and virtual money, 204, 209
CHIPS (Clearing House Interbank Payments System), 10, 41, 82, 93, 94, 155; administration/structure of, 42; amount transferred by, 7, 36, 42, 109; and control, 109, 111; and currency unification, 158; functions of, 42; and globalization, 155, 158, 168; and security issues, 223–24; and settlement, 42; and velocity of money, 109; and virtual money, 203, 205, 209
CHOICE card (Citicorp), 10, 60
CIRRUS (ATM system), 142, 146–47
Citibank/Citicorp, 10, 26, 29, 43–44, 48, 60, 219
Clandestine money, 13, 173–74. *See also* Money laundering
Clayton Act, 122
Clearing: of bank credit cards, 54; and capital markets, 159; and central banks, 168; and control, 111; of credit cards, 54, 55; definition of, 38; and e-money/e-cash, 67–68, 72; and EDI technology, 47; and globalization, 156, 159, 168; and partnerships, 134; and regulation, 129; time delays in, 38. *See also* Clearinghouses; Switching fees; *specific system*
Clearinghouses, 134, 136, 162, 168
"Clipper Chip," 182
Coates, Vary, 178
Columbia Institute for Tele-Information, 63
Commerce Department, U.S., 43

Index

Index

Index

282

Partnerships: and bank credit cards, 8, 139; benefits of, 139–40; and central banks, 134; internal strains in, 135, 137–48; and Internet, 147–48; and pricing, 137–40, 146. *See also* Joint ventures; *specific partnership*

"Payable-through-accounts," 179

Payments. *See* Payments system; Transfer payments

Payments system, 37–38, 39–40, *39,* 78–79, 109–11

Penrose, Roger, 198, 202

Philadelphia Bank case (1963), 117, 118, 120

Philadelphia National Bank, 144–45

Plastic, 46, 135, 209, 237; acceptability of, 49, 51–52, 55, 59, 62, 242, 245; and antitrust issues, 61; and bank mergers, 61–62; and competition, 50, 51, 57, 59–60, 62; cybermoney versus, 74–75; as e-money, 64, 65–66, 236; and EBT, 80–82, *80;* evolution of, 241; globalization of, 60–61; issuers of, 64; as medium of exchange, 30–31, 58–59, 60; and regulation, 123; and social class, 50, 51, 52. *See also* ATM system; Credit cards; *specific system or card*

PLUS (ATM system), 142, 144, 146–47

Point-of-sale (POS), 8, 108, 126, 139, 146–47, 182

Politics: and money laundering, 172; and regulation, 118, 119

Portfolio theory, 211

POS. *See* Point-of-sale

Predictability: and chaos, 186, 187–88, 189, 190, 195; and control, 104, 105; in the future, 244–45; and money laundering, 184

Prepaid cards. *See* Smart cards

Pricing, 16, 106, 118, 129, 137–43, 144, 146

Privacy, 181–82, 183–84, 221–23, 237, 243–44

Privacy Act (1974), 222

Private banks, 237, 242

Private networks, 43–44, 47, 158–59. *See also specific network*

Protocols, 226–27

Proton, 71, 233

PULSE, 126, 141–43, 146

Pyramid: and control, 112, 114; of money, 90–95, *91;* of networks, 128–30; of reserves, 112, 114

Quants, 190, 192, 193, 194, 212

Quantum cryptography, 231

Quantum mechanics, 213–14

Quicken program (Microsoft), 9, 30, 62, 119, 121, 122, 127–28

Rausch, Robert, 102

Reagan (Ronald) administration, 118, 126

Real-time gross settlement (RTGS), 167

Record-keeping, 220–21

Reed, John, 133

Regional card systems, 120

Regulation: of banks, 21, 67, 126, 127, 238, 240, 244; and central banks, 238; and clearing, 129; and competition, 118, 120; and consortia, 121; of conventional money, 67, 78; and credit cards, 50, 123, 124–25, 130; of cybermoney, 75, 78, 238; of e-money/e-cash, 67, 79, 238, 239, 240; in the future, 240, 244; and globalization, 161; government role in, 122–23; and home banking, 128; and information gleaning, 238; and innovation, 124; and joint ventures, 121, 123, 124, 125, 127, 129, 130; and legal standards, 123–26; and markets in flux, 238, 239; and mergers, 120–23, 126, 127, 244; and money laundering, 177; and networks, 124, 128–30; and nonbanks, 120; and plastic, 123; and politics, 118, 119; and prices, 129; and regional

Regulation (continued)
card systems, 120; and software
programs, 120; and spillover
restraints and clauses, 130; and
technology, 118; and thrift
institutions, 119. *See also*
Congress, U.S.: as regulator;
Control; Deregulation; Federal
Reserve System; Justice
Department, U.S.; *specific system
or type of system*
Reistad, Dale, 3, 4
Renaissance, 20
Reporting requirements, 172, 176,
179–80
Reserves, 77, 113, 174, 209; and
assets, 104; backing for, 112; and
comparison of conventional cash
and e-cash, 71; and control, 102,
103–4, 105, 106, 112, 113, 114;
and creation of money, 89; creation
of, 103; and cybermoney, 103; and
deposits, 67, 89, 90; "differential"
requirements for, 104; and e-
money/e-cash, 72, 76, 90, 93, 103,
104; and economy, 106; for foreign
exchange, 165–66; of gold, 24–25;
legal, 103; and money market
accounts, 102; overdrafts of,
92;pyramid of, 112, 114; and
regulation of banks, 67; and
synthesis of money, 89, 90, 91–92,
91, 93; and virtual money, 209,
210; whereabouts of, 78
Respondent banks, 77, 112, 113
Restraint of trade, 122
Retail money, 38–41, 52, 242
Rhoades, Stephen, 127
Risk: and chaos, 195; and credit
cards, 53, 55, 61; cross-system,
168; and globalization, 161, 168;
and money laundering, 173, 180;
"operational," 225; and virtual
money, 209–10, 211
Rogoff, K., 165
Roosevelt, Franklin D., 240
Rosen, Sholom, 239
Routing, 47

RSA techniques (Rivest-Shamir-
Adelman), 8, 229

Samuelson, Paul, 101, 188, 191
Santa Fe Institute, 197
Satellite transmissions, 38, 39, 42–44,
88–89, 95, 208
Savings and loan institutions, 10–11,
58. *See also* Thrift institutions
Sayers, Chera, 192, 194
Secrecy, bank, 171, 173, 180, 181,
182
Securities market: and chaos, 3–4,
192–93, 195–96, 198; computer-
aided trading in, 192–93; and
globalization, 159–61, 167; and
money laundering, 179; and
security issues, 224–25; and
settlement, 111, 167; and volatility
persistence, 195–96. *See also*
Capital market
Security issues, 39, 64, 240, 243; and
ACHs, 46; and banks, 219; and
credit cards, 50, 223–24, 240; of
cybermoney, 74, 98; and digital
glitches, 223–24, 231; and e-
cash/e-money, 65–66, 87; and EBT,
79; and encryption technology,
227–29, 230, 231; and gridlock,
225–26; innovation in, 239; and
interoperability, 226–27; and
mergers and sharing, 121; and
national database, 221–23; and
securities markets, 224–25;
shortcomings in, 229–31; of smart
cards, 82; and software, 223–25.
See also Hackers; *specific system*
Seignorage, 237–38
Settlement: and capital markets, 159,
160–61, 162; and control, 111,
112; deposits, 111; and e-barter,
237; and e-cash, 72; and e-value
clouds, 95; in EPS, 130; and
globalization, 156, *157*, 159,
160–61, 162, 167, 168; RTGS,
167; and securities markets, 111,
167; and virtual money, 235, 237.
See also Clearing

Index